# Managing common property in an age of globalisation

## Zimbabwean experiences

# Managing common property in an age of globalisation

## Zimbabwean experiences

EDITED BY

Emmanuel Manzungu

Godfrey Chikowore

Dorothy Mushayavanhu

Dennis Shoko

WEAVER PRESS

Published by Weaver Press, Box 1922, Avondale, Harare. 2002



Typeset by Fontline Electronic Publishing (Pvt) Ltd., Harare

Cover Design: Inkspots, Harare.

Printed by: Modern Press, Gweru

The editors and the publisher would like to express their thanks to the Africa Reform and Development Project, Harare for their generous support of this publication.



ISBN: 1-77922-010-3

# Contents

# Figures

# Notes: editors and contributors

**Godfrey Chikowore** holds an MSc and a PhD in regional economic co-operation and integration from Simferopol State University, Crimean Island in the then United Soviet of Socialist Republics (USSR). He is currently a research fellow at the Institute of Development Studies at the University of Zimbabwe where he heads the Department for International Relations and Social Development. His area of specialisation is regional economic co-operation and integration with special reference to the SADC, and a focus on such issues as democracy, governance, globalisation and the political economy of development in developed and developing countries. He has written on the theory and practice of regional co-operation with emphasis on the SADC.

**Patrick W. Mamimine** holds a DPhil in sociology and anthropology from the University of Zimbabwe. He is currently a lecturer in natural resource management, eco-tourism, and community-based natural resource management at the Centre for Applied Social Sciences at the University of Zimbabwe (CASS). He has published widely on socio-cultural aspects of natural resource management.

**Emmanuel Manzungu** holds a PhD in irrigation management from Wageningen University of Environmental Sciences in the Netherlands. He has written extensively on irrigation and water resources management. He has also co-edited two books on the same theme: *The Practice of Smallholder Irrigation* and *Water for Agriculture in Zimbabwe*. Currently he is a research associate with the Department of Soil Science and Agricultural Engineering, University of Zimbabwe where he is conducting research on various aspects of water resources management in southern Africa.

**France Maphosa** holds a PhD in sociology from the University of Zimbabwe. He has published widely in sociology and anthropology where his main focus has been organisational/institutional development. He is currently a lecturer and chairman of the Department of Sociology at the University of Zimbabwe. His research interests include natural resources management particularly common property management and the role of community-based organisations in natural resource management.

**Medicine Masiiwa** holds a PhD in agricultural economics from the University of Rostock in Germany. He has published a number of articles on agricultural economics, farming systems and agricultural trade. He is currently a research fellow with the Institute of Development Studies at the University of Zimbabwe. His research interests include land and agrarian policy, agricultural trade, and rural development.

**Frank Matose** is a holder DPhil in Development Studies from the University of Sussex. Currently he is on secondment to the Centre for International Forestry Research (CIFOR) from the Forestry Commission of Zimbabwe where he worked as a resource sociologist in the Research Division for twelve years. He is the team leader for the Adaptive Co-management of Forests Project in Zimbabwe. He has published extensively on forestry management. His research interest is in facilitating the adaptive capacity of resource managers and users in order to improve livelihood options within forests.

**Morris Mudiwa** holds a MSc in Agricultural Economics and a BSc Agriculture Hons from the University of Zimbabwe. He is a principal agricultural specialist in the Department of Agricultural Research and Extension in the Zimbabwean Ministry of Lands, Agriculture and Rural Resettlement. His research interests lie in the area of project planning and natural resource management.

**Phanuel Mugabe** obtained his MSc and PhD in Rangeland Ecology and Management at Texas A & M University, USA. and his Bachelor of Science degree in Politics and Administration from the University of Zimbabwe. He has been at the University of Zimbabwe since 1996 when he was appointed a Research Fellow for the Centre for Applied Social Sciences (CASS). He became a lecturer in 1998 and was appointed Chairman of the Centre in 1999 where he supervises PhD students. He has published articles on the human aspects of resource utilisation and management for journals and presented papers at conferences. His interest lies in developing social based analysis and linking them with Remote Sensing and Geographical Information Systems (GIS).

**Dorothy Mushayavanhu** holds a Bachelor of Law degree from the University of Zimbabwe and a Masters of Laws in Law and Development from the University of London in the United Kingdom. She is a lecturer in environmental law at the Faculty of Law at the University of Zimbabwe. Her research interests lie in the general area of international environmental issues focusing on water resources, land tenure and governance of natural resources.

**Ivan Farayi Muzondo** is a lecturer in Remote Sensing and Geographical Information Systems (GIS) in the Department of Geoinformatics and Surveying at the University of Zimbabwe. He obtained a MSc in GIS from the same department in 1999. His active research area is visualisation of spatial data particularly using Virtual Reality Modelling technology. He is involved in developing GIS for environmental, planning and engineering companies. He is a member of the Zimbabwe Society for Photogrammetry and Remote Sensing,

Geographical Names Standing Committee and Council of Land Surveyors are some of the associations to which he is an active member. He is also the interim chairman of Zimbabwe GIS Association.

**Rudo Angela Sanyanga** holds a BSc in Biology and Biochemistry from University of Zimbabwe, a Masters degree in Applied Hydro-Biology from Cardiff University, Wales and PhD in Systems Ecology from the University of Stockholm, Sweden. She has undertaken several consultancies on environmental impact assessment, and has also worked from the CAMPFIRE Association. She is a fellow of the Leadership for Environment and Development Programme (LEAD) and has also worked as an academic co-ordinator for the same programme. Currently she is a lecturer at Bindura University of Science Education in Zimbabwe. Her research interests include aquatic ecology applied in particular impacts of human activity on the environment.

**Dennis Shoko** is a holder of a sandwich PhD in sedimentology from the University of Zimbabwe and the Free State of Amsterdam and has published widely on mining and the environment. His research interests include small-scale mining, mining and legal issues, minerals and sustainable development, and he is a steering committee member of the Mining, Minerals and Sustainable Development Southern African project. Currently he is involved with e-learning project of the Southern Africa Network for Training and Research on the Environment and Teaching Sedimentology in the Geology Department at the University of Zimbabwe.

**Liliana Vassileva** holds a PhD from the University of Architecture, Civil Engineering and Geodesy in Sofia, Bulgaria. She was also trained in traffic and transport planning in Paris, France. She has written over 50 journal articles and three books. Currently she is an Associate Professor in Civil Engineering at the University of Zimbabwe. He research interests include traffic and transport, urban planning and development and construction.

# Acknowledgements

We wish to acknowledge with thanks the contributors who responded so positively to our initiative, the Centre for Applied Social Sciences (CASS) at the University of Zimbabwe for their input, and particularly, their Director, Dr Phanuel Mugabe, who first suggested the idea for this book. Special thanks go to Hivos for meeting the costs of production through the Agrarian Reform and Development Project in the Department of Agrarian and Labour Studies of the Institute of Development Studies at the University of Zimbabwe. Dr M. Masiiwa also deserves our appreciation for co-ordinating the necessary finances for the book. Finally we would like to thank the editors at Weaver Press for their tireless work.

Emmanuel Manzungu

Godfrey Chikowore

Dorothy Mushayavanhu

Dennis Shoko

December 2002

The authors would like to thank the

**Agrarian Reform and Development Project, Harare**

for supporting the publication this book.

# Foreword

It is accepted that common property resources (CPRs) have multiple functions, hence sustaining their productivity against a trend of increasing scarcity and growing demand is an essential task for resource users, governments, researchers, NGOs and development practitioners. It is the importance of CPRs that has resulted in many theoretical and empirical studies relevant to their management. This book focuses on some of the many local, national and global challenges that face common property management – challenges that are exacerbated within an increasingly globalised world of rapidly changing economic, social and ecological conditions.

Two key characteristics of CPRs are excludability and substractability. The difficulty of exclusion arises from the high costs of enforcing boundaries. In addition, each user of CPRs can reduce the benefits that others derive from the common resource. These two characteristics can lead to over-exploitation and depletion or degradation which Hardin has termed the 'tragedy of the commons' – a concept which has now been completely undermined. It is now accepted that under certain conditions collective management of natural resources is both feasible and enduring. Researchers have, however, struggled to explain the successes and failures of collective management. *Managing common property in an ge of globalisation* interrogates the different CPR models such as CAMPFIRE as well as institutions that govern the commons. This book is an attempt to improve our understanding of the successes and failures for herein lies the way to improving the livelihoods of many of the world's poor.

Globalisation has brought new meaning to management of common resources. It has changed our sense of time and space. There is a growing questioning of the role of government in resource management. One major impact of globalisation is the retreat or dilution of tradition and custom in the lives of many people and in the relationship between people and nature. More significantly, it has given rise to a new form of individualism. The latter is cherished because it is perceived as producing freedom – a notion that is potentially destructive with respect to management of resources such as forests where collective action by a group is required. The concept of individualism and the ethic of individual property rights implicit in democratic societies are, in many cases, inimical to effective action on shared resources.

Perhaps the greatest impact of globalisation is that it has made resource managers increasingly accountable to external constituencies, and involved external forces in national and regional affairs. National issues of poverty, unemployment, food insecurity, resource inequities, and widening income gaps have all become peripheral and subordinate to external interests.

Within a globalised world, multi-lateral processes and agreements that now form the backbone of global environmental governance are increasingly driving natural resource management. Unfortunately, the inter-governmental focus of multi-lateralism often undermines local level institutions in favour of centralised systems. There is need for a new commitment to multi-lateralism that is based on consultation and negotiation rather than a notion of absolute power.

*Managing common property in an age of globalisation* is a timely contribution to the research and study of this area now taking place in southern Africa. Its coverage of international, regional and local dimensions to the management of different natural resources makes it particularly useful in relation to both theory and practice; and the book also makes a bold attempt to explore the linkages between common property management, the environment and globalisation.

Dr Yemi Katerere
Regional Director, IUCN Southern Africa

December 2002

# Management and use of common property resources in an era of globalisation: an Introduction

*France Maphosa*

## Introduction

The management of common property resources has, for a long time, been inspired by philosophies that favoured either privatisation or central administrative control as a means of ensuring sustainable utilisation of such resources. This notion found its most eloquent expression in Hardin's (1968) now famous phrase, 'tragedy of the commons'. Current thinking and practice has, however, shifted towards an emphasis on lower levels of the state and community structures as appropriate institutions in the management of common property resources (Ostrom, 1990; Berkes and Farvar, 1989; Murombedzi, 1997; Fortmann and Nhira, 1992; Murphree, 1991).

Globalisation presents the greatest challenge to this approach as it entails the incorporation of nation-states and local communities into a global system controlled by supranational and transnational organisations. This absorption of nation states and local communities into the 'global village' undermines their influence in the management of resources. The paradox of globalisation is that it leads to both inclusion and exclusion. For instance, the inclusion of the African commons into the global world market more often than not leads to the exclusion of local people who depend on it for their livelihoods (Cousins, 2000). The challenge that the globalisation experience poses to theorists, policy-makers and practitioners in the management of commons is how to situate local nation-states and local communities within the global system. The challenge is two-pronged. On one hand, it is about how to make global policies and structures relevant at national and local community levels. On the other hand, it is about how local initiatives can influence global thinking and practice in the management of common property resources. This challenge has been referred to as 'globalisation from below'.

The overarching theme of the chapters in this volume is that globalisation will remain as rhetoric if it does not engage with local realities (Manzungu, this volume). The contributors to the volume come from various disciplines; namely politics, sociology, agriculture, geology and ecology. Using case studies from the management of different resources such as forests, fisheries, water and mineral resources, these writers tackle topics relating to local level participation, the role of technology in the management of common property resources, the management of transboundary common property resources, and the globilisation of local commons through the notion of intellectual property rights. In the following sections we discuss the concept of globalisation and its effects on developing countries, the concept of common property, and finally, we present the organisation of the rest of the book.

## The challenge of globalisation

There is growing interest among academics, particularly those in the social and ecological sciences, in the nature and effects of globalisation on the political, economic, cultural and environmental realities of developing countries. Despite this growing interest, however, globalisation is often not defined. In this book we define globalisation as 'the phenomenon of increasing integration of nation states through economic exchanges, political configurations, technological advances and cultural influences' (Henriot, 2001). It is a process that leads to the homogenisation of ideas, images and institutions (Owolabi, 2001). One of the results of globalisation is the disembedding of social relations. According to Giddens (1991:18), disembedding social relations refers to 'the lifting out of social relations from local contexts and their re-articulation across indefinite tracts of time and space'.

Although globalisation is often presented as a new phenomenon it is in fact less than particular to this new millennium. As Kurien (1998) argues, it is as old as the rise of capitalism and its overseas expansion since the fifteenth century. It is a stage in the process of ongoing outside penetration of the African continent (and other developing countries) by outside forces. The other stages are slavery, colonialism and neo-colonialism, in that order. The penetration of the African continent by outside forces has had negative social consequences on African people's development (Henriot, 2001; Kurien, 1998; Masiiwa, this volume).

Debate on the effects of globalisation on developing countries is polarised and sometimes emotional. Proponents of globalisation argue that the countries that have adopted globalisation most readily, for example the US, the UK, Australia, Singapore, and Canada, have prospered most over the past decade or so (Moran, 2000). This view, however, overlooks the unequal effects of globalisation. To developing nations, globalisation represents their marginalisation by the world economic system that is dominated by rich western industrial capitalist countries (Makoa, 2001). It is, therefore, not surprising that developing nations and other sympathetic Northerners have expressed displeasure at the ever-expanding tentacles of globalisation.

The most poignant contemporary opposition to globalisation was witnessed at the recent World Trade Organisation meetings in Seattle and Genoa. Those opposed to globalisation argue that it has caused anxiety and uncertainty among the less developed countries (Makoa, 2001: 125). As a process that is influenced by neoliberal philosophy, it puts an absolute value on the operation of the market and subordinates people's lives, the functioning of society, the policies of government and the role of the state to unrestrained free market forces. This results in a widening gap between the rich and the poor. This increasing marginalisation poses a growing environmental threat, as the poor tend to live off the environment. A fundamental fault with globalisation is that it is not embedded in the local community but organised from above and thus operates according to structures and policies that are not always relevant to the local people.

It is the all-embracing trends and challenges of globalisation in the new millennium that have attracted great attention from academic and research circles, especially in the social, environmental and ecological sciences. As issues of common property resources become international through the global reach (Mudiwa, this volume), academic interest in the relationships between the global and the local has also increased.

## Defining common property

There are two characteristics that distinguish common property resources from other types of resource. The first is that the exclusion or control of access of users to these resources is problematic. The second is that each user is capable of subtracting from the welfare of other users (Berkes and Farvar, 1989; McCay and Acheson, 1987; Cousins, 2000). For a resource to be defined as common property, it should belong to a 'class of resources for which exclusion is difficult and joint use involves subtractability' (Berkes and Farvar, 1989:7). Private and state represent other types of property (Bromely, 1989).

In 1968, Hardin, popularised the model of 'the tragedy of the commons' to describe the management and use of common property resources. According to this model, an individual resource user, as a rational being, is inclined to take as much as possible of the common property resource before someone else does. Because common property resources belong to everyone, nobody is motivated to take responsibility for them. As a result, common property resources are prone to over-exploitation. This is the tragedy of the commons. The solution is privatisation or central administrative control.

This model has influenced much of resource management thinking, especially in the West. It was premised on a number of assumptions: that there are no rules about uses of the common property resources; that common property is synonymous with open access property; that users are selfish and are not restricted by social norms of the community; that users are always trying to maximise short term gains; and that a common property resource is used so intensively that over-exploitation and depletion are possible (McCay and Acheson, 1987).

The greatest flaw of the 'tragedy of the commons' model is that it fails to distinguish between common access and common property resources. Subsequent writers have distinguished between open access and common property resources; the former is not managed while the latter are managed. In common property resources rights and duties are well defined (Cousins, 2000). Common property resources have been, and are still, subject to specific legal and/or customary arrangements that define user-groups and exclude non-users.

The model of the 'tragedy of the commons' has been criticised for its being western ethnocentric, emphasising competition rather than co-operation and assuming the supremacy of individualism rather than communitarianism (Berkes and Fravar, 1989:2; Berkes 1989:7). It underestimates the ability of resource users to co-operate towards a collective interest.

The contributions in this volume demonstrate, mostly through case studies, that the management of common property is a social not an individual concern. This is consistent with the notion of 'new institutionalism' (Bromely, 1989; Ostrom 1990) in common property resource management. Common property, like other types of property, is a social institution (McCay and Acheson, 1987:16). Common property management and use are embedded in formal and informal institutional arrangements.

## Common property management in Zimbabwe

In pre-colonial Zimbabwe, common property resources were managed through localised regimes of proprietorship (Murphree, 1990; Masiiwa, this volume). Sustainable use of natural resources was regulated through traditional institutions, which determined the intensity of grazing, the harvesting of fruit, the cutting down of trees as well as hunting and gathering (Masiiwa, this volume; Mugabe, Hamudikuwanda and Marovanidze, 2001).

Colonial policies created two types of tenure systems: private and communal lands. Private lands, comprising large-scale commercial farms and small-scale farms, were held under freehold title or leasehold while communal lands were governed by the Tribal Trust Lands Act (1979). All communal land was state land. The role of traditional structures in land and natural resource management was significantly reduced as communal land is legally state land. Coupled with the state's inability to effectively manage resource use, this produced conditions akin to those of an open access system and led to serious environmental degradation in the communal areas. As Murphree (ibid.) points out, it is not surprising therefore that the communal lands have been the scene of the greatest environmental degradation in the country. The subordination of traditional leadership to central government ensured that its role in common property management was curtailed. The role of traditional leadership was reduced to that of tax collection and the enforcement of centrally-designed environmental laws (Masiiwa, this volume). As traditional leaders became increasingly associated with the colonial regime they became alienated from their people.

At Independence in 1980, the new government created five land tenure systems, namely communal land areas, resettlement areas, small- and large-scale commercial farms, and state land comprising national parks and forest land. Communal areas remained state land with ownership vested in the President. The creation of resettlement areas saw some land taken away from private owners, largely the large-scale commercial farms, for distribution to people previously resident in communal areas. The state maintained ownership of these areas. According to Murphree and Cumming (1991), the resettlement areas are occupied under tenure systems that are more restrictive of a genuine common property regime than in communal areas.

In 1984 the then Prime Minister issued a directive aimed at decentralising the system of government. The decentralisation of local government was ostensibly meant to allow people in communal areas to participate in the development process. The Prime Minister's directive led to the creation of local government structures, the lowest being the Village Development Committees (VIDCOs). Above them were Ward Development Committees (WADCOs). The Rural District Councils Act of 1998 contradicts the ideals of participation by local communities in the development process for which these structures were purportedly created. The Act gives power to Rural District Councils (RDCs) as an 'appropriate authority' to control the utilisation and management of natural resources in these areas. The Act empowers the RDCs to '... manage everything pertaining to life in the communal areas, including trees, conservation of natural resources, bush fires, grazing, agriculture and land.' (Clarke and Katerere, 1994)

Furthermore, the Minister of Local Government is empowered by the same Act to create bylaws for the RDCs that can override any customary claims (Hobane, 1999). This gives power to the state, leaving limited options for active participation in the management of natural resources by the local people (Scoones and Matose, 1993).

This decentralised system of local government has experienced a number of problems. One of them is the tendency by bureaucrats to use the structures as convenient units of mobilisation rather than for real community participation. Instead of promoting the development of these decentralised units through various forms of empowerment, bureaucrats have tended to disempower people by using them to rubber-stamp the implementation of centrally-derived objectives. In many instances VIDCOs and WADCOs have failed to elicit popular participation of the rural population in development planning and administration (Masiiwa, this volume, Mamimine, this volume).

The other problem is that the relationship between these new structures and those of traditional authority has been problematic. The decentralisation directive did not specify the nature of the relationship between them. This was exacerbated by the efforts of the immediate post-Independence government to reduce the powers of traditional leaders for having collaborated with the colonial governments. Traditional leaders were therefore disempowered by most of the legislation passed after Independence (Mamimine and Mandivengerei, 2001). This was in spite of the fact that:

> *... chiefs, sub-chiefs, headmen and kraal heads in effect constituted the communal lands' administrative and legal institutions with historically defined areas and sets of rules and regulations clearly understood by the rural people. (*Thomas, quoted in Mamimine and Mandivengerei, 2001*)*

VIDCOs and WADCOs were therefore perceived as having been created to replace traditional authority, which resulted in conflicts and competition for allegiance between these institutions. Conflicts regarding the allocation of land, for instance. became endemic.

Despite these problems, however, the decentralised system of local government provided a basis for implementing community-based resource management policies that facilitated local participation in the management of natural resources (Murphree and Cumming, 1991; Murombedzi, 1994). It provided the framework for the implementation of the Communal Areas Management Programme for Indigenous Resources (CAMPFIRE).

CAMPFIRE seeks, among other things, to introduce a system of group ownership with defined rights of access to natural resources for the communities resident in the target areas. The programme envisaged a system of ownership which involves the creation of locally-based natural resource co-operatives with essentially the same rights and obligations as the private owners of commercial ranches, all inhabitants of the community being shareholders (Murphree, 1991).

Murombedzi (1997) argues that it has engendered complementarity rather than competition, and conflict between traditional structures and the new institutions created by the Prime Minister's directive. He concludes that the successes of the CAMPFIRE programme were, in this regard, recognised by the 1994 Land Tenure Commission (Rukuni, 1994), which recommended that a new system of village councils be adopted and implemented in the communal areas to manage communal resources.

Mamimine (this volume) argues that notwithstanding the successes of CAMPFIRE, there are still hurdles that need to be addressed to ensure that the ownership and management of natural resources is devolved to the lowest tiers of administration. He points to the tendency of power retention and lack of commitment by RDCs to devolve power to residents of communal areas, which emanates from the 'myth of lack of capacity' in the communities.

As pointed out by Murphree (1991), the tragedy of managing common property resources in Zimbabwe is the failure by both the colonial and post-Independence governments to consider the option of communally-based natural resource management. What is required is the establishment of communal property regimes by defined groups in defined areas with the rights of exclusion and inclusion. Such management would be possible if the groups involved had 'proprietorship' of the natural resources concerned. This means having user rights, including the right to decide whether to use the resource at all, the right to determine the mode and extent of use, and the right to benefit fully from the exploitation in the way they choose. This implies the state renouncing considerable authority and responsibility.

## Outline of the book

*Managing Common Property in an Age of Globalisation* is divided into two sections. Section One deals with issues of local participation in the management of common property resources. The authors in this section give primacy to local participation in dealing with issues of common property management. They search for local solutions to global common property problems. Using examples from Zimbabwe, they discuss the role of various actors such as the state, the non-governmental sector, and communities in the management of common property resources. The overall conclusion drawn by the contributions is that attempts to give local communities the power to manage their own resources have been piecemeal with very few translating into the meaningful empowerment of local people by devolving real power to the grassroots.

In Chapter One, Masiiwa asserts that due to decades of colonial rule, which created exclusion policies for rural communities, communal farmers are still marginalised with regard to decision-making about common property issues. Although the new (1980) government of Zimbabwe made attempts to redress the common property management problems by empowering communal farmers through land redistribution, reforms of property rights, and the devolution of political power to local authorities, the desired objective of empowering the communal farmers has not been achieved. Neither has management of the commons improved, as evidenced by the ever-increasing land degradation taking place in the communal areas.

Manzungu's contention in Chapter Two is forthright: 'there can be no substitute for local solutions'. He argues that the international principles of water management such as the Rio-Dublin Principles, which were adopted in Zimbabwe, are not workable and will remain global rhetoric unless or until they are embedded in local realities. For instance, the principle of water as an economic good may well further marginalise the already marginalised, as many people cannot afford to pay for the full cost of water. Furthermore, the principle of stakeholder participation remains an ideal. This is because there is no clear conceptualisation of the notion of participation or how it will work in practice given the differences among stakeholders due to variations in their socio-economic status. Effective and efficient water resource management requires local solutions that will link water management problems to the global environment.

In Chapter Three, Matose argues that access to resources around the forest reserve is complex because not only is it embedded in social and power relations, but it is also dynamic. Forest reserves are sites of complex institutional arrangements for different resources. Around each site are groups of different stakeholders for attempting to gain access to and control over the resources through enmeshed institutional arrangements. In practice, formal institutions are a reflection of different stakeholders' interests in certain resources. Institutional arrangements around forests are always changing due to the situated behaviours of these resource users at different sites, depending on the value they place on the resources at any given time. Local level arrangements and authority systems represent arenas for negotiation by different users and interests within villages on the one hand and with the state through the Forestry Commission on the other. Some resources end up being accessed through covert means while others are accessed overtly, thereby contributing to the development of different types of relationship between forest authorities and resource users.

In Chapter Four, Shoko discusses transboundary resource management with reference to small-scale mining and alluvial gold panning in the Zambezi basin. This activity is likely to cause tension and/or conflict among riparian states of the Zambezi Basin. For instance, the flooding events (two in as many years in Mozambique and parts of South Africa – 2000-01) have to a large extent been blamed on siltation resulting from such activities. The boundaries between states are therefore often tinderboxes; places where conflicts and hostilities may erupt. Shoko observes that transboundary natural resource management offers opportunities for a holistic regional and international natural resource management approach. These operations should be conducted within a legal and institutional framework that is modified to incorporate traditional and customary governance. He suggests a grassroots governance structure for the management and use of these commons. The policy framework within which this activity is carried out should be informed by the overall distribution of economic, social and environmental costs and benefits among the principal stakeholders (government, miners, and local communities) and could be based on customary and traditional laws, and other governance structures.

Chapter Five, by Mamimine, is a critique of Zimbabwe's Communal Area Management Programme for Indigenous Resources (CAMPFIRE). Despite its other successes, CAMPFIRE has not succeeded in decentralising and devolving the ownership and management of natural resources to grassroots institutions. This remains the preserve of rural district councils (RDCs), which are designated by law as the 'appropriate authority' for the management of natural resources within their areas of jurisdiction. The justification for the lack of devolution of power over natural resources to lower levels has often been related to the fact that there is lack of capacity at lower levels. Mamimine describes this as a myth, as not only is there capacity in the form of traditional values, customs and indigenous knowledge, but also the perceptions of lack of capacity at grassroots levels are only a reflection of lack of commitment to devolution. For example, substantial donor money was poured in the capacity-building projects.

The Manyuchi Fisheries Project in Mwenezi District of Masvingo province, as presented by Sanyanga in Chapter Six, is a modified model of CAMPFIRE. The project provides three alternative ways of implementing CAMPFIRE: diversifying from the traditional concern with wildlife (large mammals) to common fisheries; the involvement of all actors (local communities, local authorities, government and non-governmental organisations, and the donor) in the consultative process; and the direct involvement of local communities in the formulation and implementation of the project through a trust. The creation of a trust ensured that the council played a minimal role. Although it remains to be seen whether this project will evolve into an improved CAMPFIRE, as it is still in its infancy, the conditions for achievement are present, the most important being that the community has been given primary management of the project and thus the state's role has been reduced.

Section Two is concerned with issues of transboundary management of common property resources. The chapters in this section focus on the problems associated with transboundary common property resources and looks at possibilities for their resolution.

When dealing with issues of transboundary resource management, the unit of management should be regional. This is the point made by Vassileva in Chapter Seven. This approach should, however, include wide participation by local communities, this being the only way to ensure the sustainability of resource use. Physical planning is also a prerequisite as physical plans provide a reliable basis upon which common policies can be negotiated.

In Chapter Eight, Muzondo tackles an oft-neglected aspect of common property management, that is its geographical representation and spatial location *vis-à-vis* the population it serves. This is a result of the absence of relevant technology, such as

Geographical Information Systems (GIS). GIS is increasingly becoming one of the most important tools in common property management, especially in developed countries. Southern Africa still lags behind in its use of this technology. The SADC region can, however, use GIS applications in its forest, wildlife, pastures and water resources management.

In Chapter Nine, Chikowore observes that the challenges posed by transboundary resources in the SADC region have been addressed on a regional scale, through mutually agreed regional action plans. He argues, however, that efforts still need to be made to involve the poorer and poorest communities in the region through targeted programmes that focus on environmental challenges. While international conventions, treaties and agreements on, for instance, biodiversity conservation, have been adopted, the challenge remains to transform these into reality at the national level.

Mudiwa takes up this issue in Chapter Ten. He argues that the problem of managing common property resources globally arises from the tension between the uneven distribution of biological resources on the one hand and the technology needed to successfully exploit them commercially on the other. Developing countries possess the biological resources while developed countries have almost unlimited access to them because they possess superior technology. Thus the latter are often the first to exploit such resources, justifying acquisition through the concept of 'common heritage' used for the benefit of 'all mankind', and ownership through the concept of 'intellectual property rights'. Once the resource(s) have been processed, developed countries re-define the products as their 'private possession' and have laws (originating in developed countries) on their side to protect their interests.

The author suggests how such problems could be overcome. Developing nations must function as a voting block if they want to influence the development of international law. In this regard the nationstate should play a key role. At local level Mudiwa suggests that, the problems associated with definitions of 'community' notwithstanding, such collectivities should be constituted as 'private owners' of the resources within their environs. This could be done through registering communities as companies/trusts or having some members of the community registering a company/trust in which all members of the community have shares. Such an initiative should, however, be accompanied by awareness training among rural communities, so that they more easily understand the implications of globalisation on their resources and livelihoods.

## References

Berkes, F. and M.T. Farvar (1989). 'Introduction and overview in F. Berkes (ed.). *Common property resources: ecology and community-based sustainable development*. London, Belhaven Press.

——— (1989). 'Cooperation from the perspective of human ecology'. Ibid.

Bromely, D.W. (1989). *Economic interests and institutions: the conceptual foundations of public policy*. Oxford, Blackwell.

Clarke, J. and Y. Katerere (1994). *Building on indigenous natural resource management: Forestry practices in Zimbabwe's communal lands.* Harare, Forestry Commission.

Cousins, B. (2000). 'Tenure and common property resources in Africa', in Toulmin, C. and J. Quan (eds). *Evolving land right, policy and tenure in Africa.* London, DFID/IIED/NRI.

Fortmann L.P. and C. and Nhira (1992). *Local management of trees and woodland resources in Zimbabwe* Harare. CASS, University of Zimbabwe

Giddens., A. (1991). *Modernity and self-identity: self and society in the late modern age.* Cambridge, Polity Press.

Hardin, G. (1968). 'The tragedy of the commons', *Science*, No. 162, p. 1243-48.

Henriot, P.J. (2001). 'Africa in the age of globalisation: what is our future?' Paper presented at a conference on Land and Globalisation in Africa: Challenges for the Continent at Arupe College, 13 March.

Hobane, P. (1999). The commercialisation of gonimbrasia belina in Bulilimamagwe district: Problems and prospects. Unpublished M.Phil. Thesis, University of Zimbabwe.

Kurien, J. (1998). *Small-scale fisheries in the context of globalisation*. Thiruvananthapuram, Centre for Development Studies.

McCay, B.J. and J.M. Acheson (1987). *The question of the commons: the culture and ecology of communal resources*. Tucson, University of Arizona Press.

Makoa, F.K. (2001). 'Globalisation and democracy with reference to Eastern and Southern Africa , *Journal of Social Development in Africa,* No. 16 (1), p. 125-142.

Mamimine, P.W. and S. Mandivengerei (2001). *Traditional and modern institutions of governance in community-based natural resource management*. Harare, CASS, University of Zimbabwe.

Moran, A. (2000). Globalisation and the environment. An address to the 5th Annual Conference on International Trade and Research, 27 October.

Mugabe, P.H., H. Hamudikuwanda and K. Marovanidze (2001). *Governance of grazing lands and schemes in Zimbabwe with emphasis in Masvingo province*. Harare, CASS, University of Zimbabwe.

Murombedzi, J. (1994). The dynamics of conflict in environmental policy in the context of the CAMPFIRE programme. Unpublished Ph.D. Thesis: CASS, University of Zimbabwe.

——— (1997). *The implications of the Land Tenure Commission Rural Land Tenure Systems, renewable resources and development in Zimbabwe*. Harare, CASS, University of Zimbabwe.

Murphree, M.W. (1990). *Decentralising the proprietorship of wildlife resources in Zimbabwe's communal lands*. Harare, CASS, University of Zimbabwe.

——— (1991). *Communities as institutions for resource management.* Harare, CASS, University of Zimbabwe.

——— and D.H.M. Cumming (1991). *Savanna land use: policy and practice in Zimbabwe.* UNESCO/IUBS/CEC Workshop on Economic Driving Forces and Constraints in Savanna Land Use' Paris, UNESCO.

Ostrom, E. (1990). *Governing the commons: the evolution of institutions for collective action.* New York, Cambridge University Press.

Owolabi, K.A. (2001). 'Globalisation, Americanisation and western imperialism', *Journal of Social Development in Africa.* No.16 (2), p. 71-92.

Rukuni, M. (ed.) (1994). *Report of the commission of inquiry into appropriate agricultural systems.* Government of Zimbabwe, Harare.

Scoones, I. and F. Matose (1993). 'Local woodland management: constraints and opportunities for sustainable resource management' in Bradley, P.N. and K. McNamara (eds). *Living with Trees: Policies for Forestry Management in Zimbabwe*. Washington D.C., The World Bank.

# Section 1

# Local participation and the commons in Zimbabwe

# Chapter 1

# Common property rights and the empowerment of communal farmers in Zimbabwe: institutional legal frameworks and policy challenges under globalisation

*Medicine Masiiwa*

## Introduction

Zimbabwe, like the majority of countries in Southern Africa, has a weak industrial base. Its people therefore largely depend on the direct exploitation and use of natural resources such as land for survival. In such a situation, ownership and user rights for these resources inevitably become key political issues. Almost a century of colonial rule resulted in the systematic political and economic subordination of rural communities, who still constitute over 70 per cent of the country's population. Resource ownership patterns and political power were skewed in favour of the white minority settlers at the expense of the black majority, who account for over 98 per cent of the national population. This legacy still casts a dark shadow on Zimbabwe's socio-political landscape, as attested by the current controversial land reform programme.

The combination of lack of authority over local resources and increasing population density has resulted in serious environmental problems in communal areas. Communal areas represent areas that were formerly known as tribal trust lands, enclaves for blacks. At Independence in 1980, the new government sought to empower communal farmers through land redistribution, property rights reforms and the devolution of political power to local authorities. These measures were seen as necessary to enable communal farmers to effectively manage local resources in a sustainable manner. The empowerment strategies, however, have yielded very little. Communal farmers are still politically weak. They do not make significant decisions concerning management of the commons. Environmental degradation is a common feature in communal areas, and is exacerbated by state-inspired, inappropriate resource management philosophies and methods. In turn, this environmental degradation threatens the livelihoods of the affected communities. This chapter notes that solutions to redress the current problems have been conceived in terms of access to agricultural land and an unfortunate ignoring of the proprietorship of biological resources in general. The same issues can be said to apply to those resettlement areas where common property resources are found, such as the A1 model in which farmers have access to individual plots for cultivation but share a common grazing area.

This chapter examines the efforts, achievements and failures by post-colonial Zimbabwe to empower communal farmers through common property rights reforms. It also outlines the likely problems and challenges brought about by the process of globalisation. The focus on land is because it is the primary socio-economic resource for communal farmers. Land under common property rights is also home to various species of fauna and flora (biological resources) that are now a source of controversy and heated debate, thanks to globalisation. This chapter also takes a closer look at problems of access, use and benefit-sharing of biological resources between communal farmers, the state and transnational corporations. At the national level, biological resources can be categorised as national common property. Yet from the perspective of an international institutional framework, they can be categorised as global commons. This dichotomy, however, tends to produce contradictions in the utilisation and management of these resources (see Mudiwa, this volume).

## Property and resource management regimes

According to MacPherson (1978) property refers to an enforceable right of a person or persons to some use or benefit of something. It is therefore a political relationship between people. It is a dynamic institution, constantly changing as relationships between people change. Since property rights define the relationship between people with respect to a particular thing, they define the behaviour of persons regarding it. Thus, property rights refer to rules of access and exclusion as well as to rules regulating its use (Murombedzi, 1994). A resource is a structure of rights and duties characterising the relationship of individuals to one another with respect to that particular resource (Bromely and Cernea, 1989). In order to manage resources, a set of dynamic institutional arrangements must be put in place. These institutions must, among other things, be able to develop and define rules of access and exclusion.

It has been said that there are four distinct forms of property rights in natural resources. These are state property, private property, common property and non-property (open access). State property refers to the ownership and control over use of natural resources by the state. The state thus has the sole right to exclude individuals or groups of people from using natural resources. Examples of state property in southern Africa are national parks, national forests, rivers and dams. Private property rights (private ownership) refer to the right of an individual or corporate body to exclude other individuals or groups of people from the use or benefit of something. Private ownership is the most popular form of property rights in capitalist economies and is usually attributed to the current industrial and commercial development levels in western countries.

Open access or non-property regimes refer to situations in which there are no property rights and hence no institutional arrangements to regulate access and use (Murombedzi, 1994). Bromley and Cernea (1989) defined open access as a situation where each potential user has complete autonomy with respect to the use of the resource since no one has the ability to keep others out. Natural resources are therefore subject to the rule of 'capture' and belong to no one until they become someone's physical possession. There are no property rights in this regime; there is only possession.

Common property rights refer to private property for the group. Each and every member of the group is guaranteed the right that they may not be excluded from the use of the resources within the jurisdiction of the group. The group has the sole rights to exclude other groups and individuals from use or benefits of its resources. Informal social-legal relations usually regulate access, use and benefit rules. For instance, it is expected that people take from nature only what they need and leave the rest to nature and others. Common property rights, like private property, are individual rights because they are guarantees to the individual (MacPherson, 1978). However, if common property is not correctly administered, it can easily develop problems of uncontrolled access and use. These problems are characteristic of open access.

Communal lands in Zimbabwe do not lend themselves to easy categorisation. Legally, as will be argued below, they are state property while in practice they are common property, as traditional leaders and their subjects consider certain pieces of land as their own. However, in some cases communal lands can be transformed into open access where the traditional legal system breaks down for one reason or another.

Common property management invariably involves more than one individual, which raises the notion of a community. The controversy around the definition of a community needs no introduction. The term community in this study refers to the ensemble of a geographically specified local population, e.g. a village. Communal farmers are rural families who derive their livelihoods from farming by using family labour. In this paper, they are also referred to as farming households.

## Access to land in Zimbabwe: A historical overview

### *Before independence*

In pre-colonial Zimbabwe, both Shona and Ndebele people, the two major tribal groupings in the country, practised developed forms of government. The former group's local government was influenced by its agricultural and pastoral activities while the latter group's military organisation made a decisive imprint on its local structures. In both cases, the nucleus of the government was composed of the Chief, who was supported by councillors and headmen. Sustainable common property management methods were employed at local community level. There was informal understanding in the community as to how, when, and by whom resources would be used. Customary law regulated the timing and intensity of grazing, fruit harvesting, the cutting down of trees as well as hunting and gathering. One positive aspect to this management system was that communities were at once owners, administrators and managers of their own resources. This created a strong sense of ownership and responsibility, which fostered sustainable management methods.

The colonial conquest of the country by the British in the late 1880s destroyed these systems and subordinated the African people both politically and economically. Economic subordination began with the passing of the Land Apportionment Act in 1930, which formalised racial separation of land. Africans lost substantial economic power as they were driven to marginal areas with inherently poor soils and erratic rainfall. Although farming was part of their livelihoods, and the sole source of their food and income, a series of repressive legislation prohibited them from participating in the mainstream of the economy. While political subordination had started with the actual colonialisation in 1889, it was intensified with the passing of the Native Councils Act in 1937. This Act formalised the separation of local government into racially separated structures. The powers of traditional leaders to administer common property were significantly cut back. Traditional leadership became directly subordinate to central government through the Native Commissioner. A major impact of the Land Apportionment Act and National Councils Act was that they took away from traditional local structures the power to effectively administer land issues and allow communities to manage their resources. Common property management was no longer through community participation but through rigid and draconian measures from central government. Chiefs and headmen were given the unpopular tasks of crime prevention, tax collection, maintenance, and the enforcement of stringent environmental laws. This resulted in traditional leadership becoming less popular, and alienated it from the people as it became associated with the colonial government. Many chiefs and headmen remained on the side of the colonial regime during the liberation struggle.

### *After independence*

At independence in 1980, land ownership was skewed in favour of minority white settlers. About 4,500 large-scale commercial farmers owned about 15.5 million hectares, i.e. 39 per cent of the total land. In contrast, over one million farming households (constituting more than 70 per cent of the population) in communal areas owned only about 16 million hectares. It is against this background that the new government of Zimbabwe gave land redistribution (i.e. the transfer of land from commercial farmers to the black majority) top priority in 1980.

The first phase of land reform began immediately after independence. The government set itself the target of acquiring 8.3 million hectares from large-scale commercial farmers and resettling 162,000 families between 1982 and 1985. This target, however, was not achieved as government was only able to acquire about 2.1 million hectares of commercial land and resettle only 60,000 families. Further opportunities were lost during the period 1986-90 when only about 450,000 hectares were acquired for the resettlement of about 10,000 families. Lack of financial resources, institutional weaknesses, a dramatic rise in land prices and constitutional constraints were given as major reasons for failing to meet the targets. Land for resettlement at that time was acquired on a 'willing seller, willing buyer' basis, as stipulated by the 1979 constitution formulated at Lancaster House.

While these constraints are fact, it is indisputable that the government missed a crucial opportunity to start the process of empowering communal farmers. It is common knowledge that government could have achieved more, despite insufficient financial resources. In this respect, the government is accused of complacency, lethargy, and lack of political will.

In order to speed up the land redistribution process, the Land Acquisition Act was introduced in 1990. Government was now empowered to forcibly take land for resettlement. Despite these powers, no significant improvement was observed in terms of land redistribution as only about 79,000 families were resettled between 1990 and 1997.

The second phase of the Land Reform and Resettlement Programme was launched in 1999. The aim was to acquire five million hectares to resettle 150,000 families in five years. The programme would start with a two-year inception phase in which 118 farms would be acquired. This plan was, however, overtaken by political events, as war veterans and landless villagers started a wave of invasions of commercial farms in mid 2000. This was after the majority of Zimbabweans rejected the draft constitution, which foresaw the acquisition of commercial farms without the obligation to compensate for the land. Farm invasions were followed by the fast-track resettlement programme, which enabled government to settle people without the provision of infrastructure.

## Empowerment approaches

### *Empowerment through common property rights reform*

Reforms in property rights for natural resources, particularly the strengthening of common property rights, were identified as one of the strategies to empower communal farmers in Zimbabwe. During the colonial period, common property was often confused with that of open access. This apparently led to a general despising of the common property regime as it became associated with inefficiency, wastage and environmental degradation.

In his contribution, 'The tragedy of the commons', Hardin (1968) argued that common property regimes leads to land degradation as each individual farmer seeks to maximise their own gain at the expense of that of the community. He argued that the commons failed to provide any incentive to conserve resources: each herdsman competes at raising as many animals as possible, and in deciding whether to add another animal on the pasture, considers only the benefit that will accrue to him and not the cost that will be shared by all members of the community. Hence the rational choice for each herdsman is to put additional animals on the commons as long as personal gains outweigh personal costs, even if this reduces the number of animals others can raise. It is now no secret that Hardin's theory is based on the flawed understanding that common property is the same as open access.

It maybe in the above context that both colonial and some post-independent African governments (for example, Kenya, Namibia and Zimbabwe) undermined common property rights in their national laws. They hoped that common property rights would vanish as the largely market-driven private tenure system took over. Most African governments went further, appropriating and re-designating valuable local common properties on the assumption that the state was the only proper guardian of such properties. In Zimbabwe, the Tribal Land Act of 1979 was repealed after independence in favour of the Communal Land Act of 1982. This not only vested ownership of customary lands in the President, but also dropped the provision that he hold these in benign trust for the inhabitants of these lands (section 4). In other words, land in communal areas is state property. The Ministry of Local Government is responsible for administering communal land through the Rural District Councils (RDCs). It is, however, important to note that arable and residential land in communal areas is, in practice, held under traditional freehold tenure rights, which give private property rights to the family.

A major step towards reviewing (with the aim of improving) property rights in Zimbabwe was taken when the government formed a commission of inquiry into appropriate agricultural land tenure systems during the period 1993-95 (Rukuni, 1994). This move was generally understood by the people to be the first step towards strengthening national common property rights. It came up with some strong recommendations towards the empowerment of communal farmers, namely:

- Common property rights should be maintained and strengthened by taking the measures necessary to improve legal and administrative mechanisms for the long-term evolution of the system to meet changing needs.
- That traditional private property rights for arable and residential land are secure and this security can improve if the state relinquishes the *de jure* ownership of communal lands.

These recommended measures could have gone a long way to strengthen common property rights in the country had they been implemented. Although they were seriously discussed at the donors' conference for land reform in Zimbabwe in September 1998, nothing seems to have materialised in terms of policy implementation. The recommendations still remain a good starting point, once there is a commitment towards defining common property rights.

### *Empowerment through devolution of political power and institutional strengthening*

Political independence in 1980 came at a time when the centrally-controlled local government institutions in the country had virtually collapsed. The reputations of chiefs and headmen as traditional leaders were also severely dented by their collaboration with the colonial government in the liberation struggle. This left a power vacuum in the administration and management of common property. A lot of environmental damage (indiscriminate cutting down of trees, down-slope ploughing and settlement on water drains) followed as local communities took a free-for-all attitude towards the access and use of local resources.

As punishment for collaborating with the colonial regime, government stripped traditional leaders of some powers in favour of local government. For instance, chiefs and headmen were no longer allowed to allocate land to people. Government also took advantage of this period as the best opportunity to empower rural communities through decentralisation. In a generic sense, decentralisation is the devolution of central state assets and powers to local or private decision-making bodies, such as representative local government, local administrative branches of central government, non-state organisations (NGOs, cooperatives, associations, etc.) or private individuals and corporations. It can be split into deconcentration and privatisation. Deconcentration is the delegation of powers from central government to local branches of the government. The idea is to bring the central state process closer to the population. Apparently, this well-intended process was a contradiction of the Communal Lands Act, 1982 Section 8(2), which gave the President the power to hold communal lands in trust. This partly explains why the decentralisation process was not successful at empowering communal farmers. Privatisation of land through, for example, granting free title to land, has been ruled out by the government on the grounds of anticipated buyouts by rich people from the communal people.

Apart from the Communal Lands Act there are other legal instruments governing communal lands. The Ministry of Local Government was made responsible for administering communal lands in terms of the Rural District Councils Act of 1988. Rural District Councils would execute these functions through Village Development Committees (VIDCOs) and Ward Development Committees (WADCOs). It is noteworthy to state that these were largely party political structures that were not rooted in the social fabric of the various communities. Moreover, there was little in the way of consultation with the people involved, which underlined the undemocratic and illegitimate nature of the structures. The Traditional Leaders Act of 1998 provides for the involvement of traditional leaders in land allocation. This did not in any way empower local communities, for RDCs still remain the overall legal land authority.

It is therefore no wonder that there have been major conflicts regarding the roles of local government and traditional leaders. Whilst, on the one hand, the current national law vested powers of land administration in local government, communal farmers thought that traditional leaders, i.e. chiefs, headmen and kraal heads, were the authentic administrators of common property. Chiefs, headmen and kraal heads are viewed by communal farmers as a kind of authentic, primordial, pre-colonial, indigenous, local and thus entirely appropriate institution of community representation (Ribot, 1999). They have the status of 'administrative magistrate', allowing them to preside over local customary, civil and commercial matters. The conflict between local government and traditional leadership apparently created a power vacuum, which has severely weakened the administration of common property. Due to weak local institutions, common property took on the characteristics of an open access system. Uncontrolled access to resources and widespread abuse of these resources became the order of the day, leading to severe problems of overgrazing, deforestation, soil erosion and many other forms of environmental degradation.

Another problem facing the government's decentralisation programme was the autocratic nature of local government leadership. Local leaders were not elected by the rural communities but were appointed by central government. Political patronage, lack of transparency, and corruption in the appointments was commonplace. The institutions remained upwardly accountable to central state, rather than being downwardly accountable to local populations. A significant number of these institutions had no *modus operandi* for allowing regular elections or other recognisable characteristics of democratic governance. Central government control and the exclusion of women in decision-making was still very evident. The problems spread into the misappropriation of public funds and corruption (see Makumbe, 1998 for a thorough analysis of the decentralisation story in Zimbabwe).

Due to financial constraints, institutions could not efficiently undertake their duties in the manner expected by the local communities. As a result, local communities found local government to not be representative, and corrupt and uninterested in their welfare. As financial problems grew, a feeling that central government used the decentralisation of power as a scapegoat for abandoning its responsibilities crept into the minds of some local leaders (Mukamuri and Mavedzenge 1998). These communities alleged that despite withdrawing from its responsibilities, central government maintained the power to veto decisions taken by local authorities. This undermined working morale and sacrificed ethics. A significant number of administrators who had gained some valuable experience resigned, leaving a power vacuum in the administration.

This vacuum was, in most cases, filled by non-governmental organisations (Johansson and Mlenge 1992). NGOs often came with different philosophies and approaches to developmental issues. Unlike government, NGOs embraced the idea of participation. Participation can be understood as power sharing in decision-making. It must include real devolution of significant powers. Participatory approaches to resource management and development received a great boost from problems resulting from state-society polarity. The participatory approaches emerged from a long history of frustration with failed top-down approaches, and are now common in developmental projects.

### *Conclusion: achievements and failures*

As a way of summarising the efforts made by government to empower communal farmers and other rural communities, it is important to present the salient points that have been uncovered. A starting point is to note that the government has made serious efforts to empower communal farmers through land redistribution, property rights reforms, power devolution, and institutional reforms. However, considering their weak economic and political status, one can safely say that the desired objectives of empowering the communal farmers have not been achieved. Neither has the management of the commons improved, as evidenced by the ever-increasing land degradation occurring in communal areas.

Some of the reasons for these failures lie with the fact that the government used inappropriate strategies to empower communal farmers. The government failed to transfer power formerly vested in the President to local traditional leadership. Vesting the authority over land in the President is not widely accepted by communal farmers, who feel that they must have full authority over communal land for effective resource management. The Land Tenure Commission found out that this is the expectation of communal farmers. Communal lands are regarded as common property (Rukuni, 1994).

Despite the government's shortcomings in the selection of strategies and its lethargy in the implementation of relevant policies, devolution of power to local communities remains the best strategy to empower communal farmers and improve the management of the commons. The government should review its previous failed attempts by means of intensive consultation with rural communities in order to formulate better strategies. Communal farmers would feel respected, confident and more responsible if significant powers to administer and manage common property were vested in them. Local government institutions and institutions of traditional leadership both need further strengthening and, in some cases, streamlining.

As already noted, one such effort was the passing of the Traditional Leaders Act wherein there was an attempt to bring back traditional leaders to the realm of allocating land. Giving more power to traditional leadership should not, however, undermine the role of the state because the state remains the legitimate representative of the community at national level. Moreover, the focus should be on empowering local communities.

It is vital at national level to have a constitution, an organic code and other laws and rules that clearly spell out the division of powers among levels of government, and between representatives and administrators at each level. Local government remains crucial for the management of the commons but reforms are required for it to gain acceptance and recognition by local communities. Democratic and transparent elections should be held and local communities must be free to access the financial records of the RDCs to ensure transparency.

## Challenges posed by globalisation

Globalisation is the fourth most significant process after colonisation, de-colonisation and the Cold War. It comes at a time when the issue of common property rights has yet to be fully addressed in terms of the powers and roles of local communities *vis-à-vis* those of central government, local government and traditional leadership. Globalisation adds complexity to the issues of common property rights and the empowerment of communal farmers. The question of use of biological resources is a case in point. The commons are home to some biological resources that are often categorised as global commons. Any legal and institutional set-up regarding the administration and management of the commons must be placed within the international context of resource management. It must, at the same time, protect the interests of local communities against those of transnational corporations that pose serious threats to biological resources in the South. Zimbabwe already subscribes to multilateral environmental agreements (MEAs) such as the Convention on Biological Diversity (CBD), the United Nations Framework Convention on Climate Change (UNFCCC), the Convention on International Trade in Endangered Species of Wild Fauna and Flora (CITES), and the Convention on Wetlands.

The Convention on Biological Diversity (CBD) invests the state with sovereignty over natural resources and emphasises the importance of local communities in conservation and a sustainable use of biodiversity. The knowledge, innovations, and practices of rural local communities are considered the key to the conservation and sustainable use of biodiversity. National governments are required to respect, preserve, and maintain these elements [Art. 8(j)], to protect customary use of bio-resources [Art. 10(d)], to act according to national law to develop and use traditional and indigenous technologies [Art. 18(4)], and to adopt economically and socially sound measures that act as incentives for the conservation and sustainable use of components of biological diversity [Art. 11]. The cumulative effect of these provisions is to make it mandatory for governments to enact such laws recognising rural commons and local community knowledge systems. In any event, they are entitled to enact such laws to fulfil their obligations under the CBD. Member countries of the CBD are bound to ensure that patents and other intellectual property rights (IPRs) are supportive of the objectives of the Convention and do not undermine them [Art 16(5)]. It is also the view of the World Trade Organisation (WTO), in particular its Trade and Environment Committee, and the EC that the WTO and the CBD should be mutually supportive.

The Convention on International Trade in Endangered Species (CITES) is one organisation largely subscribed to by most Southern African countries. All Southern African Development Community (SADC) members, except Angola and Swaziland, are members of CITES. CITES makes national government recognise that wild fauna and flora, in their many beautiful and varied forms, are an irreplaceable part of the natural systems of the earth and must be protected for present and future generations. The convention also underscores the importance of the people as protectors of their own wild fauna and flora. International co-operation is deemed essential for the protection of certain species of wild fauna and flora against over-exploitation through international trade. Lesotho and South Africa are members of the Wetlands Convention.

Subscribing to these international organisations does have some significant implications for member countries because there are certain rules and obligations that each member must observe. The international rules may have a bearing on the formulation of empowerment strategies at national level. On a positive note, international organisations can provide capacity-building programmes related to the development of national legislation that supports the implementation of conventions and protocols at country level. In international forums such as the World Trade Organisation (WTO), multilateral environmental agreements must push for more favourable terms for the rural commons in Africa and in other developing countries. These organisations can also push for a balance between economic, social, and environmental concerns in order to achieve sustainable development. If used in a pragmatic way, multilateral environmental agreements (MEAs) are sound instruments for achieving the goals of sustainable development, even at national and community level.

The empowerment of communal farmers and other rural communities in Zimbabwe is likely to face serious challenges, as well as problems associated with the implementation of the WTO Agreement on Intellectual Property Rights (TRIPs). Through the use of revolutionary technology known as genetic engineering, scientists can now transfer genetic information from one organism to another, and even across species' boundaries. The resultant organisms are known as genetically modified organisms (GMOs). These are mostly used in farming and the pharmaceutical and food industries. Trade in GMO organisms is emerging as a large and lucrative business with the potential of billions of dollars in profit for the inventor. Transnational corporations (TNCs) and western universities have often taken genetic material from the South, modifying it genetically and patenting the resultant organism for commercial benefit. The controversy about this industry is that whilst the bulk of the biological material needed to create GMOs originates in the southern hemisphere, including Zimbabwe, institutions using and benefiting from GMO technology are exclusively from developed countries. The issue is relevant to communal farmers in Zimbabwe since the biological resources used for GMOs are found in common property areas, which they are supposed to own and manage. Rural communities in the South do not benefit much from GMO patents because the biological resources they conserve are regarded as non-patentable. Yet without their conservation efforts, the huge profits made in GMO technology today would not be possible. The question that needs resolution is to what extent should this conservation work be rewarded. Surely rural communities deserve acknowledgement and compensation for these efforts?

The problem is attributable to the current IPR regime, which acknowledges and rewards formal innovations at the expense of informal innovations. A patentable product, according to the current IPR regime, should meet any one of the following criteria: it should be new, i.e. it should not have been invented by someone earlier; it should involve an inventive step, i.e. it should be non-obvious and capable of industrial application. Thus, the subject of patent should be an invention, and not merely a discovery of something already extant in nature. Traditional commons find it difficult to meet these criteria, explaining why they hardly get any benefits from the patent system. The reform should expand to allow traditional and indigenous communities to apply for patents for their knowledge of the genetic resources that reside in their territory and thus obtain royalties from the use of these resources.

There is a feeling in some developed countries that indigenous cultural achievements and the abundant biodiversity in the South belongs to the common heritage of humankind. This is socially unjust and morally unfair, considering that local communities invest considerable effort and time in preserving this biodiversity. This assumption explains why the commons have become vulnerable to the greater economic and political power of multinational corporations and western universities, who seek functional genetic substances that can be modified and patented. Neem is a case in point, a typical example of such exploitation of local communities (for more examples see Mudiwa, this volume).

Some scientists have gone further, raising questions as to whether traditional and indigenous communities can be authors of intellectual property objects and thus be granted intellectual property rights to genetic resources. They find it conceptually infeasible to regard indigenous communities as capable of producing intellectual property objects and thus entitled to intellectual property rights. Their further argument is that though traditional knowledge is quite useful, it is not the discovery of a single person or group of people. Rather, it is the work of different groups of people in different generations of people who find it difficult to identify the exact person or group that first acquired the piece of knowledge concerned. As a result, it is conceptually difficult for certain communities to claim entitlement to property rights on knowledge systems and related genetic resources.

The challenge facing developing countries, including Zimbabwe, is to come up with an institutional framework that can ensure the following:

- Empowering of rural commons to effectively manage their resources.
- Empowerment policies that do not contradict international rules as stipulated by WTO, CBD, CITES, etc.
- That rural communities of the country have a satisfactory share of benefits accrued from any GMO technology that uses resources from their country.

Rural communities must contest the conventional view of patenting because it belittles the significance and exigency of investment in biodiversity by them. Khalil (1995) argues that the current patenting system is socially unjust because the developing countries derive little or no benefit from their biotic heritage after years of conservation. Rewarding the innovations of western transnational companies at the expense of those by the commons may act as a disincentive for people in the South to utilise natural resources in a sustainable manner. This could also encourage more companies from the North to further exploit biological resources in the South because the practice will be highly profitable (Mies and Shiva, 1993).

Local communities can claim compensation for the investment in another way, i.e. by separating the concepts of authorship and inventiveness within the patenting regime. Since individual creativity in the modern western sense and communal-level innovation do not easily accord, it maybe helpful to justify them in different ways. Local communities can push for a set of legitimate claims based on totally different concepts. They can claim compensation for owning the germ-plasm and technical knowledge, which together act as raw materials for those who process them into merchandisable products. This claim should also lead to compensation in the form of royalties equivalent to those paid for patents. Nonetheless, these suggestions pale into insignificance when issues of capacity are taken into account. It should also be remembered that national governments have not even acknowledged local communities as the owners of resources. Against this backdrop it has to be asked if there is any chance for local communities to benefit from indigenous knowledge.

## Conclusions

The value of natural resources in Zimbabwe is substantial because its people largely depend on these resources for their livelihoods. Equity and tenure of resources, particularly land, are therefore key political issues. The government of Zimbabwe sought to address the colonial legacy of natural resources management through land distribution, property right reforms, and decentralisation. To this extent, the country has made serious attempts to devolve more power to rural communities so that they can effectively manage local resources. However, some power devolution strategies that were used were wrong. Policy commitments have not been matched by actions on the ground. Thus communal farmers have not yet been fully empowered as government policy intended.

The globalisation process comes at a time when the issue of common property management is still problematic. Globalisation will add further complexity to the issue of common property management problems. Because the commons in Zimbabwe (land and rivers for instance) are home to various species of fauna and flora (biological resources, usually regarded as global commons), national debate on common property must develop a global perspective so that the country can prepare itself for the controversial topic of access and benefit-sharing of biological resources.

The current Intellectual Property Rights regime disadvantages developing countries in general, and rural commons in particular, because it does not offer any compensation for the role they play and have played in sustainable resource management and conservation in their localities. For centuries, the rural commons accrued vital knowledge on environmental conservation and conserved rare organisms that are now used as resource material in the food, pharmaceutical, and biotechnology industries. Conversely, western-based transnational corporations are given patents and paid royalties for modification of those genetic resources conserved by the rural commons. This practice acts as a disincentive for sustainable resource management and leads to further exploitation of the rural commons by transnational corporations. It is only through empowerment that the commons can authoritatively manage their resources and fight environmental degradation, hunger and poverty. National governments must develop clear policies that empower the communities and at the same time establish strong institutions capable of implementing these policies. Experience, however, has shown that national governments alone cannot achieve this goal due to limited financial and human capacity. Strong and sincere co-operation between the communities, national governments, and international institutions is needed in order to stop further exploitation of the commons and the marginalisation of the local people.

## References

Bromley, D.W. and M.M. Cernea (1989). *The management of common property and natural resources. Some conceptual and operational fallacies.* Washington D.C., World Bank Paper No. 57.

Chenje, M. and P. Johnson (eds) (1994). *State of the environment in Southern Africa.* SARDC/ IUCN/ SADC.

*Conservation. An Interdisciplinary Analysis of the Values of Medicinal Plants.* Edited by Government of Zimbabwe; Land Reform and Resettlement Programme – Revised Phase II, Harare, 2001.

Hardin, G. (1968). 'The tragedy of the commons' in Baden, A. and D. S. Noonan (eds) *Managing the commons.* Bloomington, Indiana University Press, 1998

Johansson, L. and W. Mlenge (1999/2). Empowering customary community institutions to manage natural resources in Tanzania. Paper presented at the SAREC workshop, People's participation in natural resources in Tanzania, October 5, 1992.

Khalil, M. (1995). 'Biodiversity and the conservation of medicinal plants: issues from the perspective of the developing World' in *Intellectual Property Rights and Biodiversity,* Cambridge, Cambridge University Press.

MacPherson, C.B. (ed). (1978). *Property: mainstream and critical positions.* Toronto, University of Toronto Press.

Makumbe, J. (1998). Democracy and Development in Zimbabwe: contraints of decentralisation. Harare, SAPES.

Mies, M. and V. Shiva (1993). *Ecofeminism.* London, Zed Books.

Moyo, S., P. O'Keefe, and M. Sill (1993). *The Southern African Environment, Profiles for SADC Countries.* London, Earthscan Publications.

Mukamuri B.B. and C. Mavedzenge (1998). 'People and big animals; an evaluation of the CAMPFIRE project in the mid Zambezi Valley'. Report to CIRAD Biodiversity Project, Guruve, Zimbabwe.

Murombedzi, J. C. (1994). The dynamics of conflict in environmental management policy in the context of CAMPFIRE. Unpublished Ph.D. Thesis, University of Zimbabwe, Harare.

——— - (1991). 'Decentralising common property resources management: a case study of the Nyaminyami District Council of Zimbabwe's wildlife management programme'. IIED Paper No. 30, London.

Murphree, M. W. (1994). 'Communities as institutions for resource management' in D. Westyern and R. M. Wright (eds), *Perspectives in community based conservation.* Washington, D.C., Island Press.

——— (1999). Enhancing sustainable use: incentives, politics and science. Paper presented at the Berkeley Workshop on Environmental Politics, Working Paper 2/99. Institute of International Studies, University of California, Berkeley.

Nhira, C. (1998). Land use planning and woodland Management: a case study of local control and regulatory capacity on household and communal woodland resources in Zimbabwe. Institute of Environmental Studies, Working paper 8, University of Zimbabwe, Harare.

Ribot, J. C. (1999). 'Decentralisation, participation and accountability in Sahelian forestry: legal instruments of political-administrative control', *Africa* Vol. 69, No. 1.

Rukuni, M. (1994). Report of the commission of enquiry into appropriate agricultural land tenure systems (vols one and two). Government of Zimbabwe, Harare.

# Chapter 2

# Global rhetoric and local realities: the case of Zimbabwe's water reform[1]

*Emmanuel Manzungu*

## Introduction

The World Water Vision, which was debated and adopted at the Second World Water Forum held in The Hague in the Netherlands in March 2000, set an ambitious global water agenda:

> *Our Vision is a world in which all people have access to safe and sufficient water resources to meet their needs, including food, in ways that maintain the integrity of freshwater ecosystems. The Vision exercise's ultimate purpose is to generate awareness of the water crisis that women and men face and of the possible solutions for addressing it. This awareness will lead to the development of new policies and legislative and institutional frameworks. The world's freshwater resources will be managed in an integrated manner at all levels, from the individual to the international, to serve the interests of humankind and plant earth – effectively, efficiently, and equitably.* (Cosgrove and Rijsberman, 2000: xxix)

By and large the Vision endorsed the Rio-Dublin principles as a vehicle with which sustainable water resource management (WRM) would be achieved. The principles espouse the philosophy and strategy of Integrated Water Resources Management (IWRM) (Chapter

[1] The chapter draws its information from official legal and policy documents. It also draws upon the author's experience as a researcher in aspects of water resource management in Zimbabwe and in southern Africa. The author has worked in three of the seven catchment areas into which Zimbabwe has been divided in order to manage its water, and has also undertaken comparative research in South Africa, Botswana, Lesotho, and Zambia.

18 of Agenda 21), which has heralded a major paradigm shift in the way water resources are supposed to be managed in developed and developing countries alike.

These international trends in water resources management have also influenced water reform processes in the fourteen southern African countries that belong to the Southern African Development Community (SADC).[2] The adoption of the SADC Protocol on Shared Watercourse Systems (1995) and the formulation of the Regional Action Programme (1998-2004) were attempts to make IWRM a regional reality.

The question, however, that we need to ask now is: can the global water agenda effectively engage with local realities in a developing country such as Zimbabwe? This is the question that we seek to address within the context of water reforms in Zimbabwe, a country that appears to have bought into neoliberalism – the doctrine currently driving the global water reform debate. The reforms are based on IWRM as the new management philosophy (Manzungu, 2001a: 99).

This chapter seeks to identify some of the problems associated with localising a global water agenda in Zimbabwe. For example, Rukuni and Jayne (1995) show that in 1999 eighty per cent of all agricultural water was used by some 4,500 white commercial farmers who also cultivated the best agricultural land, in terms of its high fertility and rainfall. In the poorer areas, where the majority of black people are concentrated, malnutrition, hunger, and even starvation were common. Inequality of access to productive resources was the main reason behind both the land and water reform programmes dating back to the 1980s. However, the government's current so called 'fast-track land reform programme', which has seen the expropriation of most white commercial farms,[3] has added a new complexity to water management. This is because commercial farmers have always made an important contribution to the water sector – about 85 per cent of revenue from the sale of agricultural water came from this sector (Manzungu, 2001a). Participants to a workshop *'The Processes and Dynamics of Catchment Management in Zimbabwe'* wondered how the water sector would be financed in the light of the shock treatment it has received (Swatuk, 2002).

The aim of this chapter is not to provide a blueprint for the application of a global water agenda in Zimbabwe, but to caution those responsible that there cannot be a substitute for local solutions in WRM. We shall, therefore, explore issues facing water reform in respect of (a) access to agricultural water by the poor; (b) stakeholder participation; and (c) the application of the notion of water as an economic good.

---

2 Member countries of SADC are Angola, Botswana, Mozambique, Zambia, Zimbabwe, Lesotho, Swaziland, Democratic Republic of Congo, Tanzania, Mauritius, South Africa, Seychelles, Namibia, and Malawi.

3 Information on the extent of the expropriation is scant. However the *Daily News* of 17 August 2002 reports that 90 per cent of white commercial farms have been seized.

It is important to note that Zimbabwe's water reform process was underpinned by two pieces of legislation, namely the Water Act [20:24] and the Zimbabwe National Water Authority Act (ZINWA) [20:25], both promulgated in 1998. The former is meant to provide for the development and utilisation of the country's water resources; the latter established a national water authority, ZINWA, a parastatal organization charged with the responsibility of managing the country's water resources on a commercial basis.

Access to agricultural water by poor disadvantaged people is the litmus test for the new water reforms. Stakeholder participation in water resource management is essentially an issue of governance,[4] one which raises fundamental issues relating to the political space accorded to water users by the state, as well as the power relationships between the different water users. The sequel to the principle of water as an economic good, i.e. water pricing, impacts on the general management of water resources and governance. Full-cost water pricing may result in the further marginalisation of already disadvantaged people, thereby negating any meaningful participation in WRM by them.

In order to discuss these questions this chapter begins by outlining the principles guiding the discourse on water resource management in the international arena as well as in Zimbabwe. The next section considers how these principles are being utilised in Zimbabwe. The final section examines what relevance Zimbabwe's experiences have for countries in southern Africa, many of which are in the process of implementing similar water reforms (Manzungu, 2002).

## Water resources management principles in the international arena

This section examines certain principles of integrated water resources management (as captured by the Rio-Dublin principles and the World Water Vision) since they reveal the origin of the discourse on WRM in Zimbabwe.

### *The Rio-Dublin principles*

As previously stated, international trends in WRM have influenced water reform processes in southern Africa in general and Zimbabwe in particular. Below is a description of key international founding principles (see Box 1).

The logic is that since fresh water is a finite and vulnerable resource, it is necessary that it be managed in a holistic manner, recognising all the characteristics of the hydrological cycle and its interaction with other natural resources and ecosystems. It is also important to realize that water as a resource has natural limits, that human activities

---

4 Indeed it has been said that the water crisis in the world is a crisis of governance (Global Water Partnership, 2000).

**Box 1: Rio-Dublin principles of water resource management**

1. Fresh water is a finite and vulnerable resource, essential for sustaining life, development and the environment.
2. Water development and management should be based on a participatory approach, involving users, planners, and policy-makers at all levels.
3. Women play a central part in the provision, management and safeguarding of water.
4. Water is of economic value in all its competing uses and should be recognised as an economic good.

Source: Global Water Partnership (2000)

significantly affect it, and that there are linkages between upstream and downstream users of water. A holistic institutional approach, which recognises that WRM involves the management of natural systems and the co-ordination between the range of human activities, is therefore needed.

If stakeholder participation in water resource management is to be effective it should be based on:

- Real participation, where stakeholders are part of the decision-making, as well as the initial consultative process.
- Consensus by all stakeholders; in its absence, arbitration and other conflict-resolution mechanisms must be put in place.
- Creating participatory mechanisms and capacity at all levels as a public responsibility.
- The lowest appropriate level, as this is often the only viable management level. The valuable role that women play in WRM should be acknowledged by involving them in decision-making at all levels. There must also be the recognition that women and men are assigned particular social, cultural, and economic roles in society. Including women in decision-making should take account of this fact.

Water is said to be an economic good because it has an economic value and is not a free good. The value of water is in its use-value as well as its intrinsic value.

The full economic cost of water is made up of the full supply cost due to resource management, operating and maintenance expenditures, and capital charges, the opportunity costs from alternative water uses and the economic externalities. The realisation of these facts led to calls for some changes to be made in the way water was viewed. For example full-cost recovery for all water uses unless there are compelling reasons not to do so was recommended. Water demand principles, where water is managed through economic instruments, were also recommended. The need to maintain a balance between financial self-sufficiency and water as a social good, was emphasised. .

*The World Water Vision*

The World Water Vision can be questioned not just on the grounds of its ownership, but also on its contents. Even if one were to believe the rather extravagant claim that the exercise of formulating World Water Vision involved 'many thousands of women and men in an extraordinary participatory exercise over an 18-month period' (Serageldin, 2000), there are still questions begging to be answered. How can such a diverse world, characterised as it is by physical, social, economic, cultural, ecological and political differences, have one vision? The question assumes greater significance if one looks closely at those actions deemed as necessary to achieve the Vision. The five key actions were given as:

1. Involve all stakeholders in integrated management.
2. Move towards full-cost pricing for all human water uses.
3. Increase public funding for research and innovation in the public's interest.
4. Recognise the need for co-operation to improve international basins.
5. Massively increase investments in water.

The relevance of some of the key actions can be doubted. For example, the suggestion of moving towards full-cost water pricing for all human water uses, as captured in action 3 (Cosgrove and Rijsberman, 2000: 54), which hails from one of the Rio-Dublin principles of water being an economic good (see above), was one of the most controversial recommendations contained in the Vision document. In fact, a number of people at the World Water Forum had hoped that water would be affirmed as a basic need and as such be declared a human right, which would put the onus on states to provide domestic water to all people, the poor in particular. There is a related concern. Determining what constitutes 'full-cost water pricing' is not a straightforward matter. Who, in fact, determines the cost structure of this 'full-cost water pricing' and ensures that it is fair for consumers? More practically, what are the consequences for poorer communities' access to water?

Actions 3 and 5 can be said to represent a 'wish list'. It is difficult to envisage massive increased investments in water, not to mention an increase in public funding for research and innovation in the public interest, actually being given priority in developing countries such as Zimbabwe. The spirit behind the intent – actions 1 and 4 – of involving all stakeholders in the management of water resources, and recognising the need for co-operation to improve international basins, is noble. However, the issues involved are complex, as is shown in subsequent paragraphs.

## Overview of Zimbabwe's water resources management principles

The principles that underpin Zimbabwe's water reform process (WRP) must be seen in the context of the rationale for undertaking them. Through the WRP, the Government of Zimbabwe intended to:

- Ensure fair access to water for all Zimbabweans
- Improve the management of water resources
- Increase protection of the environment
- Improve the administration and management of water resources (WRMS, 1998)

To this extent a number of principles were spelt out and are briefly described below. The principles have been combined for the purpose of this discussion.

### *The state owns all water*

The state owns all surface and underground water. (Prior to 1998 groundwater was not regulated.) The concept of 'private water' was prohibited, as was the riparian principle that applied under the 1976 Water Act (Bolding, *et al.*, 1999). Except for primary purposes, being domestic uses such as drinking, cooking and washing, any use of water requires a water permit issued under conditions determined by the state. All uses of water prescribed in the Act as not primary were to be registered. Furthermore, existing boreholes that fell within the prescribed specifications were to be registered as well.

### *Democratisation of the water sector*

All people with an interest in water deployment should be involved in making decisions about its use and management. People in a particular hydrological unit, defined by government officials, constitute a water constituency, as water is managed on a catchment area basis. This is because rivers do not match political or administrative boundaries. People in a hydrological unit have a right to choose their representative(s) in institutions called catchment councils. Under them are sub-catchment councils. Zimbabwe was divided into seven catchment councils made up of all stakeholder groups within a river system. In the past, only water-rights' holders were represented on the then River Boards.

Catchment councils were established in July 1999. They are responsible for (a) allocating water (a function hitherto performed by a centralised state administrative body); (b) producing catchment outline plans; and (c) supervising sub-catchment councils. Catchment councils are supervised by the Zimbabwe National Water Authority, a parastatal that replaced the Department of Water Development (DWD). DWD retained its policy-making function but not its operational responsibilities. Sub-catchment councils are entrusted with the responsibility of managing water at a local level and thus collect the government water levy, pegged at Z$40/ML, as well as rates for their administrative and management functions. The water levy is set by the government while rates are suggested by stakeholder institutions but have to be approved by the government.

*Protection of the environment*

It was stated that the use and development of water resources should be carried out in a way that protects and sustains the environment. People who pollute water resources would pay, in line with the 'polluter pays' principle. ZINWA operationalises this principle by issuing pollution discharge permits.

*Water as an economic good*

Official policy declares that water, in all its different uses, represents an important aspect of Zimbabwe's economy and as such it should be recognised as an economic good. This was viewed as the best way of achieving an efficient and fair use of water while encouraging its conservation and protection. However, the government would have to ensure that the poor and disadvantaged would continue to have fair access to water. According to the Water Act, the Minister is called upon to provide affordable water to the poor.

## Local realities in water resource management in Zimbabwe[5]

This section examines how certain principles regarding the management of water resources, as enunciated in the international arena and in Zimbabwe, are played out in practice. The three issues chosen for scrutiny are, as previously stated: access to agricultural water by poor communities (most of whom are located in rural areas), the principles and practice of stakeholder participation, and the notion of water as an economic good.

*(Poor) Rural communities' access to water*

The degree to which the new laws ensure access to water to formerly poor disadvantaged communities can be considered a barometer of the (lack of) success of the reform. The 1998 Water Act took the positive step of, for example, removing unjust clauses such as the priority date system[6] and the granting of water rights into perpetuity. Allocation of

---

5 Parts of this section draw from Manzungu, 2001.

6 Under this system earlier applications to water, registered with and granted by the responsible authority, had priority over those lodged later. During periods of water scarcity those with a higher priority were by law allowed to take their full share ahead of users with a lower priority.

water permits was decentralised to catchment councils from the Administrative Court, thus, theoretically, giving local communities a chance to participate in the allocation of the precious resource.

Nonetheless, areas of concern remain. For a start, water permits are still attached to land (though not necessarily ownership), which many people do not have. One way round this problem would have been to let communities acquire water permits that are unattached to land as was done in Chile (see Manzungu, *et al.*, 1999). People could then use a part of their water allocation in exchange for investment in irrigation facilities (Bolding, *et al.*, 1999). However, under the present dispensation, this would be in breach of the concept of 'beneficial use of water'. This states that water should be allocated to individuals who demonstrate that they have suitable land for irrigation as well as the financial means to install irrigation facilities that ensure high water use efficiency.

Section 23 (1) of the Water Act states that:

*... in considering applications for permits for the use of water, a catchment council shall:*

*a) in the case of more than one application for the use of the same water, have regard to:*

*i. the need to achieve, as far as possible, an equitable distribution of the available water resources;*

*ii. the needs of each applicant; and*

*iii. the likely economic and social benefits of the proposed use.*

*b) in granting a permit for the use of water for agricultural purposes; have regard to:*

*i. the extent and nature of all land, whenever suitable, irrigable by the water concerned; and*

*ii. the suitability of irrigation of the land concerned; and*

*iii. the efficiency of the proposed method or possible methods of using the water concerned.*

Section (b) effectively pushes the equity issue to the background and is also overly concerned with the technical issues of efficiency of water use. Given that smallholder farmers cannot afford the sophisticated equipment that ensures high water-use efficiencies, it can be said that this regulation contradicts one of the main objectives of water reform: equity. Worse still is the fact that all existing water right holders automatically have their water rights changed to water permits for periods of up to twenty years. In an over-righted catchment this translates to no immediate release of water to the smallholder sector. The only course of action available to smallholder farmers in such a situation is expensive and cumbersome. Section 34(6) of the Water Act says that:

*Before granting an application for a permit relating to water which is being beneficially used by another person, a Catchment Council shall require the applicant to pay to the person*

> *beneficially using the water concerned such compensation as may be agreed by the applicant and such person or failing such agreement, as may be fixed by the Catchment Council.*

While it is commendable that the Act permits personal negotiations concerning compensation, using the Catchment Council as arbiters, this only works in the negotiation of equals. It is unlikely that smallholder farmers can enter into any meaningful dialogue with large-scale commercial farmers and, at the end of it all, be able to provide the required financial compensation. A better approach would have been for the government, through the Water Fund, to provide the money for compensation, in which case the fund would become a genuine water development fund, as was suggested by Zimconsult (1996).

An avenue that would allow disadvantaged communities to have access to cheap water was simultaneously opened and closed. Section 30 (5) of the ZINWA Act says that:

> *... different charges may be fixed in terms of subsection (1) for the sale of water to different classes of persons or for different uses: Provided that, in fixing different charges in respect of different classes of persons, there shall be no discrimination between persons on grounds of race, place of origin, political opinion, colour, creed or gender.*

It is difficult to see any other grounds for instituting differential water pricing than those listed above.

### *Stakeholder participation*

Stakeholder participation in Zimbabwe's water sector seems to be more of a philosophy than an operational concept. This is because no attention has been paid (to the author's knowledge) to how stakeholder participation can be designed and practically effected. Below is an outline of some areas of weakness which need to be attended to if stakeholder participation is to be achieved.

Legally, stakeholder organisations have limited decision-making powers. For example, they play no part in assigning names to the Catchment Councils, determining the membership or setting levels of water rates to be paid (Manzungu, 2001a; Manzungu and Kujinga, in press). Even in cases where the law is clear, lack of knowledge and skills have compromised the stakeholders' effectiveness, particularly in the case of formerly disadvantaged people. For example, Annual General Meetings (AGMs) held in the Save and Gwayi Catchment Councils since 1999 failed to adhere to laid-down procedures and rules (Kujinga, 2001; Manzungu and Kujinga, in press; Manzungu and Manjonjori, 2001). Outgoing officials offered themselves for re-election without seeking a fresh mandate from their constituents. In the Lower Gwayi sub-catchment two meetings were held without the prescribed quorum (Manzungu and Manjonjori, 2001). Moreover, the 'representatives' did not provide any feedback to their constituents. This was worsened by the lack of money with which to undertake such activities.

The use of the English language in the debate did not help matters; there was, as a consequence, minimal contribution from disadvantaged groups (Sithole, 2000; Manzungu, 2001b). Thus, the formerly disadvantaged stakeholders were further disadvantaged through an alien language, alien procedures, lack of information, lack of advisory or educational support, and staff that treated them as if they were totally ignorant.

Another problem area, as hinted at above, was information dissemination. There lacked a good communication strategy (Marimbe and Manzungu, 2002). For example the message was that people should pay for the water. The lack of a clear demarcation of the responsibility for building capacity among the formerly disadvantaged did not help matters. Without a budget of their own, catchment councils did not have the means to spread the message. The relevant ministry had no strategy on information dissemination (Manzungu, 2002).

There was also a conflict of interests. For example, to the disadvantaged people WRM meant the provision of boreholes for clean drinking water as well as access to irrigation water not just in the form of a legal entitlement, but the provision of irrigation infrastructure as well. Incidentally, both the latter fall outside the jurisdiction of catchment and sub-catchment councils, which are mandated to deal with WRM only. Inevitably then, rural people soon became disillusioned when no attention was paid to their concerns.

There was also a failure to take into account existing local organisations that, directly or indirectly, have previously been involved in the water sector. Indeed, it can be argued that the provisions of the Act were never meant to create genuine local organisations. The Act does not, for example, have provision for water user associations below the sub-catchment level. Thus, the Irrigation Management Committees, for years without legal status, which was said to compromise their effectiveness, were not part of the institutional new arrangements.

Power dynamics were shown to influence stakeholder participation. This was demonstrated by the fact that at the sub-catchment and catchment level women were conspicuous by their scarcity or absolute absence. In the Save Catchment Council there is not a single woman representative. The same is true for the Upper Save sub-catchment Council. The Odzi sub-catchment has just one female representative. This was also worsened by the fact that the process of choosing representatives was faulty. Often the representatives were handpicked (Moyo, 2000; Latham, 2002).

### *Water as an economic good*

The reference to water as an economic good has raised both fundamental and practical issues in WRM in Zimbabwe. The problem starts with the meaning of this concept, i.e. what is actually being implied when water is said to be an economic good.

It appears that the phrase has two meanings. The first meaning is that water should not be considered a free good to which no economic value is ascribed. Rather, the use of water incurs a financial cost which has to be met. Until the promulgation of the 1998 Water Act, the popular method was for the state to provide subsidies. It is therefore crucial, according to official thought, that water users pay for the water, hence the talk of cost-recovery. This perhaps was the thrust of the Rio-Dublin principle of water being an economic good.

Another meaning could be to view water as a tradeable good, like any other commodity on the market. This view finds its ideological home among neoliberal economists (see Moore, 1989). The logical manifestation of water as an economic good is the water market. Proponents of water markets have argued that they are useful because they:

- Help users to allocate and use water more efficiently and will therefore re-assess the value of water, giving it a higher rating.
- Encourage crop diversification as they allow farmers to respond with greater flexibility to changing water prices.

In recent years, empirical evidence has shown that these claims are not supported (see Kloezen, 1998, for a fuller discussion). Water specialists have further argued that water is a difficult candidate upon which to apply market principles (Moore, 1989; Saveninje, 2001). Moore (1989), however, shows that economic instruments can provide useful signposts when designing appropriate political actions. It is not clear in which sense Zimbabwe's experts approached the water reform issue.

The lack of a clear definition of water as an economic good is well illustrated when it comes to water pricing, particularly of water in government dams. Water from these is priced in the same way throughout Zimbabwe, this being the national blend price. This represents an average price, which takes into account capital redemption, operation and maintenance costs and allows for cross-subsidies. The blend price, across all catchments, the administrative and management units of WRM, does not hail from economic principles since no cognisance is taken of its abundance or scarcity in a particular catchment. This is well illustrated in the case of the government-built Osborne dam in Manicaland Province. This water was supposed to supply water to the lowveld area as well as the nearby city of Mutare. The city instead opted for the Pungwe water project. The consequence has been that 80 per cent of the water in Osborne dam is unutilised. Despite its relative abundance the water is still priced at Z$350/ML. Arguably, the price of the water should be reduced in order to stimulate greater usage of water from the dam to the financial advantage of ZINWA.

While the Water Act extols the notion of efficiency in the management of water resources, it contains clauses that seem to directly contradict this principle. Take, for example, the principle of 'use it or lose it'. This concept states that once issued a water permit must be used to the fullest. Failure to use all the water may result in that proportion of the unutilised water being re-allocated. Taken to its logical conclusion this applies even if the user has invested in water-saving technologies. Thus there is no incentive to save water since one will be punished for so doing.

Another area of contention is water use priority, which guides water allocation between the different sectors. Priority of use in situations of water scarcity is as follows: primary water, Urban/Industrial/Mining (UIM), and agriculture. The lower rank occupied by agriculture means that industry and mining continue to have priority even if the opportunity cost of using that water lies in agriculture. A suggestion was made that domestic water be de-linked from UIM so that the productive sectors compete for water on the opportunity-cost basis (Figtree Consultants, 1998). This suggestion, which takes account of economic principles, was not accepted, for unclear reasons.

## Conclusions

This chapter began with the observation that Zimbabwe's water laws, which guide the country's water reform process, are founded on Rio-Dublin principles and the World Water Vision. The question that this chapter sought to answer was whether there was a possibility of this global agenda engaging with local realities in Zimbabwe. To answer this, the chapter discussed issues relating to access to water by the poor, stakeholder participation in water resource management, and water as an economic good.

With regard to access to water by rural communities, it was shown that the legal framework contained contradictions that were to the detriment of poor smallholder farmers accessing agricultural water. In the case of stakeholder participation it was noted that the first difficulty emanated from the Act's unclear conceptualization in law and practice. This deficiency resulted in other administrative problems, which were exacerbated by the lack of capacity among many of the stakeholders, particularly those in the rural areas.

Conceptual problems also arose with the notion of water as an economic good. This was manifested in water prices in government dams that flew in the face of economic logic. The same applied to the concept of 'use it or lose it'.

The chapter concludes that operationalising international water resource management principles in Zimbabwe is fraught with difficulties at both the conceptual and administrative level. What Zimbabwe needs are local actions for local problems. Yet the search should not be for blueprints, the focus should rather be on providing principles for local water management while taking global trends into account.

## References

Bolding, A., E. Manzungu and P. van der Zaag (1999). 'A realistic approach to water reform in, Zimbabwe' in E. Manzungu, A. Senzanje and P. van der Zaag (eds) *Water for agriculture in Zimbabwe: policy and management options for the smallholder sector*. Harare, University of Zimbabwe Publications.

Chenje, M. and P. Johnson (eds) (1996). *Water in Southern Africa*. Maseru/Harare, SADC/IUCN/SARDC.

Cosgrove, W. J. and F. R. Rijbersman (2000). *World Water Vision: making water everybody's business,* London, Earthscan Publications.

Figtree Consultants (1998). Impact of removing the priority date system and options for future water management in Zimbabwe. Paper prepared for the Water Resources Management Technical Secretariat, Ministry of Rural Resources and Water Development, Harare.

Global Water Partnership (2000). Integrated Water Resource Management (Technical paper 4). Stockholm/Harare, Technical Advisory Committee, Global Water Partnership.

Kloezen, W. (1998). 'Water markets between Mexican water user associations'. *Water Policy,* 1.

Kujinga, K. (2001). Decentralising water management: an analysis of stakeholder management of water in the Odzi sub-catchment area, Save Catchment Council. Paper presented at the 2nd Waternet/WARFSA Symposium on Integrated water resources management: theory, practice, cases. Cape Town, 30-31 October 2001.

Latham, J. (2002). 'Catchment management: a case study from the Manyame catchment, Zimbabwe' in E. Manzungu (ed.) *The processes and dynamics of catchment management in Zimbabwe.* Harare, Save Africa Publications.

Manzungu, E., A. Senzanje and P. van der Zaag (eds) (1999) *Water for agriculture in Zimbabwe: policy and management options for the smallholder sector.* Harare, University of Zimbabwe Publications.

——— and N. Manjonjori (2001a). A review of the Gwayi Catchment Council. Paper prepared for the Netherlands Embassy in Harare.

——— (2001b). 'A lost opportunity: the case of the water reform debate in the fourth parliament of Zimbabwe'. *Zambezia* Vol. 28 (1).

——— (2001c). More than a headcount: towards strategic stakeholder representation in river basin management in South Africa and Zimbabwe. Paper presented at the 2nd Waternet/WARFSA Symposium on Integrated water resources management: theory, practice, cases. Cape Town 30-31 October 2001.

——— (2002). Multistakeholder platforms in Southern Africa. Part 1:an analysis of emergence. CWP Paper 11. Wageningen University, Wageningen.

——— and K. Kujinga (forthcoming). 'The theory and practice of the governance of water resources in Zimbabwe'. Submitted to *Zambezia*.

Marimbe, S. and E. Manzungu (2002). Challenges of Communicating integrated water resource management in Zimbabwe. Paper presented at the Waternet/Warfsa symposium: Integrating water supply and water demand for sustainable use of water resources. Dar es Salaam, 30-31 October.

Moore, M. (1989). 'The fruits and fallacies of neoliberalism: the case of irrigation policy'. *World development*, 17 (11).

Moyo, M. (2000). Sharing the waters: an analysis of participation in water management reforms in the Mazowe catchment area in Zimbabwe. Unpublished MSc thesis. Wageningen University, Wageningen.

Rukuni, M. and T. S. Jayne (1995). 'Alleviating hunger in Zimbabwe: towards a national food security strategy'. Supplement to *Zambezia*.

Savenije, H. H.G. (2001). Why water is not an ordinary economic good, or why the girl is special. Paper presented at the 2nd Waternet/WARFSA Symposium on Integrated water resources management: theory, practice, cases. Cape Town 30-31 October 2001.

Serageldin, Ismail (2000). 'Word from the chairman of the World Water Commission', in W. J. Cosgrove and F. R. Rijbersman (2000) *World Water Vision: making water everybody's business.* London, Earthscan Publications.

Sithole, B. (2000). Telling it like it is: devolution in the water reform process in Zimbabwe. BASIS CRSP Project.< http://www.dec.org/pdfdocsPNACL420.pdf>

Water Resources Management Strategy (1998). Highlights of changes to the Water Act No. 41 of 1976, Harare, Zimbabwe.

Swatuk. L. A. (2002). 'Summary of discussions', in E. Manzungu (ed.) *The processes and dynamics of catchment management in Zimbabwe.* Harare, Save Africa Publications.

Zimconsult (1996). Water pricing options and implications: case studies paper .Report. Harare, Zimconsult.

# Chapter 3

# Institutional configurations around forest reserves in Zimbabwe[1]

*Frank Matose*

## Introduction

This chapter examines how state institutions seek to change values placed on different forest resources by different forest-users. It focuses on the key question: how do the situated practices of different actors – collectively as a community, or as individuals – influence relations between the state and local people in relation to utilisation of forestry resources? It also examines how institutional configurations in different contexts may influence the development of co-management systems, and which institutional contexts produce which sets of relations, and with what implications for forest management.

In considering the role institutions play in influencing access to resources in forestry reserves in Zimbabwe, this chapter addresses the ways in which different people's actions are constrained by institutions (structure) and, in turn, how actors change the nature of institutions through their actions. This conceptualisation draws from on Giddens (1984). Taking his approach renders the notion of 'community' – often viewed as a panacea for addressing natural resource-use problems in developing countries – as somewhat unhelpful in explaining the practices of different actors in situations where the state is dominant. It is argued that the approach, which give emphasis to the situated behaviour of the actors and reveals how this shapes the nature of resource regulations in relation to access, is

1 This work was supported by joint grants from the Ford Foundation and the International Development Research Centre (IDRC-Canada) to the Forestry Commission of Zimbabwe for 'Strengthening Social Forestry Research Capacity'.

better able to provide us with an understanding of what is actually happening in and around forest reserves. By focusing on 'rules in use' (after Ostrom, 1990), this chapter takes a critical look at institutions and authority systems (Robbins, 1998) around a state property from the perspectives of the social practices of different users and user-groups. Access to resources in forest reserves is complex and embedded in social and power relations; it is, however, also dynamic, due to the constant interplay between agency and structure. Power relations are manifest in many contestations concerning use of forestry resources, and often lead to factionalism and conflicts (Cleaver, 2000) at different levels. While in most cases different actors' access to forest resources in the reserves is influenced by state institutions, enforcement practices tend to be shaped by the prevailing circumstances (cf. Giddens, 1984; Long and Long, 1992; Long and van der Ploeg, 1994).

Fieldwork, on which this chapter is based, was done between April 1997 and October 1999 and was based on interviews[2] (informal, detailed and key informant) as well as from Participatory Rural Appraisal exercises, detailed case studies, and observations. In the case of state institutions, official documents were analysed to complement the interviews and observations. In analysing the role of institutions in influencing access to forest resources, the household level is presented first, followed by the community level and then the state's institutional arrangements. At every level, the evolution of both the organisations and institutions is traced before analysing their contemporary operations in mediating access to resources for different actors. The interface between community- and state-level institutional arrangements, together with the interaction of rules and practice, is critical for sustainable forest management options, and the circumstances in which co-management may or may not work. Finally, some conclusions on the roles of institutions and authority structures in relation to access to forestry resources around state forests are given.

## Background

About 2.4 per cent (9,414 square kilometres) of Zimbabwe's land area is forest land, which is managed on behalf of the state by the Forestry Commission (FC) of Zimbabwe. Two study sites from the indigenous state reserves located in the western part of the country were selected for this study. The first case study area included the Gwayi/Mbembesi Forests (hereafter, Gwayi, for convenience) and is found in the Lupane and Bubi Districts of Matabeleland North Province. To the south, the forest shares the border with Umguza District, while to the south-west lies Tsholotsho District. Each district is subdivided into several wards. It is from two such wards that the two villages for the study in the Gwayi case were selected. This case itself was selected on the basis of being the biggest and

2 Out of the 40 respondents who contributed most of the information presented in the study, twenty-two were Ndebele (55%), nine were Shangwe (22.5% and spoke Ndebele in public places), eight were Shona (20%) and one was of Malawian descent (2.5%).

Figure 1. Map of Zimbabwe showing the case -study sites (Source: VegRis, Forestry Commission)

oldest forest area, at over 180,000 hectares (combined area), having been reserved in 1931 and 1940. The area has a long history of settlement, stretching back before reservation.

The second case study area is Mafungautsi, which is found in the Gokwe South district of the Midlands Province. In Mafungautsi there has been no settlement inside the forest since 1986. However, the area is completely surrounded by communal areas. Large populations in these areas use forest resources. Originally, the forest[3] covered 105,000 hectares but it now covers an area of 82,000 hectares after the rest was ceded to

[3] The 'forests' are defined as dry forests under the Forest Act (19:05, 1949, revised 1996), i.e. not the woodlands outside the demarcated forests.

neighbouring communities in 1978. As in the Gwayi case, two villages from two wards bordering the forest were selected for the study. The first was from Ndhlalambi Ward One, in the north, where I had done previous research and the residents were working officially with the FC in resource-management inside the forest. The second village was selected from Chirima Ward in the south. Here, residents had resisted participating in the FC resource-management project because their land demands had not been recognised.

## Household institutions

What role exists for household-related institutions located around forest reserves in mediating access to resources owned and controlled by the state? Different forestry resources are brought into different homes at household level in different ways. Therefore, it is pertinent to analyse how household members gain access to which resources. In this regard, household labour and task allocation systems are central to the way in which resources are collected for the home. Institutions around the family and marriage are important in shaping who collects what resource within different household types for the purpose of securing their livelihoods.

At household level, familial institutions put pressure on different family members to undertake certain collection activities as part of their role. Family institutions give authority to parents in allocating tasks to other members of a household. Marriage institutions in general, and across the main groups in the study sites, confer authority on husbands over production decisions while wives are charged with the reproduction aspects of their families. Although this division holds generally, each household has its own nuances depending on the presence or absence of a male 'head'. A more aged family, for example, confers different authority on younger members than one that has middle-aged parents. Thus, adult women with the responsibility of cooking for their households take the lead in firewood collection and are assisted by younger females. However, in the villages of Mafungautsi South and Gwayi East in particular, these roles are changing. As the distance from which firewood can be collected increases, up to say five kilometres, young men (in rich and average households) have taken over this role. In such situations firewood is transported by scotch carts. However, for poor and average households without carts, women collect firewood and carry it on their heads. Turning to men's roles within households, young men herd animals as part of the family institutions while older men oversee the general care of the livestock. As such, the latter are involved in the politics over grazing. The case of the teacher in Gwayi East illustrates this household-level arrangement. The man, as the head of that household, is not responsible for the day-to-day taking of livestock for grazing, but when it comes to the 'politics' (negotiations over the use of grazing spaces) of grazing resource use, he is the household member responsible.

However, as state institutional arrangements supersede those at household level, changes take place with regard to access to resources by different household members. In Mafungautsi North some men are now assisting in or have completely taken over the harvesting of thatch grass from women. Likewise, women in average-to-poor households can also be observed cutting poles for the construction of their homes, with male members busy doing piecework for rich households. As distances involved in collecting resources such as thatch grass increase, men take more pronounced roles, just as in the case of firewood collection. There are, however, financial reasons arising from the value of the resource that increase the participation of men, Shangwe men in particular. Through the resource-sharing project that the Shangwe men (through the Resource Management Committee, RMC) control, they have taken over the harvesting and sale of thatch grass from women. One case from Mafungautsi North illustrates this point:

> *One settler man (from a poor household) was observed working together with his wife in harvesting grass from the collection area in the forest. The man receives a permit from the local RMC, from whom he also gets the direction to the collection area (under the project each RMC has its own harvesting areas). The next few days are then spent harvesting, as a family unit, the grass in the forest. Half the bundles (around 25), after about 14 days, are given to the RMC while the other half are taken back home. Once back home, the man then resells them to richer households in the village and beyond. From the sales, the family, through the husband, realises about $800 minimum from selling the grass at $8,00 a bundle. (Field notes)*

The state, through the resource-sharing agreements controlled by men, is thus aiding changes within households over arrangements for resource collection. Where women were the sole harvesters and collectors of thatch grass before the project began in 1994 (Matose, 1994), men are now participating and taking over control of this resource.

In conclusion, it can be said that changes in resource values (in relation to the transaction costs of its collection and, in the case of thatch grass, monetary values derived therefrom) are contributing to shifts in family and marital institutional arrangements for resource collection. More importantly, the situated practices of different actors within households are altering institutionalised patterns of household resource collection. For example, settler men in Mafungautsi North are modifying established systems of thatch grass collection in their favour, i.e. against women, as the resource increases in monetary value and becomes a major source of income for households.

In the next section, my focus shifts to arrangements at 'community'-level.

## 'Community'-level institutions

Beyond household-level arrangements, the social practices, norms, conventions, values and authority systems of the community mediate resource access for different users. In discussing these, the following subsections draw from the typology used by Bruce, *et al.*, (1993).

### *'Sacred controls'*

Within the Gwayi case-study, certain species are not used as firewood, medicines, carving materials, or even poles for constructing fences and other structures because of the beliefs surrounding those species, which are passed from generation to generation. For example, *umphafa*, *ichithamuzi*, *umqhobampunzi*, *umnyelenyele* and *ibhanda*[4] are not supposed to be used for any purpose, especially for firewood. These species are believed to bring bad luck to anyone who uses them and, sometimes, to the wider community. This type of protective institution also applies to certain wildlife species such as eland, pangolin, elephant, and buffalo, which are not supposed to be hunted. Mostly, these are 'royal' species, once reserved for chiefs and kings. However, prohibition on the hunting of these wildlife species at community level changed when the FC tightened hunting arrangements in the late 1980s and 1990s. However, there is still illicit hunting going on, with eland being the favoured species.

Notwithstanding the fact that ownership and management of forests rests with the FC, forest inhabitants and neighbours retain their own environment-related religious practices and attach great importance to the sacred sites they consider their own. These practices revolve around the holding of ceremonies and the performance of rites at certain sacred sites at certain times of the year, as was observed in the case of Mafungautsi North. One of the sites where only a few elders and village heads hold these ceremonies is near Bandakamwe on the eastern part of Mafungautsi Forest, which is also the source of the Lutope River. This area of the forest is deeply revered by the Shangwe people, even those beyond the forest perimeter. Immigrant livestock herders also respect the area out of fear of being abducted by the spirits alleged to reside within it. Legend has it that the area is sometimes awash with 'traditional' music at certain times of the year. Many former forest residents (Shangwe settlers) argue that the Lutope River no longer flows because the elders no longer perform rites at designated pools. It is said that many large pools along the river from which big fish could once be caught have virtually dried up since the eviction of forest residents in 1986. Primarily, it is alleged that all these practices are no longer performed because certain Shangwe elders are now estranged from the forest in which the sacred sites are located; they now live too far away to come and perform the rites. In Gwayi West, revered sites include those around certain trees where rain-making ceremonies are conducted. Rain-making ceremonies are performed before the start of each rainy season.

---

4 The respective Latin nomenclature is: *Ziziphus mucronata*, *Psorospermum febrigum*, *Pseudolachnostylis maprouneifolia*, *Ochna ulchra* and *Lonchocarpus capassa*.

Sacred sites are locations of contested protection systems amongst different groups of people. Authority systems around sacred controls are enmeshed in a system of cultural beliefs in which fear of the spiritual world is significant. The fear of afflictions to one's family or a wider group is an enforcement mechanism. An example from Mafungautsi North illustrates this point:

> *Rains in the 1996-97 agricultural season did not fall in one part of the village. One immigrant family was alleged to have transgressed the sacred site in the forest before the onset of the rains. At the same time, surrounding fields (not more than 2km away) had received good rains and harvested good yields. The immigrant family's neighbours were very unhappy with them to a point where they felt like 'misfits'.*[5]

While in reality that rainy season had been patchy, the coincidence served the purpose of enforcing belief systems around the sacred site in the forest, particularly among immigrants who sometimes do not follow the existing settlers' cultural norms. The case also illustrates the lack of uniformity in belief systems. Immigrants are less likely to follow the sacred controls of settlers given their differences in ethnicity and culture. Likewise, different religious groupings, particularly Christians, generally do not follow the sacred practices of settlers and sometimes even contest them. This was observed in Gwayi East and Mafungautsi North where there are many ethnic groups and cultures in the same locality, which has led to a mixture of belief systems. Settler groups use these sacred controls over parts of the forests in order to retain control over immigrant groups. The 'old' authority systems vested in the *sobhuku*[6] and chiefs also play a part in controlling access to resources such as grazing, fruit trees, thatch grass, medicine, and fibre (string obtained from the bark of trees), although these are also regulated through established social relations. These resources nevertheless lend themselves to a set of relations that are different from all others. In turn, they have their own implications for co-management, given the retention of some 'traditional' authority.

The next section turns to a different set of local-level institutions.

### *Social relations and access to resources*

Bruce, *et al.,* (1993) refer to a type of institution called 'civil contract' around which 'norms of civility' play a major part in regulating behaviour and practice related to resource use. Local versions from the study sites include *kugarisana* (neighbourliness), *ukuncedisana* (mutual assistance), and *kudyidzana* (good relations, reciprocity). These social practices, to which can be added kinship ties and obligations, are important when viewed from the

---

5 Insight from Homera, my research assistant, October 1998.

6 Ndebele. These are clan-based village leaders who are responsible for land allocation and presiding over minor cases within their villages of jurisdiction.

perspective of how different groups of people gain access to certain resources. The resources to which these institutions apply include thatching grass, mushrooms, fruits (only in Mafungautsi North), game meat (as well as other poached resources such as poles and fibre, in the case of Mafungautsi North), grazing and, sometimes, firewood. All these resources entail a level of difficulty or complexity with respect to accessing them, so much so that social practices have minimised the problems. Difficulties can take the form of long distances to collection places inside forests or, as in the case of game meat, constraints imposed by the State or the resource itself. Within such households, women and men who collect these resources rely on these arrangements in order to gain legitimate access to them.

With respect to thatch grass and fruit collection in Mafungautsi North, women group together and mobilise their networks of relations, neighbours and friends to collect resources from forests. Besides thatch grass and fruits (Mafungautsi North only), mushrooms and firewood for stockpiles are also collected through these nested networks of relations. The networks are important both for getting into the forests (either because of distance or because forests are deemed fearsome) as a group and simply for keeping each other company. Each person collects the resource for his or her own household, so collection is still at the individual level, except in the case of thatch grass where high transport costs may entail working as a group to minimise costs.

Mutual-assistance practices concerning grazing vary slightly across all four sites. The practices are carried out to overcome labour shortages in herding livestock during the rainy season, and also to look for livestock for penning in the evenings during the dry season. Thus, neighbours, kin, or friends, take turns to look after each other's livestock. Groupings around herding turns rarely exceed three households while those for collecting resources such as fruits range from five to eight. Members sometimes enter and leave these groupings for various reasons depending on the nature of relations at any time. Groupings tend to be within the same wealth category, but in cases where kinship ties are strong the arrangements cross such boundaries.

There is another set of networks that overcome constraints or difficulties imposed by state institutions over resources such as game meat, poles and fibre (in the case of Mafungautsi North). Mutual assistance is important for surveillance of the forest police's movements when entering the forest to collect and when ferrying these resources from the forest. For game meat, mutual assistance is also used in killing animals. Because the resources are all 'poached' from the forests, groupings rarely exceed five members, although in hunting, groups sometimes extend to ten. The groups tend to be very close – they usually revolve around a core group of kin members. Success in getting the resource often reinforces the strengths of grouping. If any member is caught then he or she is usually the only one apprehended by the forest police. The rest lie low for a while. Such

tactics rely on the strength of these nested networks of relations and social practices. Social practices, norms, and relations around resource use persist beyond the benefits derived because what is at stake is *ukama* (relationships). Friendship, neighbourliness, and kinship ties all last for long periods even though their strengths may weaken at times, particularly when the state becomes too overbearing about resource access.

In practice, these institutions are underlaid by factionalism (after Cleaver, 2000). Factionalism manifests itself in the behaviour of some households within these groupings, taking advantage of networks to enhance their claims on particular resources at particular times. Thus, richer women rely on such networks, for although they are built around the collection of thatching grass these networks are also used to maintain relations with poorer women whose labour they rely on for other activities. Likewise, the older Ndebele groups incorporate immigrant neighbours into their hunting networks, as in the case of Gwayi West. For the old settlers, hunting is part of their cultural identity while the immigrants participate in the networks to gain legitimacy amongst the host groups, particularly in stating the settlers' claims against the state. The fact that those with higher status within the social networks rely on their relations with those of lower status is illustrative of how these sets of institutions are characterised by 'free riding' (cf. Ostrom, 1990). In other words, those in positions of status within the groups of social networks, such as the richer women among thatch grass collectors or the older settler groups within the hunting networks, use their status within the networks to gain access to resources with the help of their lower status relations. As a result, network-related institutions last only as long as they are not underlain by divergent behaviour of a high magnitude, especially by members with higher status.

Now it is necessary to look at authority systems at 'community' level that have been recently formed through the state, and at how these mediate access to forest resources.

### *State-assisted authority systems*

In addition to cultural beliefs, sacred and other types of controls rely on the authority vested in *sobhukus* and chiefs to oversee their maintenance. These longer-established authority structures, which rely on kinship systems and cultural norms, generally play a greater role in mediating access to forest resources, particularly outside forests, than do state-assisted and the more recently established structures. The latter include the Resource Management Committee (in Mafungautsi North), the Forest Residents Associations (in Gwayi), councillors, and ruling party structures.

Those more recently established or state-aided organisations are called upon to mediate resource-access disputes between local people and forest managers. They are not resource custodians, nor do they have any authority over social practices or rules. The organisations are elected by forest residents to represent them and their concerns

before the state. Thus the Residents Associations (RAs) in Gwayi were initially formed as Permit Holders Associations in the 1970s but attained their new name in 1987 when residency permits for tenants stopped being issued. Membership is open to all forest dwellers who collectively elect an RA to represent them in liaisons with forestry officials and vice versa. The Association has a chairperson, a secretary who takes the minutes of every official meeting, a treasurer, and a number of ordinary members to represent each village in a forest area/locality. Whenever an Association ceases to be effective in articulating residents' issues to forestry officials, they are voted out of office through a general meeting. RA membership includes both men and women as well as youth. Since 1993, RAs have had to mediate and negotiate the issue of the relocation of forest residents to the east of the forest. Several meetings were held with residents in order to formulate strategies on how to articulate concerns and to discuss how to have these taken beyond local forest managers. Meetings were also held with local forest managers, the more senior members of the FC hierarchy, and Matebeleland North politicians and administrators, which were essentially against moving residents and for such residents to be 'treated better' by the FC. Forest residents' representatives also happen to be the ruling party leaders. Thus, higher level politicians are called upon when the FC 'tightens' regulations around forest residency and general forest use, as happened in September 1997:

> *Relations between forest residents in Gwayi West and forest managers at Forest Hill worsened when over 20 residents were issued with fines for offences ranging from cutting poles without permits (which were no longer issued) to settling on forest land without permission (when the land was being cleared by former tenants' children who were establishing their own lands). The chairman of RA, after failing to defuse the rising tensions with foresters, then reported the issue to the ruling party hierarchy in the province who in turn, through the governor, had meetings with two members of the FC board who were based in Bulawayo. The board members eventually convened meetings with FC management and set up a committee to look at problems of forest residents throughout Matebeleland and at the same time halted the 'harassment' of forest residents in Gwayi West. That has allowed residents to be given permits for access to several resources as well the withdrawal of the fines that had been served on the over 20 residents.* (Field notes)

Thus, community-level authority structures are called upon at such times to ensure that access to resources is maintained even when the state becomes too overbearing in applying the law. The above case also illustrates how the state has lost control over the RA to the residents since relations changed with the relocation issue (see Matose, 2002). In both Gwayi contexts the representatives are effective in articulating issues to forest administrators and beyond.

In contrast, the Resource Management Committee in Mafungautsi North plays a different role. It is supposed to act as the local monitor of forest-resource use (where the Forest

Protection Unit had that sole role) and to draw up timetables for collection of the agreed resources such as thatch grass, mushrooms and firewood. Thus, in order for a resident of the village to take a resource from the forest, he or she is supposed to first obtain a permit from the RMC. In reality, the RMC is beset with inter-ethnic conflicts and corruption as well as limited capacity due to inadequate training. Consequently, it has tended to be plagued by favouritism, shaped by the agency of Shangwe people to work in their favour in accessing resources from Mafungautsi, to the disadvantage of immigrants in the village.

Given the aforementioned, local-level social practices and authority systems therefore conjoin to mediate access to resources. However, such arrangements are riddled with disputes, conflicts and negotiations over access – a result of the inherent inequalities among forest user-groups. In practice then, rules represent arenas for power relations and politics among different stakeholders as they try to gain access to resources, as observed in the meetings over land and permits, particularly in Gwayi West and Mafungautsi North. Community-level arrangements are nevertheless important for the ways different resource-users access forests, and are reproduced by their actions. They also shape users' opportunities. This was illustrated by the withdrawal of the permit in Gwayi West, and by the several representations by the Mafungautsi North RMC to the forest officer in relation to changing the regulations regarding access to poles and arable land in the forest.

The next section explores how state institutions and authority systems add another layer of complexity to different households' access to forest resources.

## Interactions between state and local institutions regarding forest reserves

Access to resources within forest reserves is regulated by the Forest Act (Chapter 19:05, 1949, revised 1996) – the most significant piece of legislation governing state forests in Zimbabwe (see Matose, 2002). However, access to wildlife resources, which may be present in forest reserves, is regulated by the Parks and Wildlife Act (Chapter 20:14, 1975, revised 1996), which has even more powerful ramifications for forest-users. In reality, formal institutions do not necessarily have as many negative impacts on different households' access to resources as it might appear. The truth is better depicted by the ways power relations operate at the local level in response to the situated actions of different users at different sites. This in fact shapes the ways the institutions are enforced. Institutional arrangements about different resources are, in practice, different, even though formal institutions are supposed to be the same. These are discussed separately under the subsections that follow.

### *Unenforced resources*

The first group of resources are those that are accessed with relatively little difficulty, in relation to the institutional arrangements around their use. The resources include grazing, fruits, firewood, medicines, and mushrooms. In all these cases no permits are required to access them, although in terms of The Forest Act (1996), use is supposed to be with the permission of the FC. Instead, local-level institutions mediate access to these resources. For example, what places to graze and when and which species to use are actually governed through social norms and conventions rather than through state institutions.

These resources could also be placed under Bruce's (1993) typology of 'pragmatic controls' as regards the authority of the state. The resources represent either a non-threatening use, or their use may actually be complementary to state forest management, as in the case of grazing and fuel-load reduction[7]. As a result, forest managers do not issue permits for these resources, nor do they exercise as much surveillance over their use as they do for other resources. These resources are thus more amenable to co-operative management between the state and local people. However, when the economic values of the resources rise, the institutional arrangements tend to change. For example, a firewood sale scheme was devised in 1996, initially in order to mitigate the effects of the drought for forest residents in Gwayi East, but to also rid the forest of materials that would increase the volume of fires in the event of outbreaks. Some households from Gwayi East that participated in the scheme were asked to form co-operatives and were issued with permits by the FC, enabling them to sell firewood to merchants from the city of Bulawayo. The same pattern occurred over commercialised grazing leases in Gwayi forest. Whereas grazing is not normally accessed through permits, grazing leases for large parts of the forest are obtained at a price and a contract agreement is signed between the FC authorities and the lessee. However, when grazing leases were put up for tender, local forest residents were not offered the opportunity to obtain these and, due to the rich cattle owners in Gwayi East, they ended up losing access to their 'traditional' grazing area to the west of the Victoria Falls road. In turn, the loss of access to the grazing area led to the development of poor relations with the forest authorities.

In general, forest managers at local level avoid the unnecessary bureaucratic paperwork associated with the issuing of permits under formal institutions unless the resource in question either has revenue generation potential or is perceived to lead to the 'destruction' of forests. In practice, access to fruits, medicines, mushrooms, grazing and firewood is thus mediated by community- and household-level arrangements rather than through those of the state. These practical institutional arrangements can lead either to the

7 i.e., reducing the possibility of fire because of the reduction of fuel wood that would feed the fire.

development of a *laissez-faire* type of relations between local people and the state or to relations that are more fundamentally co-operative in nature.

Those resources that are mediated by more formal arrangements are discussed next.

### *Forbidden and moderately-enforced resources*

For the next group of resources, state authorities, in line with provisions of the formal institution of the Forest Act, forbid use but issue access permits to users. At the same time, the issue of permits is not regularly enforced and users do not necessarily always access the resources with permits. Poles, honey, *macimbi* (edible worms),[8] fibre, and carving-wood are resources over which such institutional arrangements prevail. The arrangements concerning use of these resources have changed over time. Main poles were for a long time, even up to independence in the early 1980s, not prohibited, except for the use of the favoured commercial tree species. However, with the increase in forestry personnel in the forest areas in the 1980s, permits to access main poles became a requirement in both sites. In Gwayi East, the issuing of permits now takes place at village level but enforcement still lies with the Forest Protection Unit (FPU), on behalf of the FC.

In Gwayi West and Mafungautsi North permits are required and sometimes enforced. A variation for the Mafungautsi North village is that the RMC is supposed to monitor pole requirements in the village and issue permits for the collection only of dry materials. In practice very few households use dry materials and most households now rely on the few settler-households who sell poles for a living. These few supplier-households are kin of members of the RMC who 'turn a blind eye' to the illegal cutting activities of their relations. In Mafungautsi South, access to poles is unfettered, in spite of the formal arrangements that completely prohibit the cutting of poles. Thus there are differences between the two forests in relation to practical arrangements for accessing poles. In Gwayi, permits are required and are sometimes monitored, with adverse effects on household welfare. This was the case in September 1997 when over 20 households were issued with fines ranging from $200 to $5,000 for having cut main poles without permits. On the other hand, the FC had stopped issuing permits to forest residents in the western part of Gwayi as a means of compelling them to relocate to the east. The following year the issuing of permits resumed after mediation by FC board members and the Forest Residents chairperson. When enforcement is low, very few households bother to obtain permits. In most cases only people from poorer households are concerned, perhaps feeling compelled to gain access legally because richer households dominate the institutional structures. Carving materials are not accessed differently from poles but, because of a lack of a peak in their collection, collectors obtain them without permits and are rarely apprehended by the FPU.

---

8 Imbreasia belina.

Honey collection has been viewed negatively by state forest managers (to the extent of being banned) ever since forest reserves began during the colonial period, given the associated use of fire. All the same, herd boys always devised ingenious ways of avoiding detection by forest authorities. One of the major offences under the Forest Act involves the causing of fire: 'Any person who – without authority, in or on a State forest ... (iii) lights or assists in lighting or uses, rekindles or adds fuel to any fire ...'.[9] Be that as it may, honey collection per se is not monitored, rather the people who cause fire without putting it out are those who face prosecution. The felling of trees for purposes of gaining access to honey is also prohibited. However, due to the limited time it takes for a collector to complete the task, it is very rare for honey collectors to be found in situ. Thus the FPU reacts only in the event of an outbreak of fire; they trace the source and if it happens to be a honey collector he is prosecuted under the Forest Act. As the head of the FPU put it, 'we are humane, we know that people also want to survive therefore these little things like honey collection, unless one causes a fire outbreak, we just let them off.'[10]

Authority systems for these resources, where permits are required, are not uniformly applied. Moreover, there are no established patterns. In Mafungautsi North, quite probably because the village lies closer to the main rivers that drain from the forest, the Forest Act – as it relates to injuring or cutting any trees in a state forest – is applied to the fullest degree. The authorities are in constant surveillance of transgressors. In the other three villages, particularly in Gwayi, users of the above-mentioned resources are under much less surveillance. There, enforcement was rather episodic and so random that households accessed the resources as if they were under the same institutional arrangements as the first group. In turn, these institutional configurations led to the development either of co-operative relations amongst different stakeholders or, where enforcement was observed, conflictual relations.

### *Strictly forbidden and highly-enforced resources*

The third type of arrangement takes the form of strict prohibition and high enforcement by and on the part of state authorities. Resources mediated by such arrangements include all commercial forest species, wildlife, arable land, and the felling of trees (in Mafungautsi). The use of these resources is perceived by state forest authorities to lead to the destruction of the forest, hence access to them is strictly prohibited and severe penalties are given to local people who try to gain access.

This group of resources are the main targets of forest conservation practice. Gwayi Forest, as the first to be reserved, was set aside to control exploitation of the three favoured

---

9 Forest Act, Chapter 19:05; Section 78, Subsection (a).

10 Discussion with the Head of the FPU in Bulawayo, October 1997.

tree species by logging companies. Thus the forest reservation, and subsequently the forest law (1949), was aimed at prohibiting the use of teak,[11] mukwa[12] and *umtshibi*[13]. Mafungautsi, on the other hand, was reserved primarily for watershed conservation, such that the removal of tree cover is highly prohibited and regulated. In both sites, settlement and farming are carried out only with the permission of the FC. In the Mafungautsi forest, settlement and farming are unlikely to take place in the foreseeable future due to the protective function of the forest (see Matose, 2002). Wildlife institutions in both sites have been changing since forest reservation in the colonial period right through to post-independence. The historical context of institutional arrangements for each of the resources is discussed next.

Commercially-valued species were first protected under the Tribal Trust Land Forest Produce Act of 1929. However, the prohibitions were applicable in what are now communal areas and commercial farms rather than on forest reserves. Use of these species by residents in and around forests was strictly prohibited, and to the extent that elder members of these communities remember how the first foresters 'educated' them about not felling these trees. In any case, prior to the arrival of foresters these species were, with the exception of mukwa (for medicines and carving utensils) and teak (for sledges, firewood and shade fields and around homes), hardly used. (The low key use of these resources was also due to fear of the colonial forestry administration. Many were afraid of being evicted from forests or being prosecuted.)[14] However, medicinal use of mukwa continued unabated.

Independence in 1980 brought with it euphoria and the feeling that rural people could now do what had previously been prohibited. This, combined with their subsequent long absence from the forests in the mid-1980s, brought about a general dearth in regulations over the use of forest resources from forest reserves. The period saw the use of mukwa for carving being reclaimed by forest residents and communities after a long period of prohibition. However, with the cessation of 'dissident activities'[15] in 1987, the FC authority returned to the forests with vigour. Permits for the cutting of poles were reintroduced and forest patrolling/policing was also increased. In Mafungautsi, the FPU

11 *Baikiaea plurijuga*.

12 *Pterocarpus angolensis*.

13 *Guibortia coleosperma*.

14 Extension officers employed by the state through the RMCs were supposed to provide support and educate, as well as control. Sometimes the emphasis was placed almost exclusively on the latter.

15 A small element of ZAPU, unhappy with the results of the election won by ZANU, purportedly engaged in acts of dissidence. In 1983, the ZANU(PF) government reacted by sending in the Fifth Brigade to Matabeleland. The resulting clamp-down, *gukarahundi*, resulted in an estimated 20,000 dead, and widespread atrocities against the Ndebele people.

was eventually introduced in 1990 and oversaw the prohibition of access to nearly all forest resources. At the same time, people started using prohibited species such as *musenya*[16] for poles, not only for their needs but also as a means of getting back at the FC. The current situation is that in Gwayi, carvers now rely on *Combretum imberbe* where they were once using mukwa, due to the tight regulations around the use of the latter as well as the policing by the FPU. In Mafungautsi covert means are now used for accessing both *musenya* and mukwa for poles and carving materials, respectively. This is in spite of the policing by the FPU.

Wildlife access regulations were fairly 'liberal' at the beginning of forest reservation, i.e. up to the 1960s. Problem animals straying into people's fields could be trapped or hunted until they returned to the forest ridges. From the 1960s, forest residents in Gwayi vividly recall the foresters prohibiting the hunting of problem animals. In Mafungautsi, the liberation war in the 1970s and the hostilities in the 1980s meant that forest authorities did not police access to wild animals for meat. Since 1987, and with the increasing value of wildlife in the 1990s, wildlife policing has been bolstered by a major increase in the size and coverage of the FPU. The main duties of the FPU now seem to revolve around catching wildlife poachers. Wildlife regulations are implemented through the Parks and Wildlife Act of 1975 and the FPU receives regular training from the Department of National Parks and Wildlife Management (DNPWM) in relation to gun use and apprehending poachers. The remaining hunters within communities in turn develop more ingenious methods to elude members of the FPU on patrol.

When forest land was reserved in 1929, at least in the case of Gwayi forest, use of that land came to be only through the permission of the FC. Forest land is still held inviolate. To this day, foresters still view forest residents suspiciously and would, if circumstances allowed it, evict them from Gwayi West. Thus in the early 1980s, in 1987, and from 1993-98, the FC management in Bulawayo burnt people's homes, stopped issuing residency permits, and employed harassment strategies, respectively, in order to move residents from the forest. Forest authorities closely monitor any form of land expansion by forest residents in Gwayi and sometimes the opening of new land by grown up children is prohibited, as happened in September 1997. In Mafungautsi, events outside forest management aided authorities in 'ridding' the forest of residents who were perceived as a threat to the watershed conservation function of the forest (see Matose, 2002). As a result, all forest neighbours' attempts to change the prohibition of farming and settling in the forest continue to be denied by the state authorities. The land issue is not part of the sharing agreement, despite the overwhelming demands by and needs of the forest's neighbours (Matose, 2002). Not surprisingly, this set of configurations has led to the development of conflictual relations between local actors and the state.

---

16 *Erythrophleum africanum*.

Two sets of authority structures are meant to ensure compliance with forest use regulations around reserves. On the ground, patrolling the forests are members of the Forest Protection Unit, who in effect are the 'forest police', while above them is a hierarchy of foresters who manage the forests on a day-to-day basis.

The FPU falls under the section of the Indigenous Resources Division of the Forestry Commission that is responsible for forest protection activities. In Gwayi forest, the unit has around six men who patrol the forest with support from the head of the section and his assistant, whose headquarters are in the forest. Mafungautsi forest also has six men who report to their head of office, who is based at Forest Hill in Gwayi Forest over 200 km to the south-west, through the Gokwe Forestry Extension office. Various members of the FPU point out that they could never possibly cope with the demands of their policing duties. They admit that no matter how many people are employed to police the activities of neighbouring and forest resident communities, people would still get into the forest to obtain whatever resources they wanted, legally or otherwise. This is because people tend to develop ingenious alternatives for gaining access to the forest in response to the unit's success at dealing with their 'old' methods. For example, in 1995 a group of women pretended to be weeping when two members of the FPU came across them in the Mafungautsi forest. When asked why they were weeping, the women claimed to be going to a funeral. However, after walking a short distance from the women, the FPU members were surprised to hear the same women laughing. Eventually, they established that the women had feigned going to a funeral to escape prosecution for collecting clay soil,[17] which they were hiding in bushes nearby. Because of such clever tactics employed by different resource-users at different times and places, the FPU sometimes exercises a policy of stopping and searching nearly everyone they meet in the forests in order to deter illegal activities.

One of the major reasons why the unit is not as effective as it could be is because of the conditions under which it operates. Members of the unit walk very long distances; the sizes of the forests are nearly 200,000 and 82,000 hectares for Gwayi and Mafungautsi respectively. These long distances walked mean that the FPU has to camp in the area of the forest that they will be policing for the duration of the watch, which is usually about three weeks. During this period, they operate like a guerrilla army in order to be as effective as possible. Despite cold winter nights, they put out their fires in order to be less detectable to game poachers. Sometimes their effectiveness is limited by lack of adequate food and water supplies, in which case their mission ends prematurely. The FPU in Gwayi is better supported by virtue of proximity to the headquarters, while those in Mafungautsi work through the Gokwe Forestry Extension office, 30 kilometres away from their base in Lutope camp.

---

17 A particular type of soil found in the forest that is a prohibited resource but favoured for painting walls.

When the FPU enter the part of the forest where they intend to police local activities, they sometimes have to blend into the local community. One of their members usually joins a beer gathering in order to scout for potential informants. Thus a network of paid informants all around each forest is maintained. It is from these informants that the FPU usually traces people's movements and activities, especially those of hunters. In a number of instances they would have failed to apprehend game poachers operating very close to their camps had it not been for these local informants. Unit members also have to walk the same long distances with the poachers they apprehend, in some cases carrying the evidence of poachers' illegal activities with them, which can be a whole carcass of game meat. However, the meat usually provides an incentive for the unit to make arrests as they take it for their own consumption. The head and legs of the slaughtered animal are then used as evidence when the FPU brings charges against the poacher at the nearest police station. Sometimes the FPU embarks on a house-to-house search of all homesteads adjacent to a particular section of the forest in which hunting is known to have recently taken place. It is not unusual for these searches to result in the discovery of many hidden kilograms of meat in granaries.

On the whole, members of the FPU wish the FC could deregulate the collection of a wide variety of forest products for use by different households. This would make their work easier, in the sense that they could focus on major resources such as wild animals and specific tree species.

Nevertheless, the results from a survey in 1994 (Matose, 1994) indicated that only 16.5 per cent of those who used the forest had ever encountered the FPU while in the forest. This contrasted with the 81.8 per cent of respondents who said that they had used forest resources, and had thus been in the forest illegally. This means that the majority of forest-users never come across the FPU, largely because of the FPU's small force in relation to the large sizes of the forests they patrol. This statement from one of the more experienced members of the FPU sums up the picture: 'At the moment people are forced to use some "environmentally damaging methods" to collect certain products because they feel excluded from the forest and it is difficult to control all of them.'[18] In the end, the FPU focuses on what they consider the most valuable resources or the most 'damaging' (the FPU's term) activities to the forest environments and let users have access to the rest.

Communities have very vivid memories of different forest managers in so far as they mediate access to forest resources. This in turn impacts on the nature of relations between the two parties. In both sites, nearly every individual forester or forest manager is remembered for the particular way in which they enforced forest regulations. A forester in Gwayi in the 1960s, for example, is infamous for having enforced the prohibition on

---

18 Discussion with Mafungautsi FPU leader in 1998.

hunting problem animals and also for being anti forest-tenants. Yet another forester in the early 1980s in Gwayi is fondly remembered for having issued permits to forest returnees (officially 'squatters'). A forest manager in Gwayi in the mid-1990s is remembered for having used an approach that was conciliatory in dealing with the issue of residency, though his successors are remembered for having pursued a policy of 'harassment' from 1996-98. As one elderly former tenant put it: 'they don't want to see us here, they want their animals (wildlife) and want residents to get out of the forest.'[19] At the time, the area forest manager and forester were officially harassing forest residents, mostly by denying them permits for all forest resources as a means to 'push them out' of Gwayi West. Similar patterns were observed in Mafungautsi, where tree felling for poles or fibre was not and is not part of the resource-sharing arrangements. However, due to their training in extension methods, forest officers in Mafungautsi tend not to push the FPU to pursue tree poachers. The FPU, on the other hand, are inclined to apprehend all forest-users who fell trees in accordance with the provisions of the Forest Act.

The latter experience illustrates that the enforcement of forest regulations, that is 'rules in practice', is shaped by the authority system and by the styles of individuals, i.e. forestry officials. The actual institutions too are shaped by those individuals charged with their execution and vice versa, depending on how each forester interprets the Forest Act or provisions therein. The more pedantic the forester, the more regulations were followed to the letter of the law and vice versa. Currently, Mafungautsi forest officers seem generally to be less concerned about enforcing forest regulations than about building 'good relations' with forest neighbours so that the neighbours can police the use of resources themselves. Thus, managing forest environments is not their strength. Officers in Gwayi, on the other hand, are more concerned about managing the forest environments, and the resources within them, than they are about managing forest relations with residents and neighbours. Here, managing human interfaces is not their strength. These differences between the two groups of officers relate to the contrasting policy contexts of the two sites. Furthermore, in Gwayi, foresters are appointed on the basis of their knowledge of forestry and the productivity side of forest conservation, while in Mafungautsi, forest managers are appointed from the Extension Division of the FC on the basis of excelling in working with rural communities. Moreover, Mafungautsi is the site of the pilot experimental co-management scheme.

## Conclusions

This chapter has shown that forest reserves are sites of complex institutional arrangements over different forest resources. Around each site are groups of different stakeholders

---

19 Discussion with Gwayi West Councillor in June, 1997.

attempting to gain access to and control over resources through enmeshed institutional arrangements. In practice, formal institutions are a reflection of different stakeholders' interests in certain resources. However, institutional arrangements around forests are constantly changing, a result of the situated behaviours of the resource-users at the different sites, depending on the values placed on the resources at a given time.

The creation of state-sponsored organisations in Gwayi West and Mafungautsi North has added new dimensions to the practice of accessing resources, overlying the existing ones. On one hand, there are mutual-assistance type institutions being used to overcome 'difficulties' in gaining access to some resources, such as game meat, and being invigorated in the process. At the same time, these arrangements are exploited for developing strategies to gain access to prohibited resources. On the other hand, new forms of community-level authority systems reflect the inherent power relations within forest user-groups. Thus, if one takes the case of Mafungautsi North RMC, Shangwe settlers have used it to extend their control over resources in the state forest, through sharing, as well as to maintain their hegemony over immigrants. In the Gwayi West case, recent authority structures have been used to assert local meanings of forest environments to the state. On the whole, local-level arrangements and authority systems represent arenas for negotiation by the different users and interests within villages and, separately, with the state (FC).

Finally, this chapter has provided insights into how, at state level, the practices around formal institutions are shaped by the behaviours of different actors at different levels. What resource is prohibited from use by law and how this translates in practice is shaped both by the actions of the different users of the resource and the vested interests of the different actors within state authority-structures. Prohibitions and enforcement patterns also depend on the policy context and values attached to a resource by forestry officials at a given time. The outcomes of the changes at state level are reflected within the strategies that different resource-users, at local level, then employ to gain access to their means of livelihood and to assert their understandings about forest environments. At the same time it can be discerned that formal institutions necessarily have to be both sensitive to local nuances and robust if they are to articulate the multiple values of different resources at local level in different places. By necessity, therefore, authority systems over the formal institutional arrangements need to be able to cope with the complex and varied needs of the diverse forest-users in different places. Whereas co-management is taking hold globally as a means of resolving conflicts involving state property regimes, the evidence provided in this chapter, from an institutional perspective, points to the addition of another layer of complexity for resource-management by communities, however they are defined. New forms of organisations are emerging that are not necessarily best placed to manage resources.

In this chapter then, it has been demonstrated how access to forest resources for different users and actors is gained through formal and informal institutions and authority systems. This, as the evidence presented herein indicates, has implications as to how certain people gain access to certain resources. Some resources end up being accessed through covert means while others are accessed overtly, thereby contributing to the development of different types of relationships between forest authorities and resource-users.

## References

Bruce, J., L. Fortmann, and C. Nhira (1993). 'Tenures in transition, tenures in conflict: Examples from the Zimbabwe social forest.' *Rural Sociology*, 58 p. 626-42.

Cleaver, F. (2000). 'Moral ecological rationality, institutions and the management of common property resources.' *Development and Change*, 31: 361-83.

Giddens, A. (1984). *The constitution of society: An outline of the theory of structuration*. London, Polity Press.

Long, N. and A. Long (eds) (1992). *Battlefields of knowledge: the Interlocking of theory and practice in social research and development*. London, Routledge.

Long, N. and J.van der Ploeg (1994). 'Heterogeneity, actor and structure: towards a reconstitution of the concept of structure', in D. Booth (ed.) *Rethinking Social Development*. Harlow, Longman.

Matose, F. (1994). Local people's uses and perceptions of forest resources: an analysis of a state property regime in Zimbabwe. Unpublished thesis submitted to the University of Alberta in partial fulfilment for a Master of Science degree.

——— (2002). Local people and reserved forests in Zimbabwe: What prospects for co-management? Thesis submitted for the degree of Doctor of Philosophy in Development Studies, Brighton, University of Sussex.

Ostrom, E. (1990). *Governing the Commons: the Evolution of Institutions for Collective Action*. Cambridge, Cambridge University Press.

Robbins, P. (1998). 'Authority and environment: institutional landscapes in Rajasthan, India'. *Annals of the Association of American Geographers*, 88 , pp. 410-35.

# Chapter 4

# Small-scale mining and alluvial gold panning within the Zambezi Basin: an ecological time-bomb and a tinderbox for future conflicts among riparian states

*Dennis S. M. Shoko*

## Introduction

The Zambezi Basin and its water resources are shared by eight of the fourteen Southern African Development Community (SADC) states. The long-term environmental well-being of the Zambezi River, its tributaries, and associated dams and lakes depend on the types and volumes of economic activity that take place within the basin. These include urbanisation, logging, agriculture, manufacturing, tourism, and mining. More recently, small-scale mining and alluvial gold panning activities have taken centre stage as a result of both the economic structural adjustment programmes (ESAPs) and recurrent droughts within the SADC region. It is estimated that up to two million people directly or indirectly benefit from small-scale and alluvial panning of minerals within the Zambezi Basin. Most of this mining activity takes place on riverbeds and banks and releases enormous amounts of silt and heavy metals into river systems, dams, and lakes. Siltation of rivers reduces river conveyance and the storage capacity of reservoirs, which in turn makes several areas prone to flooding. Other effects of siltation include the shortening of reservoir life-spans, depletion of fisheries, and diminishing of hydropower generation potential. Small-scale miners are also responsible for the clearing of extensive areas of natural forest for firewood and infrastructural construction. Deforestation directly contributes to rapid loss of soil moisture and topsoil, resulting in the disruption of climatic balances and the spread of desertification. This can lead to water scarcity and stress within the region, a sure precursor to conflict between neighbouring states.

This chapter analyses the effects of small-scale mining and alluvial panning on transboundary common property resource management (TBCPRM) and use within the Zambezi Basin. It reviews the major challenges, prospects and obstacles to TBNRM by assessing regional and local legislative and institutional regimes. A grassroots governance structure is suggested for the management and use of transboundary commons. It is argued that policy formulation should be informed by the overall distribution of economic, social and environmental costs, and benefits among the principal stakeholders (governments, miners and local communities) and could be based on customary and traditional governance structures.

An analysis of common property resource management and use has to be appropriately based on a clear definition and identification of what constitutes common property and what constitutes the community. Unfortunately, consultants' reports and project documents are often helplessly vague on these issues (Bruce, 1989). In most cases, and particularly in TBCPRM, the definition and identification of communities is both complex and intricate. Control of resources is primarily associated with geographically-bounded communities where kinship ties buttress territorial ties. Community membership is commonly defined by present or previous residence, property ownership, kinship ties, or by some combination of these factors. Communities are also broadly defined by unitary traditional and customary institutional structures. The definition of community membership determines who may or may not lay any claim to community resources. The limits placed by definition of membership, if they can be enforced, regulate pressure on the resources. Property refers to an enforceable right of a person or persons to some use or benefit from an asset or resource, and can also be defined as a benefit (income) stream, while a property right is a claim to such a benefit stream (Ciriacy-Wantrup and Bishop, 1975). Four property regimes can be differentiated on the basis of the above definitions, i.e. state, private, common and open-access. Property regimes characterised by rights of exclusion are often referred to as private. Common property is a shared resource. The sharing is, however, restricted to a well-defined group of individuals who can exclude access by others. The group shares the resource's beneficial use. Common property rights are a special class of rights that assure each individual's access to resources over which they hold collective claims.

Common property is created when members of an interdependent group agree to limit their individual claim on a resource in the expectation that the other members of the group will do likewise. For a resource to be managed as a common property, each individual confidently relies on every other member's contribution to management. Common property should be restricted to communally-owned resources – that is, those resources for which there exist communal arrangements for the exclusion of non-owners and for the allocation among owners (Gibbs and Bromley, 1989).

Common property resources have also been described as a class of resources for which exclusion is difficult and where joint use involves subtractability (Berkes and Farvar, 1989). The non-property or open-access regime is a situation where no one can lay claim to a particular resource. Every potential user has complete autonomy in respect to use of the resource and nobody has any legal right or ability to keep others out. A natural resource is therefore subject to the rule of capture and basically belongs to no one until it is someone's physical possession. There are, therefore, no property rights but there is property possession (Bromley and Cernea, 1988).

Small-scale mining and particularly alluvial gold panning, as currently structured, is an open-access, non-property regime. This is largely due to the fact that over the years central governments within the SADC region have tended to downplay the existence and/or legitimacy of this sector. Declining regional economic fortunes – caused by a variety of factors – have resulted in the small-scale mining sector employing large numbers of people in recent years. State governments are feeling the pressure to recognise the sector; something they appear to be doing reluctantly. In countries where the existence of the sector is now recognised, the state has either sought direct control or allowed partial devolution of responsibility to local authorities. The governments apply 'command and control' regulations, which are usually enacted for large-scale mining operations. These are usually far too complicated for full compliance by small-scale miners. Paradoxically, central governments have neither the financial nor the human resources to enforce these regulations on small-scale miners. Local communities are also reluctant to incur costs that go together with better management and control of their activities as there are no direct benefit-streams. The result, in the main, is a chaotic, unregulated and poorly-organised small-scale and artisanal mining sector that causes untold environmental degradation, which directly impacts on local communities.

## Overview of small-scale mining

There is as yet no widely accepted definition of artisanal and small-scale mining. The term has been used to cover a broad spectrum of activities – from the army-run Hpakant jade mines in Myanmar, for example, where up to a million miners can be working on one site, to individual *garimpeiros* panning for gold in the remote regions of the Brazilian Amazon, and to former state mining company workers or laid-off private company employees who have organised themselves into co-operatives (MMSD Global Report, 2002). At the other end of the spectrum, particularly in industrialised countries, are the many fairly sophisticated and mechanised small-scale mining activities. In developing countries, most of the small-scale miners (men, women, and children) are rural and poor. In such countries as Bolivia, Colombia, Indonesia, Mali, the Philippines, and Zimbabwe, they participate in the activity seasonally, i.e. when they are not involved in agriculture or if there is a drought.

The activity may be poverty-driven during periods of economic recession, as has happened in countries including Bolivia, Peru, Venezuela, and Zimbabwe.

It has been estimated that in China alone, up to 15 million people may be involved in small-scale mining activities, and that worldwide there are between 80 and 100 million people who have their livelihoods directly affected by small-scale mining activities.

The problems associated with small-scale mining are numerous and fairly common to all developing countries. They range from the disruption of local community life, conflict over land (which, in the case of Brazil's Yanomani Indians, resulted in the death of about 1,500 people during a gold rush in 1987), and numerous environmental impacts that affect the delivery of common property services to local communities.

It is the thesis of this chapter that given the right legal and institutional framework, as well as technical and financial support, small-scale mining can contribute to poverty alleviation through the encouragement of better mining methods for sustainable rural development. The realisation that small-scale mining is largely a poverty-driven economic activity demands a co-ordinated and collaborative approach from all stakeholders that is geared towards poverty alleviation, improving knowledge and skills, as well as improving the mining system, from production to marketing. This requires co-operation by national governments, the mining industry, NGOs and donor organisations, and local communities, as well as the small-scale miners themselves.

Small-scale mining is commonly associated with informal, unregulated, under-capitalised and under-equipped mining operations, where technical and management skills are lacking. It is also believed to erratically produce limited amounts of minerals from uncertain reserves. While small-scale mining can lead to wastage of non-renewable resources and be hazardous to human and environmental health, it can also contribute to national economies and economically empower disadvantaged groups by virtue of both its low investment costs and short lead-time from discovery to production. This sector produces minerals from deposits that are not economically viable at large-scale mining level.

Small-scale mining is labour intensive and thus provides employment and incomes for large numbers of people who are generally uneducated, poor, and living in remote areas where no opportunities exist for formal employment. It is estimated that in the southern African region alone, up to ten million people are employed or benefit directly from small-scale and artisanal mining activities, which involve more than a dozen different types of minerals – dominated by gold and a variety of gemstones. In most of the SADC countries, mining is the only known alternative economic activity to agriculture. The employment figures within this sector increase many-fold during the recurrent droughts. More than 50 per cent of those actively involved in the sector are women and, unfortunately, children. Globally, small-scale miners produce hundreds of thousands of tonnes of gold annually. In countries such as Zimbabwe and Tanzania, small-scale miners contribute up to 25 per cent of the total national gold production. As a poverty-driven economic activity, small-scale mining cannot be wished away.

As already said, small-scale mining sector plays an important complementary role to its large-scale mining counterparts. The former, due to lower overheads and non-costed labour, is able to work the smaller and lower grade mineral deposits considered sub-economic by the latter. In addition to the creation of employment and wealth within rural communities in remote areas, a viable small-scale mining sector will also stem the common rural-urban drift. Thus, a concerted global effort is required to remove the difficulties that hinder the development of this sector. Doing so will ensure that small-scale mining contributes to sustainable development in both developing and developed countries.

The major drawbacks to socio-environmental sustainability within the small-scale mining sector are poverty, population pressure on natural resources, and a lack of knowledge. Indeed, a number of bold measures have to be taken to ensure that small-scale mining is carried out in a way that is economically viable, socially acceptable, and environmentally and ecologically sustainable. The International Labour Organisation (ILO) noted, in a recent resolution, that the lack of resources, skills and knowledge on the part of the small-scale miners meant that their operations suffered from low productivity, inadequate income-generation, and poor safety and working conditions. The resolution called on member states of the ILO and on employers' and workers' organisations to adopt a range of measures that would enable small-scale miners to work more productively, more safely, and with fewer negative environmental impacts.

## *Environmental impacts of small-scale mining on transboundary natural resources*

Small-scale mining operations are always located close to, and are supported by, water bodies. Mining is a geographically concentrated activity that results in a number of negative impacts on immediate as well as distant locations. These effects include water and air pollution, river and dam siltation, and a loss of biodiversity (deforestation, over-fishing and poaching). There are today a number of threatened species within the Zambezi Basin. Others have already become extinct. Some of the negative impacts have caused considerable anxiety and tension among neighbouring countries.

The recent flooding (2000 and 2001) that affected Mozambique, South Africa, and Zimbabwe is believed to have been exacerbated by the siltation and deforestation within certain riparian states. The absence of common water standards means that there will always be disagreement as to what water quality ought to be, or how and where it should be tested. Governance issues within the small-scale mining sector will have to be harmonised in order to create a basin-wide climate of openness and co-operation over water resources and water quality.

Although the environmental impacts of individual operations are not necessarily significant, the accumulated impacts of numerous small-scale mining operations can create serious problems for ecosystems and local communities.

These problems reveal themselves in the form of deterioration and reduction in the quality and amounts of environmental and common property services within and beyond state borders. The most noticeable negative environmental impacts of mining include land disturbance, deforestation, depletion of water resources, and pollution of water and air.

*Land disturbance and siltation*

All operations of small-scale miners lead to considerable land disturbance. For artisanal alluvial gold panning operations, this involves the digging up of river channels and banks, paleo-channels and their floodplains, as well as surface trenching using picks and shovels. In some cases, the mining requires the stripping of overburden to expose the mineral-bearing horizons. The most noticeable effects of these operations are the siltation of rivers and dams, a deterioration of water quality, the reduction of grazing areas for domestic and wild animals, and an overall reduction in biodiversity.

Some of the overburden-stripping may be accomplished by using bulldozers. Rarely are explosives used in small-scale gold and chrome mining. In chrome mining, underground operations require the opening up of adits, vertical shafts, winzes and raises, as well as underground tunnels. Underground openings eventually result in land subsidence.

All methods employed by mining co-operatives result in land disturbance and serious problems of waste disposal. The digging up of river banks and floodplains for alluvial gold panning and the stripping of overburden in the tantalite and chrome operations all result in enormous amounts of waste sand, gravel and rock dumps, which contribute to siltation of river channels and dams. Siltation is reported to be increasing over the last two decades at the rate of more than five per cent per annum in Mozambique, Tanzania, and Zimbabwe (Chiwawa, 1993).

Siltation results in the reduction of conveyance and storage capacities of rivers and dams and is believed to play a major role in the frequency and magnitude of flooding affecting Mozambique, Zimbabwe, and South Africa. It is also responsible for the destruction of habitats for fish and other aquatic organisms.

### *Deforestation*

The rapid sprouting of overnight settlements in newly-discovered gold and gemstone areas leads to rapid 'urbanisation' in the form of haphazard settlements that not only result in rampant deforestation but also social ills associated with urbanisation. These include alcohol and drug abuse, prostitution, land-use conflicts with local communities, water pollution, infant and child labour, and disease epidemics. Deforestation is driven by the need for the construction of shelters, underground support props, panning dishes, and firewood. The excessive reliance on wood as a source of energy results in the reduction of biodiversity and increasing rates of desertification.

It is estimated that about four million tonnes of wood are used every year in Zimbabwe for fuel, which translates to a felling of trees covering approximately 100,000 hectares (Chiwawa, 1993). Habitat destruction and uncontrolled hunting and fishing further threaten biodiversity. The loss of biodiversity (woodlands and grasslands particularly) commonly leads to tension between miners and local communities. The introduction of an exogenous mining community always upsets local traditional and cultural common property management and use systems.

### *Water pollution and depletion*

In alluvial tin, tantalite, and gold mining operations, mineral concentration is achieved by the use of gravity separation, through the medium of water, using panning dishes and sluice boxes.

Absolute dependence on the use of large amounts of water in mining operations dictates that they be located as close to water sources as possible, and in some cases at the water source. Alluvial ore is a result of river deposition and is therefore part of a river system. The reliance on water for mineral concentration results in the accelerated evaporation of surface water, the drainage of wetlands, and the siltation of rivers and dams. As previously mentioned, the siltation of rivers, dams, and lakes has been blamed for frequent flooding of low-lying areas, especially in Mozambique, South Africa, and Zimbabwe.

Some small-scale miners use cyanide and mercury to concentrate and amalgamate gold, which end up polluting water and ecosystems. The emergence of unplanned mining compounds sited close to water-courses, with attendant poor sanitary facilities, also results in considerable pollution from human waste.

In Tanzania, for example, 78 per cent of water samples analysed in the Lake Victoria goldfields contained mercury in concentrations significantly above the drinking water standard of 1g/l (Mpendazoe, 1996). The situation is believed to be similar in countries like Mozambique, Zambia, and Zimbabwe, where the use of mercury by small-scale miners is equally extensive. Mercury is poisonous to humans and aquatic-based food chains through bio-accumulation. The use of cyanide in gold concentration has been responsible for cyanide poisoning of domestic and wild animals.

Ore and waste stockpiles established on the surface commonly contain significant amounts of sulphides and, with the passage of time, heavy metals, sulphates, and other pollutants are dissolved and leached, by precipitation, into local streams and community water sources. The impact of this mineral pollution on an ecosystem may be severe and may result in the total elimination of animal life from the receiving waters. The depletion and pollution of fresh water within the Zambezi Basin by mining activities is bound to have tragic consequences for a sub-region that not only receives relatively little rainfall, but whose extremely high air temperatures and higher rates of evaporation reduce surface water flows in rivers and streams, and provide little recharge to groundwater.

The region is already classified as being water scarce/stressed. The Zambezi Basin riparian states are already competing, directly or indirectly, for maximum possible benefits from the available water resources (for domestic, industrial and hydropower use). It is not inconceivable for water-related conflict or war to be recorded in the region in a matter of a few years, unless regional water management strategies are immediately put in place.

### *Environmental, economic and social costs and benefits*

It would appear that both the quality and degree of commitment to prudent management and use of common property resources is predicated on the overall distribution of costs and benefits (economic, social and environmental) among the stakeholders.

The socio-economic benefits of small-scale mining, which include employment and income generation, are seriously weighed down by devastating environmental costs and impacts. These negative impacts (costs) are imposed on communities downstream of the mining activities. The affected communities are neither involved in the mining activity nor are they included in the mining benefit-streams; they thus suffer the impacts of what are essentially externalities. The small-scale mining sector does not compensate the local communities for their loss of common property services.

Based on the analysis of economic and environmental costs and benefits, a study done in Zimbabwe's Mashonaland West Province showed that alluvial gold panning as presently practiced is not economic when the full range of economic, social and environmental costs are compared with the limited number of benefits (Milne and Marongwe, 1995). The distribution of costs and benefits is an important aspect for policy-makers.

Policy considerations are, in most cases, given to making the beneficiaries compensate the losers (defined in very general terms, and may include the physical environment for example) for such externalities.

It is clear that while the miners receive the lion's share of the benefits of their activities, they do not pay for the social and environmental externalities borne by communities downstream. Governments appear responsible for most of the costs, yet they recover nothing from the miners by way of taxes. This unjustifiably increases government expenditure. Increased government expenditures are not without penalties for society.

Costs to society include either increased internal and external borrowing or pressure on domestic interests rates and balance of payments, or difficult trade-offs by reducing spending in other programmes such as health or education. Where funds are borrowed, the question of debt-servicing and the impact this has on current expenditures must be raised.

Gold-panning represents a classic case of externalities caused by inappropriate natural resource extraction. Any policy formulation option for alluvial gold panning activities must take into account the fact that miners should be made to take more or increasing responsibility for their downstream negative environmental and social impacts within a more appropriate institutional and property regime.

## The Zambezi Basin: an overview

The SADC region, and indeed most regions of the world, shares a range of transboundary natural resources, most of which include river courses, nature reserves and/or protected areas. More often than not, there is no shared vision or standard legislation, nor policies or regulations for the sustainable management and use of these shared resources at national, regional or even international level. Furthermore, there are no established or co-ordinated regional or international institutions for the supervision and enforcement of transboundary resources management or for the resolution of conflicts.

Transboundary natural resource management is concerned with the sustainable use of resources that are shared by various communities domiciled in different countries. The Zambezi Basin and its water resources are shared by eight riparian states in central and southern Africa (Angola, Botswana, Malawi, Mozambique, Namibia, Tanzania, Zambia, and Zimbabwe, as shown in Fig. 1). Riparian states are countries that share a transboundary natural resource.

The total geographic area covered by the SADC countries is approximately 5.08 million square kilometres, of which the Zambezi Basin constitutes approximately 26 per cent. The Zambezi Basin refers to the total area drained by the Zambezi and all its tributaries.

Water is one of the resources most prone to transboundary environmental problems and conflicts. There are more than 300 river basins worldwide (nearly 50 per cent of the Earth's land surface) that are shared by two or more countries. Underscoring the tensions that divided basins engender, nearly 300 international treaties or protocols have been

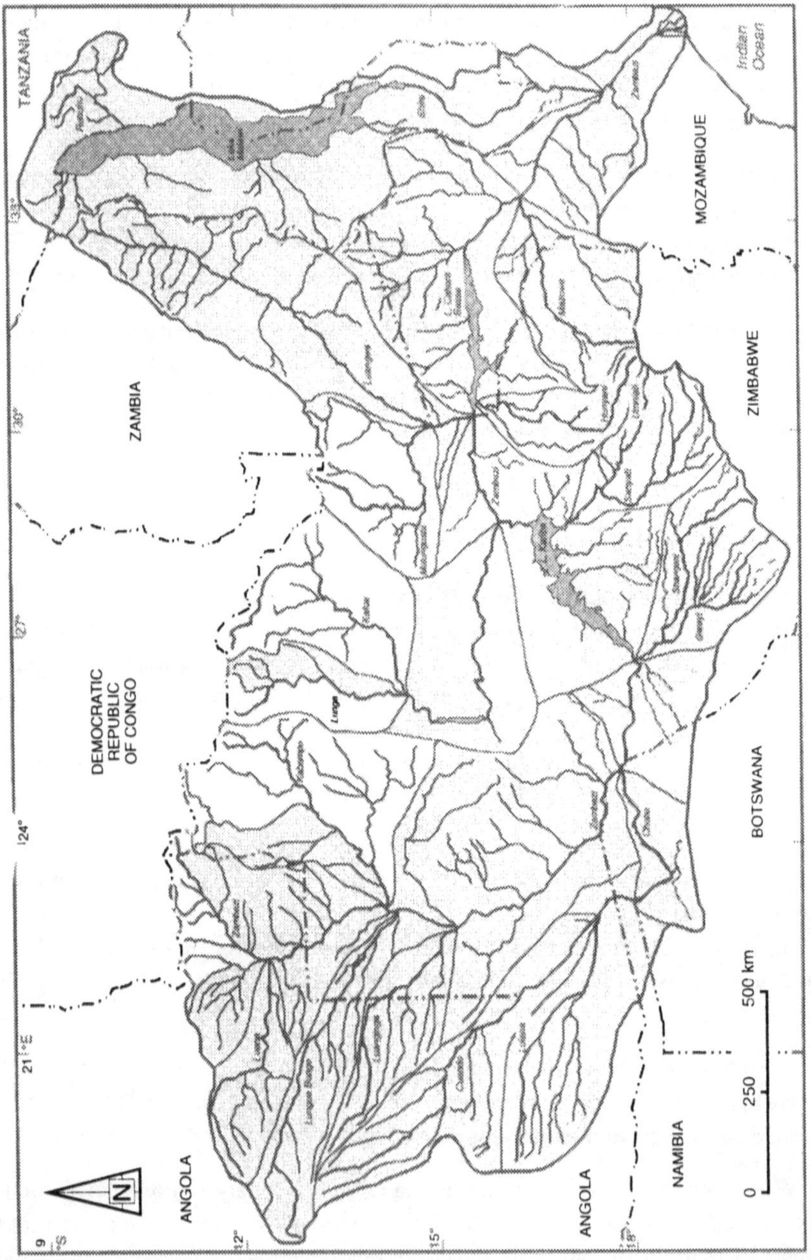


Figure 2: Sketch map showing the main rivers, lakes and sub-catchments of the Zambezi basin

adopted for the purpose of avoiding conflicts over water. (See *http://www.sadc-usa.net/reference/protocol/h2oprot.html.*).

The total population of the Zambezi Basin riparian states is estimated at 105 million. About 30 million (30 per cent) live within the Zambezi Basin itself. Its water, mineral and biological resources are deeply critical to all economic activities carried out therein. However, these activities contribute adversely to water quality and availability and also have negative impacts on most other natural resources within the basin.

Shared river courses, and their water and biological resources, are perhaps the most well known forms of transboundary common property. In terms of their management and use, shared river courses present profound and multifaceted problems and challenges to state governments and various stakeholder communities.

The resolution of these problems requires complicated definitions of 'communities' at various political levels as well as of what constitutes 'common property'.

All transboundary commons such as potable water for humans and drinking water for domestic and wild animals, fisheries, forests and wetlands are negatively impacted upon by various economic activities, which include agriculture, manufacturing, mining, tourism and logging.

These negative impacts, which include water and air pollution as well as siltation, are externalities where they affect communities other than those involved in a particular economic activity. The above economic activities are subject to varying legislative and institutional regimes within individual nation-states as well as regionally. These regimes differ in format, content, and degree of enforcement within riparian states. Most stakeholder-communities living within the Zambezi Basin have very little or no influence as to which economic activities can or cannot take place close to them.

State laws and regulations, where they exist, can be reasonably enforced in the domain of formal economic activities, some of which have been mentioned above. Informal economic activities, such as small-scale mining and alluvial panning, usually fall beyond the arm of state legislature and regulatory authority. This results in the informal sector contributing a disproportionate number of externalities to common property services.

## Challenges for transboundary natural resources management within the Zambezi Basin

In most SADC countries, small-scale mining, particularly artisanal mining, is not legally recognised and thus the sector's production and marketing figures are not always captured by national statistics. All eight Zambezi Basin riparian states have long traditions of small-scale mining, yet only a few have moved towards its formal recognition, let alone putting together a legislative and institutional framework for it. This lack of recognition largely stems from a lack of a clear cost-benefit structure or the existence of a skewed cost-benefit structure among the main stakeholders (government, small-scale miners and local communities). Experience shows that the small-scale mining sector consists of people involved in subsistence-mining who will continue their activities regardless of its legality. The financial requirements for environmental management are well beyond the reach of most if not all small-scale miners, who would also need less stringent laws and regulations to operate profitably. The migratory and scattered nature of the operations would require a very well resourced legal and institutional framework to enforce any stringent regulations, which most SADC economies cannot afford.

A further complicating factor is that the 'equitable sharing approach' has no built-in mechanism for safeguarding the rights of communities and other local users (Mahomed-Katerere, 1995). There is no recognition of the fact that local stakeholders should be incorporated into the decision-making process when it is their rights and interests that are at stake.

Often, the founding principles of the SADC Treaty and associated protocols are found to be in sharp contradiction to the overriding need to address the socio-economic issues of rampant unemployment and rural poverty. One set of competing and even conflicting values is *environmental protection versus economic empowerment/poverty alleviation.* Environmental stress has always been seen as the result of growing demand on scarce resources or the consumption of raw materials as well as the pollution generated by the rising living standards of the relatively affluent. But poverty itself pollutes the environment to a comparable extent:

> *Those who are poor and hungry will often destroy their immediate environment in order to survive: They will cut down forests; their livestock will overgraze grasslands; they will overuse marginal land; and in growing numbers, they will crowd into congested cities.* (World Commission on Environment and Development, 1987)

And:

> *Many parts of world are caught in a vicious down spiral: Poor people are forced to overuse environmental resources to survive from day to day, and their impoverishment of the their environment further impoverishes them, making their survival even more difficult and uncertain.* (World Commission on Environment and Development, 1987)

While small-scale mining is credited with the following advantages: working mineral deposits that are too small for large-scale mining; using 'appropriate' technology; creating employment in remote areas; the small initial capital and infrastructural requirements;

and the short lead time from discovery to production, the trade-off has been low incomes due to the inefficient mining, processing and marketing of minerals. This has generally led to widespread poverty among small-scale miners, and in turn resulted in over-dependency on nature for fuel, food, and infrastructural constructions. This has also meant poor housing and sanitary facilities for the miners. The net result has been increased rates of deforestation, siltation, and pollution of water bodies as well as poaching of fish and wildlife. The World Bank has singled out poverty as a major cause of environmental degradation.

While the small-scale miners are nomadic, and the alluvial panners particularly so, the effects of their negative environmental impacts are felt by local and distant users of environmental services. It is the national government and/or non-governmental organisations that have to pick up the cost. The 'tragedy' of the management and use of transboundary commons is usually rooted in the non-consultation and non-involvement of local communities in decision-making processes by central, and even local, governance structures.

> *Indigenous people are the base of the environmental security system. They are the gate-keepers of success or failure to husband their resources. They are the first to know about changes in the environment and yet they are the last to be asked or consulted. The most they have learned to expect is to be compensated, always too late and too little. They are seldom asked to help avoid the need for compensation by lending their expertise and consent to development.*

So lamented the president of the Native Council of Canada when he addressed the World Commission on Environment and Development (WCED, 1987).

## Recommendations

Small-scale mining, particularly alluvial panning, as currently practised within the Zambezi Basin, is an open-access property regime that results in uncontrolled degradation and uneven appropriation of common property services such as water and biological resources. The sector is still both largely illegal and informal in most of the Zambezi Basin riparian states and will have to be fully recognised and formalised. There is an obvious lack of interest in the sector from central government, which partly stems from their lack of capacity to collect taxes from these scattered and mobile miners.

It is clear that the sector, not to mention central government, would benefit from a well-organised, formal sector that can operate within the confines of a well-crafted legislative and institutional framework. The architectural design of this framework would have to be informed by an analysis of the distribution of costs and benefits among the main stakeholders.

As a common property enterprise, small-scale mining should be managed at local community level. This may have to be predicated on traditional and customary leadership structures in addition to appropriate revisions of existing land tenure in communal areas. It is essential, in the search for policy solutions to the problems of resource degradation in communal areas, to consider and define the tenure system operating in these areas. It is this system that ultimately defines the nature of relationships in the utilisation of common property services. In this vein, the following is instructive:

> *I think this Commission should give attention on how to look into the question of more participation for those people who are the object of development. Their basic needs include the right to preserve their cultural identity and their right not to be alienated from their own society and their own community. We cannot discuss environment or development without discussing political development. And you cannot eradicate poverty, at least not only by redistribution of wealth or income, but there must be more redistribution of power.* (WCED, 1987)

The lack of internal organisation of small-scale mining activities, their scattered and commonly remote nature, and their illegal status are factors that make central governments disinterested. Local communities are commonly in conflict with small-scale miners – due to their negative impacts on common property services such as water, forests, grazing land as well as interference with traditional and customary lifestyle – but lack the authority to control them. Local government departments are without the requisite resources to supervise these scattered activities. The cheapest regulatory route appears to be through local communities who are not only close to the activity, but have an obvious interest in controlling it. A system of penalties and levies for degradation and pollution could be introduced and policed by village committees. An added incentive for so doing would be that the money collected would be used by the local communities themselves. Conflicts between local communities and small-scale miners would be arbitrated by a committee from local government.

The regulatory framework for small-scale mining should be simple, clear, understandable, and stable. Complex regulations dissuade small-scale miners from attempting to adhere to them. More often, the widespread lack of institutional capacity to implement small-scale mining regulations means that the chances of miners being caught and sanctioned are slim. It has also been observed that where the traditional 'command and control' regulations exist for small-scale miners, they serve only to stifle the activity, trapping it in sub-optimal operations rather than promoting it as a sustainable, profitable entrepreneurial activity that can provide significant employment in rural areas. The SADC protocols on transboundary natural resources (Mining, Shared Watercourses and Wildlife Conservation) suffer from serious drawbacks. For example, the accords are top-down in nature and reflect policy decisions that are made in national capitals and ignore the needs, desires and aspirations of those they affect. This is particularly problematical when a river basin forms an international boundary and the people on the opposing banks have stronger ties to each other than to their respective states, as is the case for most of the Zambezi Basin riparian states.

Other clear weaknesses of the regional protocols are that the goals have in some cases been poorly chosen and that the organisations or government departments tasked with implementation are inadequately resourced and lack the capacity and motivation to be effective. There is generally a lack of or, at best, weak public participation in the decision-making process. Unfortunately, the exclusion of public-interest groups and local communities makes implementation of the accord difficult and expensive.

The major constraints to TBNRM within SADC are the reluctance of central governments to devolve tenure and user-rights to local communities and the reluctance by co-operating states to allow free movement of people, goods, services, and money. Differences in capacity, commitment and national policy can be obstacles to the finalisation and formalisation of transboundary agreements. Issues of national sovereignty and security, and high transaction costs may slow down the formulation of multinational policies and agreements. The lack of resources and capacity can also seriously hinder regional integration and effective TBNRM. National and regional governance structures will have to deal with issues of competing values, including openness versus secrecy, established cabals versus public values, use versus environmental protection, over-allocation versus conservation, and sustainability versus immediate economic gain in order for effective TBNRM to be realised. Competing values can be major obstacles to regional integration and programmes such as TBNRM.

Zimbabwe's CAMPFIRE (Communal Areas Management Programme for Indigenous Resources) concept has received worldwide acclaim as a clear demonstration of benefits that accrue from sustainable management and use of natural resources for local communities. The big question is: can this concept be applied successfully to the management and use of all other natural resources, including minerals? This also begs the question as to whether suitable policy and appropriate legal frameworks exist for local participation in the management of mineral resources.

From a study conducted to assess the rationale for local management of mineral resources (Manzungu and Sithole, 1999), some of the important findings were:

- It was morally wrong and undemocratic to deny people the chance to participate in issues that affected their lives. There was demonstrable decentralisation in some sectors that promoted participation of local communities, e.g. in the water and land sectors.
- A centralised system compromised efficiency and effectiveness of managing mineral resources, as the state could not effectively monitor all the mining activities due to a shortage of financial and human resources.

- Local participation reduced management transaction costs as it obviated those huge costs of transport, subsistence and salaries required for central government employees.
- Local management engenders local stewardship of natural resources, which in the end results in sustainable natural resource management.
- The negligible benefits, less than 0.01 per cent, that accrue to local authorities was enough neither to compensate for the losses suffered by local people nor to generate interest in natural resource conservation. The enhanced revenue-base would result in local authorities being able to better perform their functions.
- Prominent NGOs in CAMPFIRE were of the opinion that local management of mineral resources was the best option since this empowered local communities by enabling them to negotiate directly with mining companies and any other miners.

In Zimbabwe, the government has shown some willingness to move towards local participation through the enactment of the Mining (Alluvial Gold) (Public Streams) Regulations (1991). These regulations give the local authority the power to issue mining licences, to collect revenue for these licences, and to enforce the general provisions of the regulations, which include the need to prove residence as a condition for being issued with such a licence. The overall policing of small-scale mining activities is done by the Rural District Council (RDC) in conjunction with local traditional, village, and ward institutional structures. An explicit definition of benefit-streams to the local communities buttresses the whole management structure and engenders a sense of belonging, responsibility, and ownership in the local population.

The adoption of similar regulations by the Zambezi Basin riparian states would clearly go a long way to addressing the serious environmental degradation taking place within the basin. It would slow down the alarming rates of siltation and the deterioration of water quality and its availability to basin states. The institutional capacity-building process that such regulations require would serve as a much cheaper avenue for the administration and enforcement of the various provisions of SADC transboundary natural resources related protocols.

## Conclusions

Boundaries between and among states are often tinderboxes, places where conflicts incubate and hostilities erupt. The competition for resources, usually as a result of uncontrolled economic activities, population growth, and migration across national boundaries, has resulted in a number of boundary clashes and wars in recent years. A prime example is the war between the Democratic Republic of Congo and its eastern neighbours (Uganda and Rwanda) since 1998. Most of the problems concerning transboundary natural resources management and use commonly arise from the arbitrary political boundaries that apportion natural systems and resources to two or more nation-states.

Small-scale mining is a widespread activity in all the eight Zambezi Basin riparian states. The economic activity is haphazard and poverty-driven, and ever-increasing numbers of people within the basin are turning to it due to recurrent drought and the economic hardships accompanying economic reforms within the region. Alluvial panning activities are illegal and therefore go unmonitored, and have largely been blamed for the siltation of rivers, dams and lakes, deforestation and poaching of wildlife. The greatest losers in this unfolding drama are the local communities, whose common property services are being negatively impacted upon. Some of these common property services, including water and wildlife, are of a transboundary nature. Siltation resulting from mining and panning activities in one part of the basin (one or more countries) results in the deterioration of water quality or flooding in another part (other countries). With worsening water scarcity within the SADC region and the increased incidence of flooding affecting particular countries, tension has been rising and could easily lead to future conflicts. The SADC region is duty-bound to take firm and binding co-operative action to arrest the slow drift towards regional conflicts arising from economic activities such as small-scale mining and alluvial gold panning.

The SADC protocols on the management of shared resources are a bold attempt to co-ordinate and harmonise the use of shared resources. Their effectiveness is, however, considerably watered down by a plethora of problems and challenges that are specific to regional circumstances. Some of these problems are: a lack of institutional capacity as well as financial and human resources to monitor and implement protocol provisions; competing values and priorities among riparian states, and the overarching issue of rampant poverty within the region. Perhaps more important is the issue of translating the spirit embodied within these protocols into practical legislation within individual countries. The legislation should provide effective institutional arrangements for their implementation.

Most of the control mechanisms (legislation) derived from regional protocols are in the form of 'command and control' legislation and regulations (Shoko and Kinabo, 2001). 'Command and control' regulatory approaches involve the state's prescription of desired changes that are then promoted and enforced through laws. The major weakness of this regulatory regime is that it requires intensive monitoring and thus a strong and well-resourced enforcement mechanism. Successful prosecution of offenders will also require reliable and efficient analytical laboratories to prove wrong-doing. Indeed, as regulation becomes more sophisticated, monitoring requires human resource skills that are far beyond the technological and managerial capabilities of many developing countries, and frequently beyond their budget capabilities too. Tapping into local communities and traditional leadership structures not only offers the best solution but is the most cost-effective. The basic requirement is that demonstrable benefits should accrue to local communities in order to ensure that they are either sufficiently motivated to be involved in small-scale mining activities or do not suffer negative consequences therefrom.

Innovative policy-formulation strategies will be required for the adoption and adaptation of customary laws and traditional institutional structures in respect of small-scale mining. Custom, when understood as shared norms and values that have evolved over time and provide a basis for decision-making on matters of common interest and concern to communities or segments thereof, will always remain an organic system that responds to both internal and external stimuli, despite initial capture in contextual form (Murombedzi, 1990).

## References

Ashton, P. J., D. Love, H. Mahachi, and P. H. G. M. Dirks (2001). An overview of the impact of mining and mineral processing operations on water resources and water quality in the Zambezi, Limpopo and Olifants catchments in southern Africa. Paper prepared for Mining, Minerals and Sustainable Development (MMSD), Southern Africa. Johannesburg.

Berkes, F. and M. T. Farvar (1989). 'Introduction and overview' in F. Berkes (ed.) *Common Property Resources*. London, Belhaven Press.

Bromley, D. W. and M. M. Cernea (1989). *The Management of Common Property Resources. Some Conceptual and Operational Fallacies*. Washington, World Bank Discussion Papers, No. 57.

Bruce, J. W. (1989). Community forestry rapid appraisal of tree and land tenure. Rome: Food and Agriculture Organisation (FAO), Mimeo.

Chiwawa, H. (1993). *Environmental impacts of co-operative mining in Zimbabwe*. 4th Congress , Organisation for Social Science Research in Eastern and Southern Africa, Debra Zeit, Ethiopia.

Ciriacy-Wentrup, S. V. and R. C. Bishop (1975). 'Common Property as a concept in Natural Resource Policy'. *Natural Resource Journal* 15, pp. 713-27.

Gibbs, J.W. and D.W. Bromley (1989). 'Institutional managements for management of rural resources; common property regimes' in F. Berkes (ed.) *Common Property Resources: ecology and community-based sustainable development*. London, Belhaven Press.

Gumende, A. (1995). 'In Search of Water'. *Southern African Economist*, Vol. 8, (4).

Manzungu, E. and E. Sithole (1999). *Towards local management of mineral resources in Zimbabwe: an analysis of opportunities and constraints*. Harare, CASS Occasional Paper – NRM; CPN 105/2000.

Mahomed-Katerere, J. C. (1995). 'International and regional agreements for environmental management: implications for sustainable development in southern Africa' in N. Steytler (ed.) *Democracy, Human Rights and Economic Development*. Johannesburg, Lex Patria Publishers.

Milne, G. R. and D. A. Marongwe (1995). 'The costs and benefits of gold panning', in: G. R. Milne and D. A. Marongwe, (eds), Small scale gold panning in Zimbabwe; Economic costs and benefits and policy recommendations. Zimbabwe, Unpublished report of the Ministry of Mines, Environment and Tourism.

MMSD (2002). A global report, *Breaking New Ground*, London, Earthscan Publications.

Mpendazoe, F. M. T. (1996). *Towards sustainable small scale gold mining in Tanzania*. Proceedings of the First World Mining Environment Congress. Rotterdam, Balkema, pp. 105-119

Murombedzi, J. (1990). *Communal Land Tenure and Common Property Resource Management. An evaluation of the potential for sustainable common property resource management in Zimbabwe's communal areas*. Harare, CASS Publications.

Okoth-Ogendo, H. W. O. (2001). 'The tragic African commons: A century of expropriation, suppression and subversion'. *The Common Property Resource Digest*, No. 57, 1-3.

Shoko, D. S. M. and C. Kinabo (2001). Legal and Institutional Framework for Mining and the Environment in the SADC region. Paper prepared for MMSD (London): *Breaking New Ground*, London, Earthscan Publications.

World Commission on Environment and Development (1987). *Our Common Future*. Oxford, Open University Press.

# Chapter 5

# How far the destination? Decentralisation and devolution in governance of the commons under CAMPFIRE

*Patrick W. Mamimine*

## Introduction

The current measure of the success of CAMPFIRE in involving communities in wildlife management and other natural resources in Zimbabwe is principally revenue-centric (see Murombedzi in Hulme and Murphree, 2001; Bond, 2001). The failure of the success index to see beyond revenue collected misrepresents the reality on the ground. It also, however, ignores the necessity of interrogating the extent to which the programme has attained its cardinal goal of decentralising and devolving natural resource ownership and management to grassroot institutions or communal proprietorial units.

Meinzen-Dick, *et al.,* (1999:3) use the term devolution to denote the transfer of responsibility and authority over natural resources from the state to non-governmental bodies, particularly user-groups; and decentralisation to refer to authority and management transfers to lower levels of government. Over the years, there has been mounting support for development policies and projects that aim to transfer rights and responsibilities from central government to more localised bodies (Meinzen-Dick, *et al.,* 1999:4). Within the context of community-based natural resource management, one of the key elements of governance is the capacity of communities to participate and contribute to decisions on access to and use of natural resources (Mohamed, 2001:3).

For some scholars, associating decentralisation with increased efficiency, equity, popular participation, and accountability in governance remains debatable (see Agrawal and Ribot, 2000). However, the centrality of decentralisation to good governance and development cannot be over-emphasised. Decentralisation is the quintessence of democracy in its strictest sense of 'government by all the people, for all the people and of all the people'. Although there is increasing support in many countries for the devolution of natural resource management to local users, numerous policy constraints exist that can fracture the process by preventing it from taking off, impede its progress, or contribute to its outright failure (Meinzen-Dick, *et al.,* 1999:17). In many Third World countries, where decentralisation has been attempted, lack of capacity to exercise the devolved powers has been harped on by some scholars as one of the stumbling blocks to sound natural resource management (see Winter, 1998:23). However, the argument is not only simplistic but overlooks the fact that capacity-building is part and parcel of the devolution process.

This chapter explores the hurdles faced by CAMPFIRE in anchoring ownership and management of natural resources at the lowest tiers of administration, with particular reference to the 'myth' of lack of capacity. Using examples from literature, this chapter examines issues of legislation, autonomy, benefits sharing, and accountability to illustrate that the claim of lack of capacity at the local level is, on its own, indicative of a lack of serious commitment to decentralisation by central and local government authorities. As a point of departure, it is necessary to revisit the fundamental goal of CAMPFIRE and the lack of capacity argument.

## Whither CAMPFIRE?

The CAMPFIRE (Communal Areas Management Programme for Indigenous Resources) in Zimbabwe has been a subject of many evaluative studies. The studies, *inter alia,* focused on local institutional development (Murombedzi, 1992; Thomas, 1991), the effect of migration on the CAMPFIRE (Dzingirai, 2000), opportunities and constraints of Community Based Natural Resources Management (CBNRM) under the CAMPFIRE model (Madzudzo, 1996), the contribution of CAMPFIRE to rural development (Child and Peterson Jr., 1991), the issues and constraints of the rapid implementation of CAMPFIRE (Murphree, 1991), and membership, costs and benefits in CAMPFIRE (Nabane, *et al.,* 1996). This preceding list of studies is primarily concerned, in the broadest sense, with the extent to which CAMPFIRE has reached its intended target, the local level management units, as envisioned from inception.

CAMPFIRE was conceived in 1982 by Zimbabwe's Department of National Parks and Wildlife Management (DNPWM) and was incorporated into the National Conservation Strategy in 1987 with, *inter alia,* the following goals:

(i) To achieve management of resources by placing the custody and responsibility with the resident communities.

(ii) To allow communities to benefit directly from the exploitation of natural resources within the communal areas.

(iii) To establish the administrative and institutional structures necessary to make the programme work.

The mission statement succinctly summed up the *raison d'être* of the programme as:

> *To enable rural communities in Zimbabwe to effectively manage their natural resources. We aim to see rural communities in Zimbabwe freed from the vagaries of poverty and enjoying the benefits of the sustainable use of their natural resources.* (CAMPFIRE Association Annual Report ,1999-2000)

CAMPFIRE was designed as a remedy to the shortcomings of its predecessor – the Wildlife Industries New Development For All (WINDFALL) of 1978, which stalled due to lack of devolution of funds to local communities, and absence of local participation in decision-making, control, and ownership (CAMPFIRE, 2000:7).

WINDFALL failed to ensure that communities participated in the generation of wildlife revenues rather than simply be passive recipients of revenue (Murombedzi, 1992:13). The objectives of CAMPFIRE are clear in regard to central government's commitment to decentralise the management of natural resources to the lowest tiers of administration, which Jones and Murphree (Hulme and Murphree [eds], 2001:45) refer to as 'communal proprietorial units'. Nevertheless, the policy statement seemed to have put too much trust on the 'benevolent' RDCs, who were to cascade the 'Appropriate Authority (AA)[1] ' status conferred upon them by central government to communal proprietorial units (CPUs). According to Murombedzi (in Hulme and Murphree [eds], 2001:244), the problems of natural resource management in the pre-CAMPFIRE period were 'a result of a lack of both the institutional *capacity*[2] and the incentives to effectively manage natural resources.' CAMPFIRE was therefore conceived to deal with, *inter alia,* the capacity problem. Nevertheless, in a CAMPFIRE Association Annual General Meeting attended by the author in year 2000, most Rural District Councils' Chief Executive Officers argued that they had failed to fully devolve authority over natural resource management due to the CPUs' lack of capacity. This 'capacity excuse' was being raised more than a decade after the official launch of CAMPFIRE. One of the prime elements of devolution is the strengthening of

---

1 In broad terms, Appropriate Authority refers to the conferment of authority over natural resource management such as wildlife and others to a particular lower-stream administrative unit.

2 My emphasis..

sub-units of development management by a higher office such as central government or Rural District Council. This is implied in CAMPFIRE goal number (iii) specified above.

### *Devolution in CAMPFIRE: a blurring vision*

A 1982 amendment to the Parks and Wildlife Act mandated the then Minister of Natural Resources and Tourism to designate Rural District Councils (RDCs) as the 'appropriate authority' for wildlife on land for which they were responsible. Of late, central government has extended the 'appropriate authority' status (AA) to cover other non-wildlife natural resources such as fish, forests, and sand. By being granted an AA, a Rural District becomes a member of the CAMPFIRE association. The delegation of proprietorship to RDCs, on the basis of intent and with guidelines for further delegation to producer communities, gave RDCs too much power to act however they deemed fit. The threat of the withdrawal of appropriate authority status in cases of non-conformity was relatively hollow, as RDCs soon realised (Jones and Murphree in Hulmes and Murphree [eds], 2001:49). Seemingly, it is in this arrangement that the foundation of the devolution problem in CAMPFIRE is situated.

Kasere (Johnson and Mbizvo [eds], 1999) points out that the role of RDCs should be mainly facilitatory and custodial, since CAMPFIRE principles require full participation and decision-making by producer communities, that is those benefiting from wildlife-generated revenue. Principally, the rationale for this was that the unit of utilisation (UU) should be the unit of management (UM) and the unit of responsibility (UR). A closer examination of the devolution thrust in natural resource management points to the fact that there is little synchronicity between rhetoric and practice. RDCs are largely serving as gatekeepers in the devolution of authority over natural resource management to grassroot level.

Stockil noted that although the devolution of authority, legalised hunting, and the appropriate distribution of financial benefits were starting to have the desired impact on wildlife management under CAMPFIRE in the Mahenye area of Chipinge District, the lack of participation by local communities in the management of the adjacent park area was creating a great deal of tension (Stockil in Johnson and Mbizvo [eds], 1999:11). He emphatically observed:

> *Do not devolve expenditure, devolve authority.*

A study recently conducted by Chitsike (2000) is revealing in terms of the problems faced by producer-communities as a result of the RDCs' failure to devolve authority of natural resource management to lower-tier structures of administration, such as Ward CAMPFIRE Committees and Village CAMPFIRE Committees. The most critical problems are that some RDCs have a tendency to:

- Dictate to wards and villages management and benefit issues.

- Delay paying producer communities proceeds from wildlife.
- Have CAMPFIRE officers living far away from the producer-communities making it difficult for them to attend to urgent matters such as Problem Animal Control (PAC).
- Enter into contracts with safari operators without involving producer communities.
- Withhold feedback to producer communities on deliberations of Council on CAMPFIRE issues.
- Make game guards and scouts answerable to Rural District Councils rather than to the communities they serve.
- Withhold interest accrued from CAMPFIRE fund accounts.

## The capacity issue

In light of the constraints discussed above, can CAMPFIRE communities be justifiably criticised or blamed for the lack of capacity to assume stewardship of natural resource management? Bhatta (Jreisat [Guest editor], 2001) observes that:

> *Decentralisation per se does little to enhance good governance. It must be combined with empowerment, involvement and access to essential resources for local economic needs. This is what is meant by 'capacity'.*

At the 2000 CAMPFIRE Annual General Meeting held in Victoria Falls, the issue of devolution was very topical. Almost all Rural District Council officials present registered their commitment to the devolution process. A few claimed to have started the devolution process but most of them admitted to having failed to devolve authority over natural resource management to the wards and villages. The failure was attributed primarily to the producer-communities' lack of capacity to handle various key functions. The key functions identified were, *inter alia*, negotiating contracts with safari operators, managing the large staff complement associated with problem animal control, the supervision of CAMPFIRE staff at ward and village level, preparing tender documents, and making decisions pertaining to the planning and management of CAMPFIRE projects.

In other words, if there were capacity at village and ward level to deal with various functions of critical importance to the execution of CAMPFIRE, all RDCs would have devolved most of the responsibilities to lower-tier administrative units. This argument is untenable. After the launch of CAMPFIRE in 1985, the governments of Zimbabwe and the United States of America forged a bilateral relationship in which the latter committed itself to financing CAMPFIRE under the Natural Resources Management Phase I (NRMPI). The funding was channelled through the United States Agency for International Development

(USAID). The aim of this phase was to develop the human and institutional capacity needed to run the programme at RDC and local community level. On the assumption that Phase I had, to a large extent, achieved its goals, Phase II was then introduced to focus on infrastructural development. Therefore, the argument of lack of capacity is a tacit admission that the USAID capacity-building grant failed to achieve its purpose.

Evaluation reports on the impact of the capacity-building grant indicate that local communities gained basic skills in book-keeping, conducting meetings, controlling poaching of resources, supervising resource monitors, originating concept papers for project proposals, quota setting, and bylaw formulation, amongst others (see Mamimine, 2000). Essentially, local communities fared well with the skills to which they were exposed. Thus it would appear that their lack of skills, if this holds true, in areas regarded as crucial to enabling the devolution of authority over natural resource management to the local level, was a deliberate strategy by RDCs to continue to dominate in the management of natural resources. Ribot (2001:190) observes the following:

> *Capacity is a chicken and egg problem. There is reluctance on the part of central government to devolve powers before capacity has been demonstrated, but without powers there is no basis on which local authorities, can gain experience needed to build capacity and there is no basis on which they can demonstrate [that] capacity has been gained.*

The same situation seems to apply to local authorities and communities under them.

## Prohibitive legislation

Prohibitive legislation is at the forefront of the perpetuation of the 'myth of lack of capacity' on the part of local communities. Legal constraints have inhibited success in CAMPFIRE (Hulme and Murphree [eds], 2001:190). The devolution of Appropriate Authority to district level has been portrayed as a strategic compromise by the Department of National Parks and Wildlife Management (DNPWM), without which CAMPFIRE would have been stillborn (Maveneke, *et al.*, 1999). It is a pity that further devolution of Appropriate Authority (AA) to sub-district levels has not taken place, despite the fact that this proposal has been in the pipeline since 1992 (ibid.). Since 1996, national policies have tended to re-centralise the control of wildlife with central government (ibid.). This could account for the current lack of commitment by RDCs to decentralise and devolve powers to the lower tiers of administration.

In a case study of ecotourism development in the Mahenye area of Zimbabwe, Murphree noted that, as things stand in Zimbabwe's current legislation, formal authority over Mahenye land and natural resources is vested in the Chipinge Rural District Council, and not with the people in the wards and their leadership. The inference is that the community cannot formally interact with its client, Zimbabwe Sun Limited (ZSL), but must deal with it through the Council (Hulme and Murphree [eds], 2001:191). Murombedzi observes that community participation in CAMPFIRE can therefore be seen as constituting little more than the receipt of handouts (in Hulme and Murphree [eds], 2001:247). This smacks of a deliberate ploy to incapacitate local communities and give the Rural District Councils an upper hand in any business transactions involved. As Murphree noted, this arrangement has negative repercussions for the Mahenye area. The arrangement is administratively ponderous, and formal interaction sometimes does not take place when it is critically needed. The Management Committee, which under normal circumstances should have comprised the Ward Wildlife Committee and the ZSL but consists of the latter and the Council, should meet on a regular basis. However, 'the Management Committee has not met with regularity and cannot address the functional needs for which it has been designed' (Murphree in Hulme and Murphree [eds], 2001:191).

A befitting comment on the conferring of AA status to RDCs is Ribot's (2001:5) observation that:

> *Empowering local authorities who are not held accountable to local populations can imperil the long-term environmental well-being expected from more accountable local management. It can imperil democracy by taking resources away from emerging democratic structures while strengthening and helping to entrench the very non-democratic institutions that democratic reforms aim to replace.*

The statement above aptly describes the current situation of CAMPFIRE.

## Autonomy

The claim that communities lack capacity is primarily premised on the fear of local autonomy in natural resource management. Such autonomy would leave RDCs with little or no basis for intervening in natural resource management.

Yet devolution does not imply the transfer of all functions to lower-tier administrative units. It should be guided by the principles of 'maximum possible autonomy' (Matimba, 1994) and 'subsidiarity' (Chitsike, 2000). The former principle implies that central government functions should be devolved only to the lower-tier institutions' limits of self-governance. In the case of the latter, devolution is premised on the assumption that decision-making, especially in the area of natural resource management, should be the responsibility of people living closest to the resources in question (see ILO, 2000). Ribot (2001:6) envisaged that the principle of subsidiarity would call for decisions to be located at the lowest political administrative level possible, without any negative effects at a higher level. But, he was also quick to point out that the principle does not appear to be followed in most African environmental decentralisations (ibid:7). In the case study of Sunungukai Camp of Uzumba-Maramba-Pfungwe, Zimbabwe, Odero and Huchu (1998:4) argue that:

> *Community-based management of natural resources presupposes that local capacity will be mobilised to effectively assume management responsibility. Serious human resource constraints, inadequate financing arrangements, inefficient management structures and weak management systems variously contribute to CBOs' [Community-Based Organisations] inability to effectively and sustainably manage natural resources. Accordingly, the decentralisation and devolution process would be incomplete without investment in human capital, institutions and practices.*

Perhaps the most important point to heed in their argument is that for complete devolution to take place, RDCs must realise that they have an obligation to develop human capital. In any case, without human capital, to whom would the authority be devolved?

Despite an availability of capacity, autonomy at the local level seems to be dreaded. Most RDCs cannot imagine Ward and Village CAMPFIRE Committees receiving proceeds from wildlife directly from safari operators, independently setting quotas and making decisions on problem-animal control, negotiating and entering into contracts with safari operators, and being in charge of game guards and scouts. In a study carried out by Murombedzi (1992) in Nyaminyami, he observed that although the Nyaminyami Rural District Council (NRDC) was granted 'Appropriate Authority' status in November 1988, and the Nyaminyami Wildlife Management Trust (NWMT) was subsequently formed to devolve authority to locals, the latter has increasingly come to function as a subcommittee of the NRDC. The NRDC controls the budgeting and finance allocation of NWMT as well as transport, it also issues permits to hunt, signs all contracts, generally administers projects, and requires that NWMT be directly accountable to the Senior Chief Executive Officer of NRDC for its routine operations (Murombedzi, 1992:18). Murombedzi strongly criticises the adamancy of Rural District Councils as giving maximum possible autonomy to locals. He argued that:

> *Since Nyaminyami District Council controls the daily operations of Nyaminyami Wildlife Management Trust, the initial intention of some degree of autonomy for the NWMT has not been realised because Appropriate Authority was granted to the District Council and not to the NWMT. Local authorities in Zimbabwe today are inherently non-participatory institutions given the nature of their accountability to the centre rather than to the people. (18-19)*

The argument to 'justify' this unwillingness to give local people autonomy is that they lack the technical know-how required to execute the 'technical' functions. If technical know-how is an acquired skill and not inborn, then CAMPFIRE Committees at Village and Ward levels can also be trained to handle these 'crucial' functions. The extension and training of communities in resource governance acts as an epoxy to strengthen the local institutional environment in order to support devolution of natural resource management (Meinzen-Dick, *et al.*, 1999:24). Ramboll (2001) highlights that capacity development in environment initiatives builds on principles of partnership between equals, access to and sharing of information, stakeholder involvement and ownership, subsidiarity, and dynamic learning process orientation.

The reality is that most RDCs are not fully committed to implementing devolution in natural resource management in accordance with the principle of maximum possible autonomy. The systematic marginalisation of grassroots CAMPFIRE committees by RDCs, through depriving committees of training in handling 'strategic' functions of the programme, has resulted in the proliferation of the fallacy of lack of capacity. Primarily, this fallacy is peddled in order to protect what is perceived by RDCs as a major source of revenue (see Murphree and Jones in Hulme and Murphree [eds], 2001). The fear is that once Ward and Village CAMPFIRE committees are capable of taking over most of the responsibilities of natural resource management it will then become difficult for RDCs to justify the current position, where part of the proceeds from natural resources reach local communities via Councils.

## Devolution of benefits

The effective devolution of benefits to producer-communities is a prerequisite for building the local communities' capacity for efficient natural resource management. Benefits encourage communities to take an interest in acquiring skills that are essential for the sound management of natural resources, which are the source of the benefits they enjoy. Taylor noted that the devolution of benefits to communities living with wildlife is intended to stimulate both collective and individual resource management, thereby providing rural communities with an alternative or complementary land use to agriculture and livestock (Taylor in Hulme and Murphree [eds], 2001:267). Numerous studies have documented the resistance of Rural District Councils to disbursing wildlife revenue to sub-district levels (Maveneke, *et al.*, 1999). This has been attributed to the perception, within the RDCs, that revenue from wildlife is a panacea to a myriad of fiscal problems that they face. In addition, more recent studies show that councils are reluctant to allow producer-communities to benefit from wildlife other than through money RDCs give them. What this implies is that in certain cases, the devolution of Appropriate Authority to district level might have resulted in greater external control over the wildlife resources than previously existed under the poorly-enforced state management systems (Maveneke, *et al.*, 1999).

Kasere, the then director of CAMPFIRE, acknowledged that the issue of who benefits under CAMPFIRE has been very controversial (Kasere in Johnson and Mbizvo, 1999:52). In an honest assessment of CAMPFIRE, he confessed that:

> *[The] problem rocking CAMPFIRE at the moment is with regards to devolution. For a considerable time now, CAMPFIRE Association has been battling with the whole issue of further devolution of power to lower echelons of the Rural District Council. This has been necessitated at times by bottlenecks experienced at RDC level where some of the local authorities have been holding on for too long on money intended for distribution to producer communities.*

It is an axiom in business circles that money delayed, especially in the wake of galloping inflation in contemporary Zimbabwe, is money denied. The actions by some of these RDCs, as reported by Kasere, are tantamount to blocking the process of devolving benefits to local communities. It suffices to say, too, that as holders of the Appropriate Authority status, Rural District Councils are not obliged to devolve revenue to sub-district levels but are encouraged to do so in the 'spirit of CAMPFIRE' (Bond in Hulme and Murphree, 2001:232). What this implies is that devolution of benefits to wards is a privilege and not a right. More often than not, it is the local communities who are the ultimate losers. No wonder why Mandondo, in Ribot (2001:11), advocated transparent and timely disbursement of CAMPFIRE revenues to local communities, in tandem with more community representation in the RDDC (Rural District Development Committee) and, more importantly, effective participation of locals in bylaw formulation at RDC level.

Under the current arrangement, RDCs retain at least 50 per cent of revenue realised from natural resources, such as trophy hunting. Once grassroot committees are capable of negotiating contracts with safari operators and making the operators pay proceeds directly to their coffers, RDCs would lose an important source of revenue. Rural District Councils in Zimbabwe lack their own financial resources[3] and are characteristically cash-strapped organisations whose responsibilities usually exceed their total incomes (de Valk and Wekwete, 1990; Owen and Maponga in Hulme and Murphree [eds], 2001:233). Therefore, it is in the interest of RDCs to perpetuate the myth of 'lack of capacity'. Through this myth, RDCs can continue to benefit from the proceeds of CAMPFIRE. Nhira, *et al.*, aptly stated that:

> *Where commercially valuable resources are concerned, community interests are likely to be sacrificed by Councils starved of central government funding (1998:95).*

It has also been noted by scholars that central government is likely to be wary of devolving authority to more local levels for various reasons (Nhira, *et al.*, 1998:91). One of these reasons is the fact that the more that communities are able to control land and natural resource use, the less government can prevail in installing its approach to economic development in local contexts.

A complicating factor in CAMPFIRE is the limited nature of the empowerment granted to the rural communities directly involved with wildlife (Turnham, 1999). The party empowered with Appropriate Authority under the legislation is the Rural District Council, not the Ward(s). District Councils negotiate with private operators and receive revenue from them, yet, in overall terms, they will be purporting to represent communities who are hardly consulted prior to the negotiations with operators. There is considerable uncertainty as to when RDCs pass on the revenue to producer communities and numerous

---

[3] www.undp.org/hdro/oc15.htm

diversions of revenues before it gets to local communities. Statistics indicate that the latter receive a little over 50 per cent of the gross revenues (see appendix A). In some cases, the districts attempt to assert direct authority over wildlife management, limiting the role of the Ward-level organisations and, in effect, reducing them to passive receivers of rents (Turnham, 1999).

## Accountability

Lonsdale (in Ribot, 1999) observed that 'rulers claim to be responsible to their people; people try to hold them to account.' Accountability is thus the measure of responsibility. The question is, are RDCs in Zimbabwe accountable to their respective constituencies? The presumed benefits of decentralisation become available to local communities only when empowered local actors are accountable and the key to effective decentralisation is increased democratic participation in local decision-making (Agrawal and Ribot, 2000).

Accountable representative authorities with meaningful powers constitute the basic institutional elements from which one should expect the local efficiency, equity, and development benefits that decentralisation promises (Ribot, 2001:2). This is not the case with the RDCs' role in natural resource management under CAMPFIRE. They are generally upwardly accountable. This is indicated by the formulation of bylaws without adequate consultation with people at grassroots level. The bylaws are then hurriedly sent to the sector Ministry for approval without the consent of those who will be governed by them. Essentially, this has raised serious questions as to whose interests the Councillors serve. There is a big gap between what Councillors deliberate over or bring to Council as bylaw propositions and what the communities perceive to be concerns requiring urgent formulation of bylaws. Successful decentralised natural resource management tends to be associated with transparent processes and people are more likely to stick to the rules when they know how rules are made (Winter, 1998:7).

Since only in small communities is it possible for all voices to be heard, community-based decision-making requires that the population in question be represented in an accountable manner (Ribot, 1999). In the absence of such representation, there is a danger that decision-making could be taken over by elite groups; dissent swept under the carpet; and women, and lower castes and minority ethnic groups, religious sects and other marginalised social groups be excluded from the forum (Painter, Sumberg and Price in Ribot, 1999:1). Moreover:

> *Authority and responsibility should be linked. When they are de-linked and assigned to different institutional actors both are eroded. Authority without responsibility becomes meaningless or obstructive; responsibility without authority lacks the necessary components for its efficient exercise. (Murphree cited in Mohamed, 2001:25)*

In the same vein, Ribot (2001:3) contends that, without powers, representative authority is empty. Community-based and decentralised forms of local natural resource management often lack representation, downward accountability, or sufficient powers. It is also widely acknowledged that accountable representation without powers is empty, and the devolution of powers without accountable representation can be dangerous. Zimbabwe's CAMPFIRE has not escaped this trap.

## Discussion and conclusion

Effective devolution is far from being attained through CAMPFIRE. Results of the literature review indicate that the devolution fiasco of CAMPFIRE has nothing to do with lack of capacity on the part of local communities. It is largely a result of RDCs ignoring the CAMPFIRE principle, which suggests smaller, territorially discrete, social units (CPUs) as being the programme's fundamental building blocks (Collins, 2001). The issue of lack of capacity being raised by some RDCs is nullified by the fact that part of the earliest obligation of CAMPFIRE was to build the capacity of rural communities to assume ownership and management of natural resources in their localities. This was supposed to have been achieved through the capacity-building grant provided by USAID. The reality is that RDCs are not content with playing a merely facilitatory role in natural resource management -- promoting the local communities' judicious management and utilisation of natural resources. The claim of lack of capacity is just one major strategy for frustrating and retaining appropriate authority status. Ironically, RDCs overlook the fact that capacity-building is the first step in the process of devolving authority to lower tiers of administration. They imply that capacity is only found at RDC level. This erroneous view is peddled to create a dependency syndrome on the part of local communities, which buttresses the communities' perception of the Council as an indispensable player in rural development and, more specifically, in natural resource management.

RDCs are adamant that they hold the 'appropriate authority' status in trust or as a transient status destined for CPUs. This manifests itself in the RDCs' resistance to extend autonomy over natural resource management to local communities, remaining obstinate to downward accountability and taking advantage of legislation that makes further devolution of ownership and management of natural resources to local communities discretionary rather than mandatory. Above all, the recognition of the transient status of the appropriate authority is impeded by a fear of losing benefits in the form of revenue from natural resources in their areas. This naturally ignores the wisdom that sustainable natural resource management is based on the devolution principle of subsidiarity, i.e. that people living closest to the resource should shoulder the management burden and that the securing of meaningful benefits is central to the motivation to conserve.

Essentially then, the point of departure in facilitating devolution to the local level is to acknowledge that the democratisation of natural resource management, through CAMPFIRE, has hit a snag. Once this acknowledgement is made, the next step is to deal with the root cause of the problem. It is not enough to amend the Parks and Wildlife Act in order to force RDCs to devolve authority over natural resource management to the local level without addressing the basis of the current malady, that is, the RDCs fear of losing revenue. Central government and local authorities should come up with alternative sources of revenue to ensure that RDCs continue to fulfil their mandate, despite the loss of a substantial amount of revenue from natural resources to local communities. Indeed, the CAMPFIRE model of natural resource management has managed to motivate local communities to take an interest in the management of natural resources around them. However, as long as natural resource management is not fully devolved to the local level, the programme risks losing ground gained to date.

A bold move would be to give appropriate authority to local committees. The formation of community trusts, currently being facilitated by CAMPFIRE Association and USAID, to take charge of community ventures in ecotourism, fisheries and others, seems to provide an opportunity for taking appropriate authority to grassroots level. However, it is important to realize that along with strong property rights devolution, will come considerable internal conflicts and challenges. Devolution will relocate some of the toughest and most fundamental questions to local decision-making, which should ensure that corruption is not the order of the day in all transactions with outsiders, such as private operators and others, for example (see also Wilson, 1997). The greatest challenge will be to ensure that all business transactions on behalf of the communities are conducted in a transparent manner, and for the benefit of all and not just a few local elites. Otherwise it will be nothing more than a matter of having replaced one type of elite with another.

## References

Agrawal, A. and J.C. Ribot (2000). Accountability in Decentralisation: A Framework with South Asian and West African Cases, cf p. 137. Bogor, Centre for International Forestry Research. Working Paper.

Bond, I. (2001). 'CAMPFIRE and the Incentives for Institutional Change' in M. Murphree and D. Hulme, (2001), *African Wildlife and Livelihoods: The Promise and Performance of Community Conservation.* Oxford, James Currey.

CAMPFIRE Association, 1999-2000 Annual Report. Harare, CAMPFIRE Association.

Child, B. and J. H. Peterson [Jr.] (1991). CAMPFIRE in Rural Development: The Beitbridge Experience. Harare, DNPWL and CASS Working Paper Series.

Chitsike, L.T. (2000). *Decentralisation and Devolution of CAMPFIRE in Zimbabwe*. Harare, University of Zimbabwe. Centre for Applied Social Sciences (CASS) Technical Publication.

Collins, M.E. (2001). An Investigation of the Role of Institutional Dynamics in Promoting Popular Participation and Co-operation in Common Property Resource Management in the Zambezi Valley. Unpublished MSc. thesis, UCC.

de Valk, P. and K. H. Wekwete (eds) (1990). *Decentralisation for Participatory Planning? Comparing the Experiences of Zimbabwe and other Anglophone Countries in Eastern and Southern Africa*. Aldershot, Gower Publications Ltd.

Dzingirai, V. (2000). *Migration and the Future of CAMPFIRE in the Zambezi Valley, Zimbabwe*. Harare, University of Zimbabwe, Centre for Applied Social Sciences (CASS).

Hulme, D. and M.W. Murphree (eds) (2001). *African Wildlife and Livelihoods: The Promise and Performance of Community Conservation*. Oxford, James Currey.

International Labour Organisation (ILO) (2000). *The Reform of the European Union*. Geneva, International Labour Office, Bureau for Workers' Activities.

Johnson, S. and C. Mbizvo (1999). *CBNRM and its Contribution to Economic Development in Southern Africa: Proceedings of the Exchange Visit Workshop for Directors*. Harare, Africa Resources Trust.

Jreisat, J.E. (Guest editor) (2001). 'Governance in Developing Countries', *Journal of Developing Societies*, 17(2). Special Issue.

Madzudzo, E. (1996). Community-Based Natural Resource Management in Zimbabwe: Opportunities and Constraints. Harare, CASS Occasional Paper.

Mamimine, P.W. (2000). Gwanda Rural District Council (RDC) Capacity Building Grant Evaluation Report. Unpublished Report.

Matimba, K. (1994). Welcome Speech by the President. In, Proceedings of the Association of Rural District Councils entitled: The Role of Local Authorities in Devolution of Functions from Central Government and Sector Ministries to Rural District Councils. Kadoma Ranch Motel.

Maveneke, T., V. Dzingirai, and I. Bond (1999). 'Local Participation as an Instrument of Conservation and Development: the Case of CAMPFIRE in Zimbabwe.' in *African Perspectives: Practices and Polices Supporting Sustainable Development*. Gentofte/Harare, Scandinavian Seminar College/Weaver Press.

Meinzen-Dick, R., A. Knox, and M. D. Gregorio (1999). *Collective Action, Property Rights and Devolution of Natural Resource Management: Exchange of Knowledge and Implications for Policy*. Proceedings of the International Conference held from 21-25 June, 1999 in Puerto Azul, The Phillipines. Feldafing, Deutsche Stiftung für Internationale Entwicklung (DSE).

Mohamed, N. (2001). *Co-Governing Natural Resources in Southern Africa: Lessons from Fisheries Co-management, Malawi, and Conservation Co-Management, South Africa*. Western Cape, University of Western Cape, Programme for Land and Agrarian Studies (PLAAS).

Murombedzi, J. (1992). *Decentralisation or Recentralisation? Implementing CAMPFIRE in the Omay Communal Lands of the Nyaminyami District*. Harare, University of Zimbabwe, Centre for Applied Social Sciences (CASS).

Murphree, M.W. (1991). *Communities as Institutions for Resource Management*. Harare, University of Zimbabwe, Centre for Applied Social Sciences (CASS).

Nabane N., V. Dzingirai and E. Madzudzo (1996). Membership in Common Property Regimes: a Case Study of Guruve, Binga, Tsholotsho and Bulilimamangwe CAMPFIRE Programmes. Harare, CASS Occasional Paper.

National Conservation Strategy, April 1987. Harare, Government of Zimbabwe, Ministry of Natural Resources and Tourism.

Nhira, C., S. Baker, P. Gondo, J. J. Mangono, and C. Marunda (1998). *Contesting Inequality in Access to Forests*. Policy that Works for People Series No. 5. University of Zimbabwe, Centre for Applied Social Sciences (CASS), Forestry Commission Zimbabwe, and International Institute for Environment and Development (IIED), United Kingdom.

Odero, K. K. and P. Huchu (1998). *Community-Based Ecotourism Venture: the Case of Sunungukai Camp, Zimbabwe*. World Bank/WBI's CBNRM Initiative.

Ramboll Group (2001). *Natural Resource Management – Capacity Development in Environment.* http://www.ramboll.dk/development/uk/natural/capacity_development.htm

Ribot, J. C. (1999). *Accountable Representation and Power in Participatory and Decentralised Environmental Management.* Washington D.C. ,World Resources Institute.

———— (2001). *Decentralised Natural Resources Management: Nature and Democratic Decentralisation in Sub-Saharan Africa. A Summary Report Prepared for the UNCDF Symposium on Decentralisation Local Governance in Africa.* Washington D.C., World Resources Institute.

Thomas, S. J. (1991). The Legacy of Dualism and Decision-Making: The Prospects for Local Institutional Development in CAMPFIRE. Harare, CASS Occasional Paper.

Turnham, D. (1999). 'Sustainable Development and Community Mobilisation: An SSC Overview Paper' in *African Perspectives: Practices and Polices Supporting Sustainable Development*. Gentofte/Harare, Scandinavian Seminar College/Weaver Press. http:www.cdr.dk/sscafrica/tur2-ssa.htm

Wilson, K. (1997). 'Community-Based Natural resources Management in Theory and Practice in Southern Africa'. Yale University, *The Common Property Digest*, No. 41, p. 7-9.

Winter, M. (1998). *Decentralised Natural Resource Management in the Sahel: Overview and Analysis.* London, International Institute for Environment and Development (IIED).

## Appendix A

### The Allocation of Revenue by RDCs between 1989 and 1996

*Source: WWF, CAMPFIRE database as quoted by Maveneke, Dzingirai and Bond.*

| | Disbursed to sub-district levels | Wildlife and programme management | Council levy | Other | Unallocated |
|---|---|---|---|---|---|
| 1989-1996 US$million | 4.9 | 2.1 | 1.2 | 0.2 | 0.99 |
| 1989-1996 Z$million | 35.2 | 14.4 | 8.8 | 1.3 | 8.3 |
| % of total activity | 53 | 22 | 13 | 2 | 10 |

# Chapter 6

# In search of a better CAMPFIRE: The case of the Manyuchi Dam fisheries project

*Rudo A. Sanyanga*

## Introduction

Following adverse reviews of the Communal Areas Management Programme for Indigenous Resources (CAMPFIRE) (for a summary see Mamimine in this volume), the programme sought to address some of the issues of concern by diversifying the focus from wildlife, particularly large mammals, to other natural resources. It also shifted from the original CAMPFIRE approach, where Rural District Councils (RDCs) more or less owned the projects, to a situation where communities were directly involved from project formulation to implementation. The Manyuchi Fisheries Project, in Mwenezi District of Masvingo Province, represents an example of such a thrust.

The Project has so far drawn together the local communities, the responsible local authority (Mwenezi Rural District Council), a non-governmental organisation (CAMPFIRE Association), and an international donor (USAID) in an intricate web of relationships. The expectation was that these relationships would be managed in a way that would both shape and change the practice of the management of common resources, in this case the common fisheries in Manyuchi Dam. The project was designed in such a way that management of fisheries would be brought in line with the global development paradigm of sustainable development, which emphasises a balance between human needs and the conservation of resources, and strong local participation by the affected people. This chapter reports on attempts at such a process by examining the space created for the local communities to bring about the effective management of common fisheries in Manyuchi Dam.

The chapter does not undertake an evaluation of the project since it is still in its infancy; rather it searches for clues that might result in a better CAMPFIRE.

The Manyuchi Dam Fisheries Project was conceived to show that a community fisheries project run under the CAMPFIRE philosophy can succeed, provided some of the well-documented shortcomings of the original CAMPFIRE concept are addressed. The fundamental difference from the original CAMPFIRE was that the community, in the form of a trust, owned the project, with Mwenezi Rural District Council (RDC) acting as a facilitator. The RDC would provide technical advice and administrative assistance if and when required. It was envisaged that the critical parameter for success of the project would be community organisation and participation. This explains why elaborate efforts were made to ensure participation of the local communities.

USAID, through the CAMPFIRE Development Fund (CDF), provided the funds required for the procurement of construction material, project equipment and initial operating capital. Local people provided labour for construction and some of the locally-available materials, such as bricks and water.

The expected major positive impact of the project was the restoration of the sustainable management of fisheries, which would result in ecological as well as economic benefits. On the economic front, the perceived benefits included employment and income-generating opportunities for the local people. Local social services were expected to improve because of the money initially invested in the project as well as from its proceeds. With benefits accruing to the local people, it was expected that a sense of resource ownership would increase among the local community. This would lead to a reduction of poaching activities, especially if it was supported by a participatory-based monitoring system.

The success of the project was seen as highly dependent on good fish harvests, effective marketing strategies, stakeholder collaborative effort, and durable social relationships within the community. In many respects the project was forward-looking, based as it was on seeking to ensure that the problems hitherto associated with CAMPFIRE were not repeated, but were used as practical lessons in implementing the project. The project description in the following paragraphs gives details of this new alternative. The chapter concludes with a discussion of how the new approach differed, and whether it holds promise for a better and viable community-based natural resource utilisation and conservation, which represents the main tenet of CAMPFIRE.

The information upon which this chapter is based was collected during a study commissioned by Mwenezi Rural District Council, which was carried out in January 2001. For data collection the study employed key informant interviews, a literature review, community meetings and ecological surveys.

## Background

Mwenezi Rural District Council helped to establish a fishery project on Manyuchi Dam. The idea of establishing the fisheries project under CAMPFIRE was mooted by Mwenezi RDC in 1999, on behalf of communities in Wards 4, 6, 9, and 10. These were Negari, Masaverema, Makuwerere/Chizumba and Nyamhondo II. The project was aimed at conserving the Manyuchi environs as well as providing income to the local communities. The project sought to allow local people to maximise benefits from their natural resources through sustainable management and utilisation. USAID funded the project through the USAID Natural Resource Management Project (NRMP) under the CAMPFIRE Development Fund (CDF). A critical requirement for this fund was that both a feasibility study and an environmental review and environmental impact assessment be undertaken. More details of the project are provided later in the chapter.

### *Overview of the Study Area*

Mwenezi Rural District is in Masvingo Province and shares borders with the Rural Districts of Beitbridge, Bikita West, Mberengwa and Chivi. The four wards participating in the project border Manyuchi Dam. When the project was proposed they had already established Ward CAMPFIRE Committees (WCC) (CAMPFIRE report, 2000).

The land around Manyuchi Dam is largely communal, and comprises Mberengwa, Maranda and Matibi Communal Lands. These lands are controlled according to the Zimbabwe Communal Lands Act [Chapter 20:04], which gives communities the right to occupy and use land but not to own it. Like most other communal areas in Zimbabwe, the major economic activity of Mwenezi district is subsistence agriculture, although there is a relatively significant small-scale commercial cotton-farming enterprise. The region has generally inhospitable climatic conditions, characterised by low and highly irregular rainfall (450-650 mm), and occasional dry spells and extremely high temperatures during the rainy season. The mean maximum temperature is around 31°C and the mean minimum is 23°C. The District falls in the dry and hot agro-ecological zone V, which makes it one of the most arid regions in Zimbabwe.

As already said, local people are engaged in subsistence agriculture, producing traditional crop combinations that generally include maize and sorghum for household consumption. However, because of the poor climatic conditions that prevail in most of the area, these crops usually fail. In times of recurrent droughts, as has been the case during the last decade, this area is most vulnerable. Consequently, people rely on food handouts from the government and other charity organisations. At the time of the survey there had been a significant turn to production of cotton as a cash crop. This produced average annual incomes of Z$15,000 per household.

Cattle and goats, in that order, dominated the types of livestock kept in the area. The cattle herds were large for the area resulting in inadequate grazing land. As a consequence, livestock grazed within the defined conservation belt, on the shorelines of Manyuchi Dam. During dry seasons the grazing areas turned into dusty grounds.

The community placed a great deal of value on their cattle herds. Some families owned as much as sixty head of cattle but the majority had none. There was a general shortage of draught power among the poorer families, which negatively affected agricultural production.

The settlement pattern in Mwenezi was dense, with an average of 35 persons per square km (Dept. of Physical Planning, Ministry of ..., Harare, 2000). Most of the settlers originated from surrounding commercial farms and communal lands. Hence, the community was made up of Ndebele, Shona, Shangani and Venda tribes. There were four languages spoken in the area, although most people understood both Shona and Ndebele. Some of the people in the area had been there for less than 40 years.

### *The Manyuchi Dam Shoreline*

The shoreline of Manyuchi Dam is hilly. The terrain is rugged, with several rivers upstream, and low-lying plains along major tributaries and in between mountains. The area east and downstream of the dam has gentle modal slopes, small hills and rock outcrops. The altitude ranges from 540-600m above sea level. There are small pockets of gently sloping land close to the shores of the dam.

The dam is situated on the border between Midlands and Masvingo Provinces, more specifically between Mberengwa and Mwenezi Districts. The dam has a capacity of 303 million cubic meters at full supply level. It is the fifth largest inland reservoir in the country, with a total surface area of 4,290 hectares.

Manyuchi Dam was constructed mainly to provide water for the irrigation of oil palm, a crop that failed to materialise. The dam is now used to irrigate sugar plantations by the Triangle Sugar Estates. An estimated 100 families were moved to higher ground to make way for the dam. Compensation was paid to these families. However, some families on the Mberengwa side have since moved back to their original sites, which are within the conservation belt.

Most of the catchment area is degraded communal land within the Midlands province. The reservoir lies in the hydrological area of the mid-Mwenezi catchment and drains into the Limpopo River. The Mwenezi River and the Mundi River form two of the four major tributaries. Currently, the Mwenezi Development Corporation (MDC) abstracts only 1% of the water for irrigation purposes. Other activities in the reservoir include commercial and sport fishing. There is hardly any documented information regarding pre-impoundment or early studies on the dam.

**Table 1 Some characteristics of Manyuchi Dam**

| | |
|---|---|
| Height of wall | 41 m |
| Length of wall | 240 m |
| Altitude | 540 m.a.s.l. |
| Catchment area | 5,166 $km^2$ |
| Mean annual run-off from catchment | 138,000 m litres |
| Capacity of reservoir | 303 x $10^6$ $m^3$ |
| Effective capacity | 319,000 Ml |
| Surface area | 4,290 hectares |
| Maximum depth | 35.7m |
| Mean depth | 7 m |
| Purpose | Irrigation |
| Yield | 59,000Ml |

Source: Zimbabwe Commission on Large Dams (ZIMCOLD) n. d.

*Dam ownership*

Mwenezi Dam was financed by the MDC on the 'Build, Operate and Transfer' principle. This scheme will run for 40 years (1989-2029), during which time the MDC will draw water at no cost. The operations, maintenance and regulation of the dam are the responsibility of the Zimbabwe National Water Authority (ZINWA). Over the 40-year period, 80% of the water is meant for MDC while 20% is to be for the communal lands of Mberengwa (10%) and Mwenezi (10%). ZINWA's functions are to maintain the dam wall, distribute water at cost, regulate water release, and monitor pollution.

Manyuchi, by virtue of its size, qualifies as a national dam and could have been so designated. According to the National Parks Act (1975), the dam should have been designated 'national'. Its management would then have fallen to the state, through the Department of National Parks. The likelihood of the dam being declared national was and is remote (personal communication, National Parks Masvingo Provincial Warden). This would add to the financial responsibilities of National Parks, whose mandate has shifted to concentrate on cost centres. Since it was built on communal land it also qualifies as a regional dam, under the authority of Mberengwa and Mwenezi Rural District Councils in terms of Statutory Instrument 40 of 1994. Until declared otherwise by government, the dam belongs to the two local authorities and, at the time of the study, all stakeholders had informally agreed that the dam was regional.

*Dam management*

When the study took place there was no organised management of the reservoir. ZINWA confined its operations to the maintenance of the dam wall and water releases. There was no authority enforcing any regulations. Nor was there any monitoring of fish off-take, pollution, or siltation levels. This may have been largely due to the uncertainty about the ownership status, and a lack of funds and capacity of the Rural District Councils and National Parks. It also appeared that the Rural District Councils were not clear as to what management of the reservoir entailed.

Initially, the Department of National Parks and Wildlife Management had assumed that the dam would come under its jurisdiction and thus had occasionally policed the dam and carried out fish assessment surveys. The last of these surveys was undertaken in 1997. The Department of Agricultural Extension (AGRITEX) had carried out the initial surveys before the commercial fishery was started up by the three co-operatives in 1992, and had given training in gillnet fishing techniques, net mending, and record keeping.

*Previous fishing activities in the Manyuchi Dam environs*

Prior to commencement of the fisheries project there were four categories of fishermen operating in the reservoir. These included co-operatives, poachers, anglers from the community, and sport fishermen, specifically bass fishermen.

Three co-operatives instituted in 1992 by the ministry responsible for co-operatives were partially operational. Due to problems related to management, lack of group cohesion, and poor entrepreneurship, the fishing co-operatives failed to function properly. They then disintegrated into five smaller groups, namely Tinechido, Torima, Madziva, Tinogona and Chomufudze. Although there were 58 individuals formally registered as members of the five groups, only 22 were active. One group, Madziwa, had stopped functioning altogether. Many of the fishermen were not permanently based on the fishing camps, working instead on their respective homesteads during the agricultural season.

There were a total of eight boats, two of which were motorised. However, due to fuel shortages and lack of maintenance, the motorised boats were being operated as rowing boats. Each individual in a group owned an average of three 45m nets of mesh sizes 3.5-4". National Parks and Mwenezi and Mberengwa Rural District Councils collected license fees from the groups every year.

Of the four groups present, only two had some savings. Originally, each member was required to contribute Z$100 per month towards boat maintenance, group welfare and equipment replacement costs. However, since the collapse of the co-operatives individual members had not been making contributions.

The level of fishing was calculated at 10-20kg per group per day, based on average daily catch records kept by some of the groups. The co-operatives faced problems of limited nets, thefts of nets, and destruction of nets by crocodiles and hippos. Ninety per cent of the co-operative members were willing to join the community fisheries under the new project. The remainder, especially those not belonging to the wards, were not happy with the suggestion. They felt insecure. During the initial stages of the project formulation Mwenezi RDC had passed a resolution that the current co-operatives be dismantled and integrated within the community groups. At the time of the field survey some of the co-operative members claimed not to be aware of this resolution.

The second category of people engaged in fishing were illegal fishermen, who used stolen nets, sacks, traps, baskets, and nets of illegal mesh sizes to harvest fish. In the main, they were people who came from outside the community, further away from the dam or even from other districts. They lived in bushes or were housed in the homes of some community members, engaging in fishing activities very late at night or in the early hours of the morning, when few people were around. The catch comprised very small fish, mostly juveniles. The illegal fishermen were not willing to join co-operatives, claiming they had no money to pay membership fees and fear of existing co-operative members, as there had been clashes before.

The third category of fishermen was that of the community members themselves, who engaged in rod and line fishing. There was little problem with this activity except that it was not regulated, and thus could easily become uncontrollable. For instance, there was no catch size limit. Reports claimed that as many as 53 per cent of the people around the dam, both in Mberengwa and Mwenezi, participated in rod and line fishing.

The fourth category comprised those bass anglers who came from other parts of Zimbabwe and from South Africa. They last visited Manyuchi Dam in December 1998. They used to arrive in groups of ten or so and paid daily camping, boat and fishing fees for the duration of their stay to the local authority, which kept all the money. These visits encouraged the local authority to start to construct a campsite for such visitors. This was not completed as the visits have now stopped because of the political situation in the country.

## The Manyuchi Dam fisheries project: a description

### *Project Goals*

The goals of the project were as follows:

- To alleviate poverty through creation of employment. The 1995 Poverty Assessment Study survey ranked Mwenezi district amongst the poorest in the country, with 86% poor households. The high level of poverty was due to the fact that the district lies in the driest part of the country, which is characterised by periodic droughts. Not surprisingly therefore, agricultural performance was poor and blamed as the underlying cause of low incomes in the district, contributing in turn to the persistence of poverty.

- To capacitate the community with relevant skills in community-based fisheries. Traditionally, the community members were not fishermen, but peasant agriculturists. The general attitude had been to regard fishing as a pastime, to be taken up commercially when agriculture was not thriving. Fishing was normally abandoned during the rainy season in favour of agriculture, and therefore was not regarded as a business.

- To enhance the conservation of Manyuchi catchment area by preventing poaching and grazing along the banks. It was believed that when communities had a stake in the fisheries it would be an incentive to discourage poaching. They would, it was hoped, take steps to protect the catchment area from siltation, and practices which would pollute the dam.

- To strengthen the local institutions and promote the people's participation in their own development. The project was intended to bring the community together to work for a common cause. It was believed that a sense of togetherness would help develop local institutions.

It was estimated that a total of 9,384 households would benefit from the project, directly and indirectly; 28 households would directly benefit from employment. It was perceived that the rest of the Mwenezi district population would benefit indirectly through improved infrastructure and social services. Other benefits would be in the form of skills-transfer and knowledge in natural resource management, mainly to those directly involved with the project.

### *General institutional arrangements*

The community unanimously agreed, during the Participatory Rural Appraisal (PRA) meetings, that the project should become a community project, and one that was wholly owned and managed by them. These meetings were carried out prior to the study. The Manyuchi Dam Fish Project Trust was formed to run the project. Details about the trust are contained in sections that follow. The Trust would be the highest authority within the management hierarchy (Figure 1). The RDC and CAMPFIRE Ward Committee, with technical assistance, were expected to take an active role in its establishment. The Board of Trustees was responsible for holding the assets of the project in trust and was the overall guiding body of the project. The CAMPFIRE co-ordinator was not only expected to take up the active role of co-ordinating activities (including training) between the four wards but also to take responsibility for the work of the individual managers of the four camps. The Ward CAMPFIRE Committees were to institute subcommittees that would be responsible for monitoring and auditing the project. Reporting to the CAMPFIRE co-ordinator, the individual camp managers were to oversee the day-to-day activities of the project. The project site staff were to be composed of the fish camp managers and two fish processors/ marketing staff per ward.

Figure 3 gives the organisational structure of the project. The structure below the level of the CAMPFIRE co-ordinator was to be replicated in each of the four wards.

## *Institutional actors and their responsibilities*

### *The Trust*

The Trust was to be formed and legally registered. The RDC, or an external facilitator, was to be hired to assist in the formation of the Trust. There was need to consult with the community over the formation of the Trust and to draw up the terms of reference and the constitution with the community. The PRA meetings recommended that the Board of Trustees be composed of the traditional leadership of the area and the WCC chairpersons from the four wards. It was also recommended that the RDC and other development institutions be included in the Board of Trustees as ex-officio members.

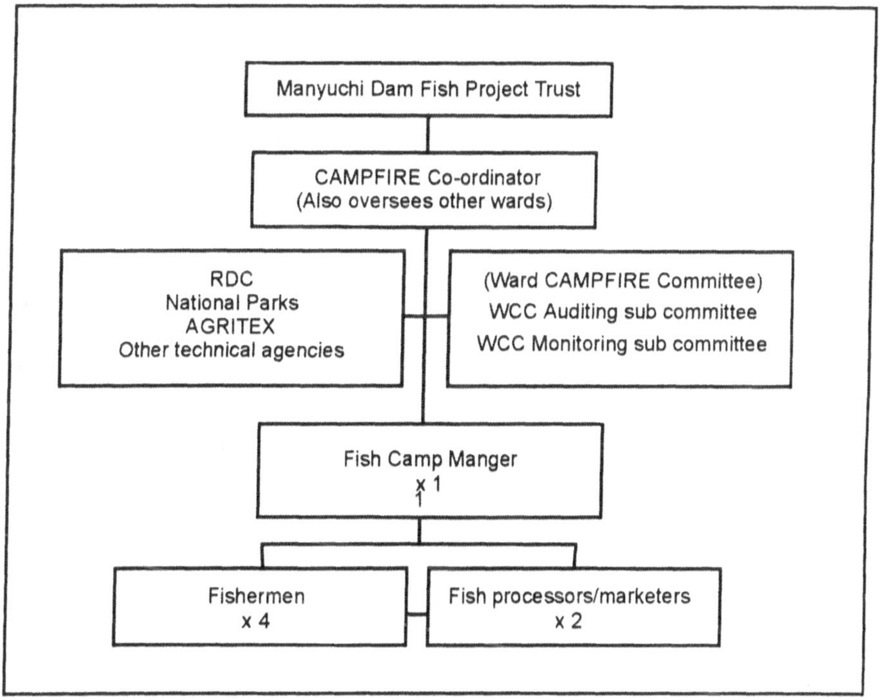


Figure 3: Manyuchi Fish Project Management Structure

This was the legal institution of the project, which was meant to ensure safe trusteeship of community assets, finances and investments on behalf of the community. One or two members of the Board of Trustees would be signatories to the project. The Board of Trustees was the umbrella body of the four fishing camps.

*Ward CAMPFIRE Committee (WCC) and monitoring and auditing subcommittees*

The WCCs were already in place in each ward before commencement of this project. According to the Ward CAMPFIRE constitution, WCCs are responsible for monitoring, evaluation and auditing through their subcommittees. They are also responsible for exploring opportunities for further CAMPFIRE-related investments that might spin off from the fisheries project. These could be investment in tourism development in the area. The WCCs from the four wards are supposed to closely liase on issues relating to fishing quotas, and on the enforcement of rules and regulations around the dam. They are also to assist the CAMPFIRE Co-ordinator in the initial phase of project establishment, in recruiting staff, and drawing up terms of reference.

Monitoring subcommittees are to be responsible for monitoring project impacts according to the monitoring plan given in the environmental review report. The auditing subcommittees are to work closely with the RDC in auditing the project in their wards.

*The CAMPFIRE Co-ordinator*

For this project the CAMPFIRE co-ordinator was to be responsible for co-ordinating activities between the four wards, recruiting staff, maintaining liaisons with the RDC, service providers, camp managers and the Board of Trustees, identifying training needs and facilitating training.

*Rural District Council*

The RDC was a key player in the project as it had been responsible for its development and the sourcing of related funds. It was expected to play the role of key advisor regarding the use of the CDF funds and to monitor financial use as well as conduct audits in collaboration with the WCC subcommittees. The RDC, through its engineer, CEO, and administrator, was expected to supervise construction of related infrastructure and the early phases of the implementation of the project.

*The managers*

The managers, who were to be recruited locally, were to have responsibility for the day-to-day planning and implementation of project activities and staff supervision in their respective wards. The managers were to be the key liaison persons between the project, the CAMPFIRE Co-ordinator, and the WCCs. They would receipt cash sales, supervise staff, ensure quality control, and keep financial records.

*Fish processors/marketers*

These were responsible for the processing and storage of fish and were also to assist with marketing.

*Fishermen*

They were to have the role of fishing, mending nets, maintaining fish catch records, cleaning the boats, general maintenance of the site, and law enforcement on the dam.

*Other actors*

Other stakeholders, including AGRITEX, National Parks and the South Eastern Dry Areas Programme (SEDAP), were to be technical advisors to the project. The survey conducted to assess the current and potential support for the project indicated that it could be supported technically, but not financially, by several Government and non-governmental organisations. However, it was indicated that services would have to be hired or have the costs covered by the project. Table 2 below summarises the potential support from these stakeholders.

*Benefit Sharing*

Benefits from the project were to be shared between the community, CAMPFIRE Association, and the Mwenezi RDC. The benefit sharing was as follows: the community would receive 83% of the profit, Mwenezi RDC 15% and CAMPFIRE Association 2%.

The community, through the Board of Trustees, would own the facilities. On decommissioning, if any sale of assets were conducted, 100% of the revenue would go to the community. The benefit-sharing differed from CAMPFIRE projects in that the community would pay the RDC and not vice versa. Other projects stipulated a minimum of 25% of the revenue to the community. In this case not more than 15% would go to the RDC.

*Monitoring*

The monitoring and auditing subcommittees would be responsible for regular monitoring. As indicated in the Environmental Impact Assessment (EIA), it was recommended that the following factors be monitored or audited: fish catches, financial, social, economic and ecological impacts. The detailed monitoring plan was given in the environmental review report. The Trust was to have the project audited yearly by council or independent auditors.

The catch records were to be taken daily as fish were landed. AGRITEX or DNPWLM could be hired (at costs to cover their subsistence) to carry out stock assessment surveys annually and also to analyse the annual fish catches. A report showing catches and catch trends was to be produced annually. These assessments would indicate the progress of the project. The monitoring subcommittee was responsible for ensuring that this was carried out.

**Table 2: Potential support from other stakeholders**

| Stakeholder | Possible areas of contribution |
|---|---|
| RDC | • Manpower<br>• Project administration<br>• Vehicle maintenance<br>• Supervision and tendering contract construction |
| SEDAP | • Complementary activities in support of sustainable agriculture and conservation |
| National Parks | • Carry out fish stock assessment surveys<br>• Provide training in fish technology<br>• Monitor and enforce bylaws |
| CARE International | • Training and extension in catchment management<br>• Restocking, if required |
| National Affairs | • Training in business and general management<br>• Periodic evaluation and auditing of the project |
| Physical Planning | • Developing master plans and ensuring adherence to plans |
| ZINWA | • Monitor pollution levels and water quality<br>• Certification of siting and location of sanitary facilities |
| MDTC (Mwenezi Development Training Centre) | • Training in business management and relevant skills as requested |
| AGRITEX | • Technical assistance – surveys and training in fishing methods and gear mending<br>• Assist in licensing<br>• Collect returns |
| Veterinary Department | • Can analyse samples in cases of fish kills<br>• Role otherwise unclear |
| CADEC (Catholic Development Corporation) | • Support social development projects.<br>• Injection of funds or fishing equipment |

## Ensuring project success – analytical points

Several factors could affect viability of the fishing project and these needed to be guarded against. The EIA had a monitoring plan to ensure an early diagnosis of these factors so as to take mitigating measures whenever possible. Some of the points indicated in the EIA that the study also found pertinent are discussed below:

- It was recognised that there was a possible danger of a *decline in fish stocks*. Previously, fishing on Manyuchi Dam had not been closely monitored. There had been no substantive quantification of levels of fish stock, neither had a sustainable level of fishing been estimated and applied. Impact on stock levels can only be realised after a number of seasons and by making regular fish stock assessments.

- The EIA recommended that fish stock assessments be undertaken yearly. The annual stock assessments were to be augmented by use of catch records. Hence it was also imperative that catch records be accurate and kept throughout the fishing periods. Based on current estimates of potential and actual catches, there was no immediate threat of failure for the project.

- The community groups were to discuss the yearly catch levels together with results from stock assessments. Recommended fishing regimes needed to be adhered to and closely monitored. An annual survey should be conducted by technical experts to assess the level of effort and a controlled catch-return system implemented by the fishermen.

- *Open access* was seen as posing a danger to the project since Manyuchi Dam is surrounded by communal land, which made controlled access difficult to achieve. The open access nature of the shoreline had been a major cause of poaching in the past and therefore the community needed to create a law enforcement unit. There was need for strict law enforcement, only allowing access to those with a permit. Rod and line fishing could be permitted but with controlled bag size. Alternatively, the traditional chief's hands (police) could, with some basic training, be used for that activity. Any attempts to curb poaching should solicit the full participation of community members, as they will be benefiting from the project.

- Project viability could also be seriously affected by continued *poaching* within the breeding sites and the fishing of juveniles. For the community to actively curb poaching they needed to be aware of the adverse impacts and also realise what they would gain from the project. Therefore, awareness campaigns in the CAMPFIRE wards were needed.

- Personnel in the management structure needed to be trained to enable them to manage the enterprise efficiently so as to neutralise *poor management*. The community would entrust a small group of people with the management of a common resource-based enterprise. Lack of transparency, misappropriation, and favouritism would affect viability. The whole process needed to be monitored to iron out any problems that might arise. A change of attitude was needed so that the community would play an important role in the project. The first year of the project included training of the community, especially of those managing the project. The training was regarded as crucial since the type of management structure and capacity of the actors could pose a danger to the success of the project.

- The Manyuchi catchment is mostly communal and the likelihood of *siltation* cannot be ruled out if proper catchment management practices are not instituted. This necessitates monitoring.
- The possibility of *conflicts* arising between the old and new fishing groups, between the wards' fishing groups themselves, or even between non-fishers and fishers, was a threat to the project. It was imperative that the original co-operative members be incorporated into the project structures, for their exclusion could be a cause of serious conflict. This could result in the co-operative members turning to poaching and threatening the viability of the project. The project handled this issue by giving those current co-op members who were still fishing the option to be employed by the community projects. It also bought out their equipment after an assessment and at negotiated prices.
- Any successful management structure had to clearly show decentralisation of power from local government structure (RDC) as community members had already indicated their mistrust of the RDC. According to the community, the RDC had to take a less dominant role. Formation of the Trust ensured that the RDC's role was reduced to a level required by the community. The success of the project would, to a large extent, depend on the organisational capabilities of the communities. The degree of organisation would translate to efficient production and hence profit.
- The project could be jeopardised by inadequate infrastructure. The project could be affected by a poor road network, the overall poor infrastructure in terms of telephones, power, and other services. There was no electricity in the area, although the dam exhibited great potential for power generation. Although an impediment, this was not seen as crucial. Alternatives such as solar power could be employed later on in the project's life.
- The processing methods of the produce needed to be attended to. Shelf life of fish is limited, and without good processing and storage facilities the fish spoil easily. The project could establish a large, central distribution warehouse away from the fishing camps, preferably at Neshuro Growth Point. The problem of the poor transport system would be solved as traders could easily access the warehouse, which would broaden

the market base. The distribution centre could also target the more established fish dealers and reduce dependence on an ever-changing trader population. Due to the initial high demand for fish, there was not much effort required to develop the market.

- Most community members were already involved in other projects (gardening, irrigation, soap-making, conservation activities, etc.). Household interviews showed this figure to total about 80%. There was need for careful screening of the members to be involved in the fisheries project, as some may become over-burdened and their commitment be negatively affected.
- Cotton growing and other agricultural activities within the area were also viable options. These alternatives would result in a more even distribution of the income base, as the fisheries project was limited by the number of community members it would be able to absorb.

In sum, the main factors for success in the project would be a constant availability of fish (the most crucial), available markets and a well-organised community.

## Conclusion

The Manyuchi Dam Fisheries project differed from previous CAMPFIRE approaches in that the community was put in the forefront of running its own project as well as participating fully in decision-making. Furthermore, the project was only funded after feasibility studies and a positive Environmental Impact Assessment were carried out.

A structure, in this case the Trust, was put in place to ensure that project goals were met. Components such as training, campaigning, and technical assistance were used to give capacity to the community and the individuals involved in the project. To avoid major collapse, safety nets were devised for almost all the activities. These included soliciting technical assistance from other organisations, such as Government institutions or non-governmental organisations.

In its infancy the project required assistance from the other actors, not with actual decision-making but to empower and inform the communities so that they were able to make independent decisions without fear of reprisals from the RDC or donor. In this regard, the study showed the donor had played a very useful role, removing itself from the daily running of the project and limiting its involvement to the provision of funds.

Registration of the Trust with the Government and making it a legal institution renders it liable for any misuse of funds and assets as well as being subject to audits. Community members had been given sufficient information for them to realise their role and the role of the Trust. However, it was resource availability rather than administrative issues, which normally cause many projects to fail, that needed to be nurtured until the community felt confident enough to take responsibility for the project.

The potential of the local people to handle the project existed. All they needed was the motivation, which seemed to be there at the beginning. This, in turn, needed to be supported by good and effective institutional support mechanisms. It does, however, remain to be seen if this will indeed evolve into a better CAMPFIRE.

## References

CAMPFIRE (1999). Project Constitutions for Ward 4, 6, 9 and 10 in Mwenezi Rural District. Harare, CAMPFIRE.

Department of Physical Planning, Masvingo and Midlands (2000). Manyuchi Dam and Environs. Local plan report of study.

Ministry of Lands (1994). *Communal Lands Act*. Statutory Instrument 40 of 1994. Harare, Government of Zimbabwe.

Ministry of Natural Resources, Department of National Parks and Wildlife Management (1975) *National Parks and Wildlife Act*, 14 of 1975, Salisbury, Government of Rhodesia.

Ministry of Public Service Labour and Social Welfare (1995). 1995 *Poverty Assessment Study Survey main report*. Harare, Government of Zimbabwe, Social Development Fund.

Ministry of Mines, Environment and Tourism (1997). *Environmental Impact Assessment Guidelines*, Harare, Government of Zimbabwe.

Mwenezi RDC (1999). *Project Concept Paper on Community Based Fisheries at Manyuchi Dam*.

# Section 2

# Transboundary issues in common property management

# Chapter 7

# The role of physical planning in the management of transboundary natural resources in Southern Africa

*Liliana Vassileva*

## Introduction

Local communities, provincial and national governments and international bodies have, in their various ways, established rules for the use and management of common property resources (Dellapenna, 1993; SADC, 1995; UNEP/UCMC, 2001). At local level, practical aspects are dominant and, although the definitions are not perfect, they are at least useful in setting up boundaries and parameters within which local communities can gain from the commons, for example through equitable access to the resource, sharing monetary gains, and in some cases obtaining much-needed food. However, in most cases, local communities do not have a free hand in the management of resources; the rules are usually established elsewhere. Thus local communities have to abide by regulations that are more or less imposed upon them.

At national level, the established practice is to centrally determine the use and management of the commons. In this scenario the commons are treated in the same way throughout the country. At this level, while discussions and, in some cases, innovations may be technically sound, the communities that are supposed to gain from these interventions often find little merit in them, and thus do not identify with them. Even in cases where local communities are involved the problems do not disappear. A good example is the Communal Areas Programme for the Management of Indigenous Resources

(CAMPFIRE), where problems resulting from inflexible management systems imposed by the state have been reported (see Mamimine, this volume). As a result the anticipated participation by local communities, to ensure the sustainability of the resource use, has been compromised.

The success of global projects appears to be most doubtful. The commons seem to be worst treated at this level due to the difficulties associated with reaching consensus, particularly between developed and developing countries. The problem surrounding the Biodiversity Convention is a case in point (see Mudiwa, this volume). Perhaps the most illustrative case is the Kyoto Agreement concerning the quality of air as related to greenhouse gas emissions and global warming. Not only the politicians, but also the researchers too, are disunited in their understanding of the so-called 'global warming'. The problem is compounded by insufficient data. This, however, did not stop a small group of meteorologists in the United States of America arguing that global warming is not of such a frightening extent. The European Union nonetheless ratified the Kyoto treaty while the US administration took its cue from its scientists and rejected it.

Comparatively speaking, the best chances of ensuring the sustainable use of common property resources are at the regional level. The principal reason is that at this level common property resources are within transboundary ecological systems, which have stabilised over a long time in both the physical and social realms. Convincing examples are the Zambezi and Limpopo Valleys, where there are many similarities in their geographical, ecological, social, demographic, historical and ethnic aspects (Gates, 2001; Manyanga, *et al.*, 2000; Mutembwa, 1998). The patterns of population resettlement, the models of housing, and community development are almost the same in the respective countries.

While co-operation at regional level is most promising in relation to sustainable management of common property resources, this is not to say that it is without problems or challenges. Regional projects in geographic areas characterised by transboundary ecological systems, such as the Mediterranean Sea, the Nile River, the Black Sea and the Danube River, carried out by special task forces and appointed authorities have, by their technical orientation, tended to exclude local communities in decision-making processes. Moreover, some projects tend to be too sectored. In such instances attempts to selectively exploit the common resource with no regard to other related aspects, such as taking into account the economic and social welfare of people living around the resources, may succeed in the short term but are not sustainable. This chapter argues that sustainable utilisation and management of transboundary common property resources is best achieved at regional level and that physical planners should play a leading role in this regard. We also suggest that regional level co-operation has the potential to avoid the problems of hegemony and marginalisation in the management of common property resources that fall within the boundaries of more than one nation-state.

In addition to comparative and analytical approaches, this chapter uses an explorative approach in order to recommend the best management practices. Some examples are mentioned briefly to emphasise the advantages of other practices that identify and redress existing deficiencies.

## The challenges of managing commons at the regional level

### *The regional level – hope for sustainable development*

Management policies for transboundary common resources must ensure the sustainability of the resources, which among other things, should ensure fairness in the utilisation of common resources for present and future generations. A dynamic management strategy, which includes a long-term perspective and is holistic and multifarious, should be adopted. The strategy should also address the issue of poverty alleviation through the promotion of measures that are locally best understood, as well as policies that ensure access to national and international capital. To achieve this, science and technology must take a leading role in formulating and instituting strategic developmental frameworks as a common basis for negotiations and decision-making by politicians.

At the national level, which is logically assumed to represent a summary of local levels, national policies towards common resources are in most cases based on leading sectoral interests with few lessons being drawn from local experiences. The national level is seen as easily transforming to local community levels, although this is often not the case. This is why we argue for a regional approach to the management of the commons where technological and social dimensions are taken into account.

Cultures and traditions are strongest among local communities. However, technological and information advances may force them to succumb to the pressure of globalisation. As a result, hegemony or marginalisation may affect both the local and national levels. A typical example is Africa. The world would like to protect and enjoy African wildlife as a global property. Yet the needs of growing populations for homes, transport, services, land, and employment are often downplayed. Moreover, national aspirations such as economic growth may not be safeguarded by the global conventions. In southern Africa, the banning of trade in elephants and their products through The Convention on International Trade on Endangered Species (CITES) has robbed the region's countries of this much-needed revenue for economic growth.

As already stated, the level that gives significant hope for sustainable and beneficial management of commons is the regional level, where common property resources are usually found within transboundary ecological systems. Such resources have often long-influenced the development of the areas concerned, as is the case with the Limpopo River valley. People on both sides of the river have used the land for growing similar crops. They have built and lived in the same type of housing, and produced similar patterns of settlement. The people know when the water in the river is diminishing and have also experienced dramatic incidents of cyclones, floods and heavy rains. These riverine communities act upon their experience and are thus able to manage the available common resource sustainably. For example, Jaarsma, *et al.*, (2001) report that local communities in Mozambique observe ants' behaviour for flood forecasting and take appropriate measures as a result. Ideally, official administrative and institutional structures for the management of natural resources must widen people's participation in this important activity by incorporating their knowledge systems.

### *Information is power*

Challenges in the management of common property resources are frequently underestimated because of the assumption that there is an intimate knowledge of the common resources concerned, garnered through research studies. The problem is that in some cases the information is not available, and even if it is, it might not make any difference. One such example is the Nile Water Agreement. The Parliament of Kenya wanted a review of the agreement because of the obsolete ban, in place since 1929, on three countries regarding use of the water of Lake Victoria for irrigation. This agreement was originally set between the British High Commission in Cairo and the Egyptian Government, and was based on erroneous knowledge – that the source of the Nile was Lake Victoria. Today it is known that the river has sources in two areas, being the area of the Blue Nile and the area of the White Nile. This information ought, one would expect, to result in changes being made to management regimes of the resource concerned. Issues like the re-allocation of water in terms of quantity for use to all countries concerned, as well as environmental protection and monitoring water utilisation, should also change in line with the new knowledge. That is to say, available information should lead to decisions that are more informed, thereby ensuring sustainability of what is clearly a strategic resource of common interest to the member countries.

The second example, which shows other dimensions to the management of common resources, is the so-called Black Sea Partnership in Europe. The Black Sea project aims to reverse toxic pollution of the Danube River and Black Sea Basin and recover the ecosystem's conditions to the state they were in the 1960s. It involves more than 15 countries, including Bulgaria, Georgia, Romania, Russia, Turkey, the Ukraine, and ten countries upstream from the Danube River. A Global Environment Facility (GEF) of US$100 million was meant to enable six years of studies and policy reforms, agricultural reforms and wetland restoration. The team included participants from the United Nations Environment Programme (UNEP), the United Nations Development Programme (UNDP) and the World Bank (WB). The structure of this facility, from the outset, was such that decision-making was the preserve of these three organisations. The result was that those who know the situation better or best, such as the local communities and researchers, were disregarded. In Bulgaria, for example, extensive research work had already been carried out on the wetlands and the conservancies along the Danube. About two decades ago, a team of researchers from the Bulgarian Academy of Sciences and three reputed national universities suggested management solutions, but no actions were undertaken. One would recommend that this work be appreciated and incorporated into the existing project.

Another project based on a transboundary ecological system is the tripartite park that includes national parks of three countries, i.e. the Kruger Park of South Africa, the Gonarezhou Park of Zimbabwe and the Limpopo Park of Mozambique. This excellent project, which will boost tourism in southern Africa and benefit the three countries, is a serious step ahead in regional co-operation for the use and management of commons. The expectations are that management policies, methods of monitoring, maintenance and future development shall be common in all the countries. Initially, innovative approaches in the management of transboundary tourist activities will be related to immigration and custom matters, fees, transport, institutions and other issues. After some time other aspects of co-operation and management will probably arise, which may be related to local service industries, to the development of housing and other related labour and social policies. However, this project makes a lot of assumptions about a number of elements. It is only through the contribution of experts, including physical planners, that the project can succeed.

### *Some lessons*

Some important lessons from the above examples can assist in formulating a framework for guidelines for future actions in the management of common property resources. Most probably, a common approach to commons' management would occur at all hierarchical levels (MMET, 1998), although the actual contents of policies and their richness will differ according to formulated objectives and goals.

The lessons that can be gleaned from the above examples are that:

- The growing influence of globalisation in economic, social, environmental and intellectual activities is accompanied by many contradictions (Dellapenna, 1993) and it is becoming difficult to achieve consensus on global treaties. In order to avoid hegemony and marginalisation, the management of commons requires an evolutionary approach, rather than a revolutionary one. Some nations may not cope because of economic, social and financial reasons at the agreed times.
- Information on common resources has a dynamic nature due to natural and man-made forces exerting pressure on the resources, and the ever-developing technological

and scientific methods of collecting data and acquiring additional knowledge. The dynamic nature of knowledge makes a case for the decision-making process to be a staged one, which sets out staged outcomes within a suitable strategic framework for the realisation of sustainable objectives.

- Transboundary common resources affect the development of all sectors and sub-systems, despite some differences in the degree of effect. The dominating and leading common resources, such as water (Staley Consultants, 1995), wildlife, land and forests, cannot be considered irrelevant even in areas where they are not easily visible. A holistic approach to analyse and understand the interactions of all sub-systems in the commons under consideration could lead to reliable and sustainable decisions being taken.
- Institutions in the management of common resources are usually hierarchical. Although there is nothing intrinsically wrong with this, imposing stiff conditions pregnant with vested interests, such as models for decision-making, from upper levels upon lower levels is not justifiable. Such practices may give rise to conflicts over the resources thereby diminishing the desired management regimes as well as killing off the local initiative. Local knowledge and experiences must inform the new initiatives.

## Physical planning and the management of transboundary resources in practice

### *The planning-management link*

Management is by all definitions a process that involves four formal activities, namely planning, organising, directing and controlling. Irrespective of which type of management structure is adopted for a particular case, without planning there there can be no management. In the process of management, planning is most extensively done at the top level, whether the level itself be global, national, regional or local. Planning is measurable in relation to the specific nature of a project or undertaking and the relevant achievable objectives that are linked to time. Since transboundary commons fall within specific ecological systems the aim should be to achieve a balanced ecological protection and beneficial use (DEAT, 2000). Therefore, sustainability in management is related to strategic planning, which at the same time must be comprehensive and sufficiently flexible to respond to long-term challenges.

There is a belief that sustainability in the management of transboundary common property resources comes from applying scientific and technological approaches. Technology in general and Information Technology in particular are playing an increasingly important role in the management of commons, particularly in recent times (see Muzondo, this volume). Past, present and future information about commons, collected by traditional and advanced methods and relevantly stored, can also be used for various analyses in response to general and particular physical and social phenomena. Historical data also play a part, providing developmental profiles that can be used to assess the impact of various policies. However, for sustainability, all parties should be involved in the use and management of commons and should be equitably informed so that they have equal chances of negotiating the exact utilisation and management regimes of the resource. The possibilities of storing and analysing huge quantities of data, networking, conferencing and exchanging ideas and concepts, enhances the prospects of better management of the commons. This is the area where physical planning plays a role.

## *The art of physical planning*

Scientific approaches are capable of guaranteeing that the scope of management and respective policies are sustainable within a dynamic context. The dynamism of both the resources and the methods of factoring these resources exercise the minds of physical planners. 'Physical planning' is a term used for the planning of man-made environments for human and social activities and of specifically measurable sizes and land areas. The latter may concern geographic, ecological, administrative and rural or urban regions of varying sizes, for instance at province, district and town level. The term is used in the titles of official governmental agencies and institutes, including the Department of Physical Planning of Zimbabwe. It is part of the official terminology in relation to issues of planning for development.

Some specialists are of the opinion that this term implies an insufficiently flexible approach to land use, infrastructure and structural development, and prefer the term 'spatial planning' (MALA, 2001). However, the term 'physical planning' is consistent with the contents of plans based on demographic, socio-economic, cultural and other characteristics that set strategic and measurable recommendations or limitations in physical development. The terms 'physical planning' and 'spatial planning' can therefore be used interchangeably. Physical planning implies the extent to which existing natural resources can be used for creating man-made values, such as environments for fundamental human activities, including agriculture, industry and social services. It is used to integrate socio-economic planning with the development of land use and built environments. It sets out recommended physical parameters and/or limiting values according to statutory, ecological, socio-economic and political considerations.

For the purpose of the management of commons, innovative and comprehensive physical planning is needed for areas within specified boundaries, which must include typical forms of land use, acceptable ranges of densities, and recommended forms of physical development. The leading strategic decisions must be localised, must have recommended parameters (volume, density or other unit) and suitable formally-built structures. There should be space for flexibility in formal arrangements within the proposed concepts of use of the common resources. The degree of flexibility is a matter of suitably formulated policies and properly defined parameters of implementation.

Comprehensive physical planning can be carried out by multidisciplinary teams headed by physical planners trained and experienced in dealing with the multifarious problems of commons. Physical planners, as well as architects, can play a valuable role in the use, development and management of commons. Fortunately for Zimbabwe, there is a strong generation of highly-trained physical planners and a very experienced Department of Phyrical Planning. The same is true of South Africa.

Expert teamwork combined with participatory approaches can help to incorporate and integrate traditional community knowledge and culture with innovative scientific research and concerted management programmes aimed at sustained development of common transboundary resources.

There are, however, several important issues that need to be addressed:

- What are the expected outcomes from an innovative and comprehensive physical planning of specified areas in relation to the use and management of commons?
- What are the advantages of a participatory approach in the planning and management of commons at regional level?
- Who selects and negotiates strategies and establishes the framework for sustainable management, monitoring and implementation (and taking action if something goes wrong)?

Planning for the use of commons within or beyond national boundaries is a political process, which ideally takes account of the science involved. Science in this process must be deployed to assist in finding the right political decisions rather than to justify certain political positions. This is why physical planners and other experts should take time to understand the political process. Politicians on their part should recognise the role of physical planning in their endeavor to balance the protection and sustainable use of the commons.

Collected data for facts and processes from studies and analyses, and knowledge about the behaviour of ecological systems and sub-systems that is based on long term experience, are important for physical planning. Consistent and reliable information in various professional areas is needed in physical planning and should be collected as a desk study and as also from the field. What is more difficult is to correctly interpret this information in the context of a particular common property resource.

Comprehensive decisions about the use, development and management of transboundary common resources are based on interpretations of collected information and analyses. These are integrated as a complex database, accompanied by relevant maps and graphic materials. Multidisciplinary teams – of planners, historians, economists, sociologists, geographers, meteorologists, engineers, biologists and other experts – are supposed to complete the profiles of commons within the various national boundaries.

These various interests may influence the process of collecting information and tend to vary according to the purpose for which it is collected (MALA 2001; MMET, 1998; SADC, 1995). It also depends on the nature of the common resource. However, it is important to realise that the links with the surrounding region may include various existing as well as potential functional and physical connections. The following information needs to be included:

- Ecological profile and identified ecosystems, based on geographic data such as location, size, topography, orientations and altitudes; climatic attributes, such as general climate zones, sun, winds, temperatures; water sources and basins such as rivers, lakes, ponds, evaporations, rainfalls; soils; flora; fauna; scenic views and natural resources.
- Historical profile with identified development periods and achievements, including ethnic traditions, major national and regional events, persons and places of heritage.
- Demographic and social profile by periods, factors of growth and growth constraints, current population, patterns of settlements, migrations, age and gender groups, health, and education, in qualitative and quantitative terms.
- Economic profile, focusing on economic use of resources, current and future trends, industry and agriculture – analyses by sectors, productions, employment etc., infrastructure by sectors, tourism and specialisation (locations, capacity of facilities), economic significance of links with surrounding areas, co-operation projects.
- Built environment on generalised land uses and real estate development in industry, services and housing, locations, densities, potential for upgrading.
- Infrastructure and communications, including roads of various classes, railways, waterways and water systems including sources, branches, supply and waste (MMET, 1998) telecommunications, and other infrastructure systems with a meaningful impact upon their establishment.
- Cultural profile to reveal typical traditional and contemporary arts, historically-defined aesthetic values, traditional scientific and technological approaches in daily life, local industry, mining, agriculture and current trends.
- Administrative and political overview, including periods, policies, organisations, national and local legislation for implementation, monitoring and management.

- Analysed, summarised and mapped information to form the database, which backs up the negotiated strategies and decisions that will be taken.

Such comprehensiveness guarantees that disadvantage and fractured policies are avoided. A multidisciplinary and multisided approach of interested parties across the border and in adjacent areas provides for equally-informed decisions that are critical. In conclusion, it can be said that when knowledge is shared through co-operation at regional levels, the use of commons is potentially sustainable.

### *Participatory approaches*

The participatory approach has gained momentum in almost every kind of activity that involves local communities. To reap the maximum benefit it must be regarded as a process, one which integrates indigenous local knowledge with the knowledge of professional experts and assists in decision-making that is not detrimental to the communities' livelihoods. Traditional knowledge is a result of long and intuitive experience and a heritage of traditional attitudes. Expert knowledge is acquired through contemporary and sophisticated methods of data collection and analysis. Local communities should not be viewed as data sets during the planning process but rather as active participants. The greatest advantage of this participatory approach lies in the merging and blending of two groups of information when generating concepts for solutions to problems and for management policies, which are context specific and community-oriented.

The participatory approach to planning in Zimbabwe is statutorily recognised under the Regional, Town and Country Planning Act (revised edition 1996). However, the application of the clauses of this Act must be seen beyond the Act, at a broadened horizon in the interest of both the local people and planners. Environmental Impact Assessments, mandatory for all development projects in Zimbabwe, provide another avenue for active local participation.

Local communities are interested in the best possible management policies because of the effect on their daily lives. Planners are interested in the same, as their professional expertise is at stake as is their professional duty – to advise politicians in negotiations and decision-making. The practical problems that communities face during implementation may be quite different from those of the professionals not to mention differences within the user communities themselves. Along a river that is a national border, the communities upstream and downstream, or those on the left bank and the right bank, may face problems that do not have similar solutions. In such cases local concerns must take centre stage.

Simple but consistent questionnaires, meetings, workshops and other forms of participation can be chosen (SADC, 1995). Replicating some techniques and methods is possible, but the outcomes should be carefully observed in order to obtain useful insights.

If this process is carried out in all areas of transboundary commons, and the local communities share experience and knowledge, learn about each other and about the difficulties and problems met by their neighbours, the chances of sustainable management of the commons are good. Explanations given to communities by authorities and professionals may assist in a better understanding of the behaviour of a given ecosystem, which might help to disseminate ways to overcome problems. This could include communities being updated about the relevant regulations and other applicable laws.

The education of local communities should be considered as a factor in the participatory approach. Education is the cornerstone for participatory actions, which are supposed to come naturally when implementing a management strategy. It is important that local communities appreciate the need for balancing the economic use of common resources against the protection of the environment as a key to sustainable development. Ideally, the concept must become a reality for people in the communities as then they can understand that breaking the balance results in mutual vulnerability. In this way self-control can be established as the most valuable form of management. However, it should be broadly socially-defined rather than enforced.

Affected communities must take part in a process of co-operation and work in mutual trust, especially in an environment of ever-increasing competition over natural resources. This provides for the development of local leadership talents, which are very much needed in community participation in planned activities. Out of this process it is often possible to expect new ideas about diversification of the use of commons and related activities.

Knowledge about capacity limitations and vulnerability in specific areas is important, not only for specialists who are expected to advise politicians and managers, but also for the communities that live within the agreed conditions of common properties use. It is logically expected that conscientiously adopted policies and activities are more manageable and successful than activities driven by a list of prohibitions. The education of those who are supposed to carry out stipulated activities guarantees that the users are responsive to the setting up of management policies and techniques, as well as to the dynamism of prioritising and strategically updating information and practices.

## The Limpopo Basin: a model for transboundary resource management in southern Africa

### *A description of the basin and the economic potential*

The Zambezi and the Limpopo, two great rivers, are, in relation to socio-economic, environmental, cultural and tourist concerns, extremely important examples of common property resources for the following riparian countries: Zimbabwe, South Africa, Mozambique and Botswana.

The example of the Limpopo Valley is used here to illustrate innovative suggestions related to the management of commons for the benefit of nations and communities. The large area north of the Limpopo River, referred to as the Limpopo Basin, includes the confluence of the Limpopo and Shashe Rivers and extends northward up to the Birchenough Bridge, which crosses the Save River. The area known as the Limpopo Valley is that adjacent to the river, including the National Park between the Limpopo and the Save rivers. In this general area the concept of a Peace Park, regarded as a way of securing regional stability and stimulating economic growth, mainly through the enormous tourist potential based on the rich natural heritage, has been mooted. The concept is expected to uplift the living standards of people in rural communities and will contain some elements of CAMPFIRE.

The concept has become a reality, as attested by the recently announced Limpopo Peace Park, which comprises three national parks of the three neighboring countries, i.e. Kruger National Park of South Africa, Gaza National Park of Mozambique and the Gonarezhou National Park of Zimbabwe that is just over 5,000 $km^2$. The newly formed Peace Park includes the largest and richest South African Park and the second largest national park of Zimbabwe. It promises to be the most interesting game reserve and a good tourist attraction in southern Africa. Its size, 35,383 $km^2$, is larger than the nation of Portugal. The Park is the first undertaking of this character in Zimbabwe. Adjoining the core of the Peace Park are areas that are managed as conservancies and self-sustainable natural resource areas. The total of this broader area is more than 95,000 $km^2$.

An agreement between the three countries (Mozambique, South Africa, Zimbabwe) was signed on the 10th of November 2000. A number of political and legislative issues are to be solved at governmental level, such as border posts, visas, managing authorities, etc. It was expected that the Park would be fully operational by April 2002, although this has not happened for reasons that are unclear.

In a similar manner, a proposed Dongola-Limpopo Valley Peace Park will include parts of South Africa, Botswana and Zimbabwe and will be formally announced soon. This makes the issue of transboundary common resources quite important for the region. Despite the existing experience of about 100 transboundary parks worldwide, the challenge of the sustainable management of these parks remains.

Managing the Limpopo Peace Park (as well as the Dongola-Limpopo Valley Peace Park) as a transboundary ecological system as a unit has the potential not just to boost the national economies of the member countries but can also bring benefits to rural communities living along the borders of the Park. There is need for more comprehensive studies of the area in order to come up with strategic guidelines for development. Here, physical planning can contribute valuable and innovative management instruments. It can offer solutions for the resettlement and re-structuring of these areas as well as ways of overcoming the enormous requirements for housing and infrastructure.

### *Management gains and expected outputs*

In order to uplift the life of rural communities, strategic physical planning must properly set out the priorities of the developmental issues related to the establishment of the Limpopo Park. One of the critical issues is to clarify how the local population will gain from ecotourism. A number of studies could help in this respect. Though powerful, the Transborder Park Ministerial Committee should not decide on issues without the help of a strategy set by a regional physical planner. These issues, which need thorough study and planning concern, are:

- Number and settlement/resettlement structures of people who live inside the Park and outside but within the adjacent area, and the land required and availability of resources for development and upgrading of settlements.
- Potential for agriculture, tourism and supporting activities, including service industries, and social services as forms of employment creation, relating to the core business of the National Park.
- Intensity of upgrading and new development, specified by densities, estimated economic growth, priorities in development, and types of rural housing and other built structures.
- Technical infrastructure, including roads, small airfields, water sources, water supply (and possibly irrigation), sewerage, electricity supply and telecommunications.
- Social infrastructure, including education, health care and cultural facilities.
- Tourist infrastructure and related wildlife safari systems and other entertainment facilities.
- Opportunities for diversification and spread of tourism activities, based on natural (landscapes and wildlife conservancies) and man-made local resources (e.g. the Birchenough Bridge).

A dynamic strategic approach for the entire region should be linked with management approaches to provide a framework for co-operation and conflict-resolution among the three nations. A regional plan may be split into smaller ones, which may be based on identified administrative units. As a major requirement, such physical plans must be sufficiently flexible. The plans, as parts of the management process, must suggest development priorities.

A valuable aspect that must be emphasised is that of fairness, which partially overlaps with the issue of the equitable use of commons. Equitable use is related to specific measurable parameters and ecological limitations. The issue of fairness is related to the possibility of some signatories taking advantage of an official agreement and may be associated with the protection of vested interests facilitated by better-developed physical facilities or greater availability of funds. Comprehensive planning of transboundary commons can serve as a guarantee of fairness.

The resources that are needed for the physical planning of transboundary commons and related areas are:

- Manpower – specialists needed for multidisciplinary planning teams.
- Information technology -- available methods and techniques for collection, analysis and interpretation of relevant data.
- Equipment for collection of data and research, mainly computers.
- Funds for carrying out scientific research and participatory activities at relevant scales by governmental agencies, institutes and private consultants.

If Zimbabwe is to get its fair share of benefits it needs to put its house in order, so to speak. The resources needed for the physical planning of commons in the Park and adjacent areas are manpower, information technology, including computer equipment, and finance. With regard to funding, it makes sense to give the Peace Park top priority in the national budget for physical planning of the commons as it will soon be active.

Some social, economic, and environmental problems that require attention are:

- What is an acceptable capacity for resettlement in the areas adjacent to the Park and how does it link with the needs of further development of tourism?
- What is the potential for the generation of employment and self-employment in the Park's internal and adjacent areas?
- What constitutes a measurable impact of the new opportunities for boosting tourism?
- Considering the existing state of the infrastructure and the potential for development, such as water sources, transportation, etc., what are the limitations?

Quite probably, some additional issues may be justified in the future, depending on the availability of more public funds and attraction of private investment.

## Conclusion

The management of transboundary common property resources at the regional level provides good prospects for co-operation in an age of globalisation, particularly where co-operation involves ecological and social systems that cover more than one country.

Despite the difficulties that may arise, which are dependent on particular international agreements and existing national administrative structures, the benefits that can be derived justify the effort.

To a great extent transboundary commons as natural ecological systems dictate the types of management suitable for the protection and sustainable preservation of such resources. The parties involved should share innovative forms of integration in order to stimulate the growth and welfare of the local populations. There will also be a positive impact on the nations, who will 'learn' not only how to protect the environment but how to stimulate development equitably and fairly at the same time.

Physical plans of the areas concerned have the potential to contribute to both the regional and national strategic vision. They provide a reliable ground upon which common policies can be negotiated. Planning of commons as dynamic physical, ecological and social systems ensures sustainable management of resources by preventing the negative consequences of fractured policies. In this scenario, local communities should not be forgotten or treated merely as data sets but should be regarded as participants, as it is their livelihoods that are at stake.

## References

Dellapenna, J. W. (1993). 'Treaties as Instruments for Managing Internationally Shared Resources: Restricted Sovereignty versus Community of Property.' *Columbia Journal of International Law*, Vol. 18.

Department of Environmental Affairs and Tourism (DEAT) (2000). *Users Guide to National Environmental Management Act, South Africa.*

Gates, J. R., (2001). *Wonders of the African World*. New York, Alfred A. Knopf.

Jaarsma, M., H. Bos, C. Vijfhuizen and A. Ganhane (2001). The credibility of an ant flood forecasting, hydrological models, credibility and communication in Mozambique. Paper presented at the 2nd WARFSA/WATERNET Symposium on integrated water resources management: theory, practice, and cases. Cape Town, 30-31 October 2001.

Manyanga, M., I. Pikirayi and W. Ndoro (2000). Coping with Dryland Environments: Preliminary results from Mapungubwe and Zimbabwe Phase Site in Mateke Hills, Southeastern Zimbabwe. *The South African Archeology Society Goodwin Series*, Vol. 8.

Ministry of Agriculture and Land Affairs (MALA) (2001). *White Paper on Spatial Planning and Land Use Management Bill, South Africa*.

Ministry of Mines, Environment and Tourism (MMET) (1998). *Strategic Direction for Environmental Research in Zimbabwe.*

Mutembwa, A. (1998). Water and the Potential for Resource Conflicts In Southern Africa. Occasional Paper No 3, Global Security Fellows Initiative, University of Cambridge.

SADC (1995). *Protocol on shared watercourse systems in the Southern African Development Community (SADC) Region*. Gaborone.

Staley Consultants (1995). *Southern Africa Regional Water Assessment: Final Report*. Lamont.

UNEP/UCMC (2001). Protected Areas Programme – Parks for Peace. (Mimeo).

# Chapter 8

# The influence of Geographical Information Systems technology on the management of common property in Southern Africa

*Ivan Farayi Muzondo*

## Introduction

The future of sustainable environmental management in Southern Africa is delicately poised given the high average annual population growth rate that exceeds 3 per cent and the low economic performance (SARDC, 1994). Ordinarily, the environment is stable, but tends to be disturbed by the human factor through mismanagement practices such as cultivating marginal lands, and through natural disasters (e.g. drought, floods). As attested by a number of agreements and protocols, the Protocol on Shared Watercourses (see Chikowore, this volume) for example, countries in the Southern African region have realised the need to communally protect the common property resources that are part and parcel of their environment. Critical aspects of common property management that are neglected in the region include geometrical representation and the spatial location of resources in relation to the population subsisting on the environment. This is largely a result of the difficulty of modelling spatial reality without advanced technology, which is made worse by the high cost of the technology.

The role of technology in common property management cannot be overemphasised – improved technological innovations have made it possible to incorporate computerised systems in the management of private and common property in the developed world. These innovations, coupled with rapid changes in the global information order, have improved the preservation and conservation of common property resources. Unfortunately, Southern Africa, like many developing regions, is lagging behind in this regard, a situation that has created and continues to create a 'digital divide', which threatens to further widen the social and economic gap between developed and developing countries. It should be noted that while Southern Africa suffers from a lack of research funding for the development and application of innovative technology, it will benefit in the long run through adoption of technology such as Geographical Information Systems (GIS). This paper examines the applicability of GIS technology to the management of natural resources such as forests, wildlife, pastures and water resources.

## The nature of Geographical Information Systems (GIS) technology

Taylor (1991) argues that definitions are more than just an exercise in semantics – they are important in focusing attention on what are regarded as the major aspects of a discipline or subject. GIS developed from the concept of the map, which allows relationships between a wide variety of both quantitative and qualitative data to be organised, analysed, presented, communicated and used in a way no other product can match (Taylor, 1991). To define GIS, one needs to understand what it hopes to represent (the Earth) and how people (users) perceive that earth. Cassettari (1993) views GIS as a tool to integrate spatial dimensions with other information handling technologies, which has been the problem of the cartographer for many years.

### *Material level of appreciation*

#### *Processes*

Figure 4 illustrates how people view specific themes depending on their interest, background and level of education (*knowledge base*). Their perception of the same 'earth' is correspondingly varied. With such diverse views, there cannot be a universally accepted definition of GIS. Several closely related terms have been used, namely Environmental Information Systems, Pollution Information Systems, Automated Mapping/Facilities Management and Resource Information Systems. In this chapter, GIS is viewed as a broad and complex set of tools for collecting, storing, transforming, retrieving at will, and displaying spatial data from the real world for a particular set of purposes (Burrough, 1990; Taylor, 1991; Cassettari, 1993; Kennedy, 1996). A tool is something that gives humans the ability to alter a system (human creativity, money and labour) in order to achieve predetermined goals. Thus, tools are more than just technology (Savory, 1991). It is important to note that GIS is a tool not a discipline, unlike Computer Science, Cartography, Surveying, and Geography. It can be used to manage common property resources at various levels, including the global level.

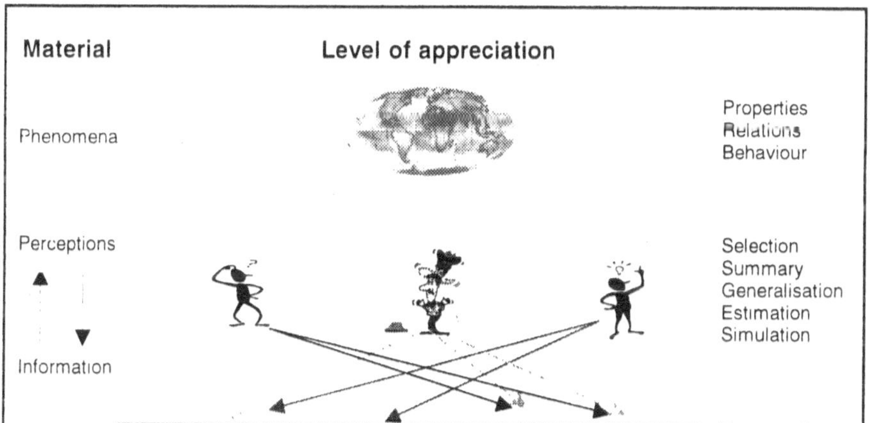


| Country | | Population (millions) | Density (per km$^2$) |
|---|---|---|---|
| Botswana | 581883 | 1 501 000 | 2.5 |
| Lesotho | 30 354 | 1 971 000 | 64 |
| South Africa | 1 219 411 | 43 327 000 | 36 |
| Swaziland | 17 367 | 1 032 000 | 59 |
| Malawi | 118 515 | 9 609 000 | 81 |
| Mozambique | 812 593 | 18 165 000 | 22 |
| Namibia | 825 336 | 1 727 000 | 2 |
| Zambia | 752 813 | 9 350 000 | 12 |
| Zimbabwe | 390 860 | 11 723 000 | 29 |

Figure 4: Differing interest about the same real world *(Modified from Laurini and Thompson 1994)*

In common property research GIS is generally under-utilised, particularly in environmental issues in Southern Africa. This is mainly due to the lack of awareness of the potential of GIS, the location of digital data and the myth of it being a difficult technology. GIS technology is nonetheless quite useful in this respect, as it has brought about an information revolution such that formerly remote lands can be accessed without a physical visit. Not only is the Windows environment, on which most GIS software runs, user-friendly but expertise in GIS is also becoming increasingly available locally. These developments are a result of historically separate disciplines (Geography, Cartography, Surveying, Computer Science, etc.) being merged and redefined, thereby generating benefits to society because of more efficient and effective ways of managing natural resources. GIS requires knowledge and use of various disciplines that do combine easily. For example, in analysing catchment flows, positions of streams are determined using Survey techniques (Photogrammetry, Terrestrial Surveys etc.) and the information represented using cartographic tools (map symbols). The resultant information can then be analysed using flow models in Geography via graphics programmes developed in Computer Science (for example, ArcView GIS).

## The common property resources and the global view

Common property resources (CPRs) in developing countries form part of the natural resource endowment of rural communities and, unlike the situation in developed countries, constitute a significant component of the land resources base, which makes them vulnerable. This vulnerability is more pronounced in drought-prone areas, such as the arid and semi-arid regions of Southern Africa, where the majority of the population lives. In the Southern African region, land resources are held in various forms, such as private, public (government) and traditional. CPRs differ from open access resources where everyone has unregulated access to the resource. Sustainable management of common property depends in part on the availability of relevant information as well as on wise decisions taken on the basis of the supplied information (Phillips, 1986). Technology is also a critical element in the management of common property resources and can be utilised to manage data, as this chapter attempts to show. Ownership patterns of land, however, determine how technology can be applied since technology operates in a social setting and not in a vacuum.

The management of resources has increasingly taken a global perspective because of developments in technology and the availability of global data through the Internet, for example. GIS as a technology has largely been driven by technical developments, not by social needs (Cassettari, 1993). Hence it has developed more rapidly than IT applications, and software or hardware developments (Davis and Williams, 1989). How such a technology can be deployed to solve problems of sustainable resource management is the million-dollar question, especially against a backdrop of a rising world population and declining resources because of increased extraction.

Since the extraction of resources has assumed global proportions through, for example, world trade and has negative global side-effects (e.g. global warming), there is need to manage resources from a supra-local perspective. In this regard technology plays a part. In developing countries, the problem is that most technologies tend to originate from the developed world thereby giving researchers in the former a sense of being alien to the technology. This explains the delay in the adoption of the new GIS tool by African researchers. They are now realising, however, that the challenge of sustainable natural resource management makes it impractical to ignore modern tools designed for this purpose.

## The seamless connection of GIS technology and common property resources

Since early civilisation (the Stone Age) applied science has increasingly been used to represent the earth's complex resources and today, there is a need to integrate the abundance of spatial (maps, images) and attribute (statistical history) information available from various sources. With GIS technology, essential information on CPRs and the environment is readily displayed (Phillips, 1986) and can be readily integrated for effective decision-making. The technology is employed at several levels before the consolidated information is made available for the purposes of planning and management.

*1. Acquisition of common property resource information*

In the 1980s, the major problem in natural resource management was obtaining sufficient information. However, with information revolution of the 1990s, there has been an explosion of available data (Taylor, 1991). Common property acquisition tools include field surveys (spatial and questionnaires), Global Positioning Systems[1] (GPS) (figure 5), Remote Sensing and Photogrammetry[2], existing maps, reports and publications. This all results in more informed decisions about the management of common property. Among the acquisition tools, space technology[3] has been dominant, particularly Remote Sensing and GPS, as we move away from the age of photogrammetry and terrestrial surveys. GPS is another system that is easy to use (Kennedy, 1996). Space platforms have the unique capability of simultaneously seeing and interacting with large parts of the earth, thereby acquiring a global picture of resources. Furthermore, there is significant increase in the

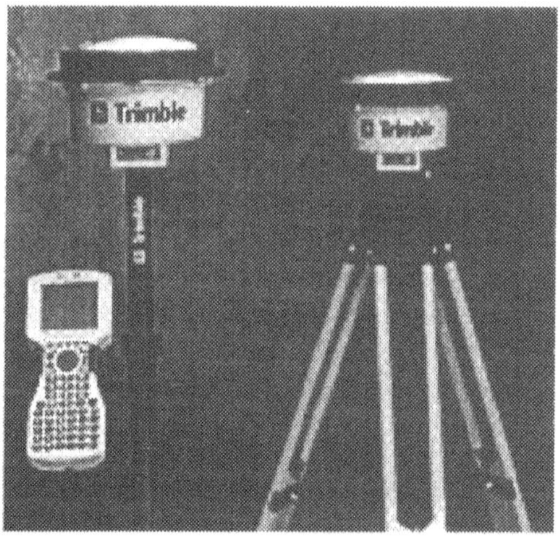


Figure 5: GPS is a popular acquisition tool in the common property domain.

1 **Global Positioning Systems** is a data acquisition technique that uses a constellation of 24 satellites orbiting the earth which broadcast data to users to allow them to determine their spatial locations.

2 **Remote Sensing and Photogrammetry** is the science and art of acquiring information on the earth without coming into contact with the earth, object or phennomenon. Photogrammetry is a subset of remote sensing that uses only visible and near visible parts of the electromagnetic spectrum, while remote sensing covers all wavelengths.

3 **Space technology** is system that uses satellites that have been launched above and orbit the earth.

speed of acquisition and repetitive coverage with minimal loss of accuracy (resolution). Previously, the utilisation of Remote Sensing in developing countries was limited by the lack of ground receiving stations (Phillips, 1986), but recent coverage has extended to the whole world and with broader spectral sensitivity[4] and temporal resolutions[5]. Spectral sensitivity, a function of wavelength of propagated wave, affects the features that can distinctly be studied in a single scene, while temporal resolution allows researchers to monitor changes over time. Scenes have recently been availed (CCRS, NASA) for civilian, research and management use at reasonable cost.

*2. Storage and management of common property resource information*

The proliferation of data as experienced today normally results in several problems:

- Redundancy and inconsistency from multiple sources of data
- Accessing of data by users who are not familiar with the locations of data required is difficult
- Difficulty in data isolation in order to select suitable data for the required application
- The need to manage concurrent use for faster response time by multiple users
- Security problems results in data that lacks privacy, e.g. available over the Internet
- Integrity constraints normally vary with applications for the same data set, hence problems occur in predefining constraints for multi-user applications

The database component of a GIS is a structured collection of related spatial and non-spatial information that attempts to solve these problems. The sets of tools ensure safe and efficient access to the data stores and subsequent display of solutions. The essential components allow definition of content, modify/insert/delete of data, and query (select) content as management tools (Star and Estes, 1990). Systems developments have made database technology a common tool for common property management.

Several management technologies exist today, from the navigational databases[6] (network and hierarchical) of the 1980s, to the relational databases[7] of the 1990s, and the object-oriented models of today's world. Relational databases have established themselves as the *de facto* standard in the world and most established GISs are based on relational systems.

---

4 **Spectral sensitivity** is the range of the electromagnetic spectrum wavelength that can be used

5 **Temporal resolution** is the rate at which data of the same area is reacquired.

6 **Navigational databases** have information that follows predefined tree or inter-linked routes to access information.

7 **Relational databases** have data stored in the form of interrelated tables.

## 3. *Analytical tools in common property management*

Complex resource-planning decisions at a regional view (large scale) require that information be structured in order to shape the local reality (user view) (e.g. to ascertain how many people a particular ecosystem can sustain per square metre for 20 years). Both scientific and social uncertainties constrain decision-making in assessing, planning, and re-mediation of projects by common property managers. The quality of decisions, which have wide-ranging impacts, depends on the depth and accuracy of data and how they have been combined using the analytical tools at hand. In GIS, individual maps, composite maps, or spatial overlay, and analyses are produced to meet unique requirements. Each map produced with GIS software is actually a layer of information. The different layers are displayed on the same map, in combination or individually, giving the user the ability to display relevant information on request. As Mather (1993) noted, data collected in the field by different methods, when integrated together on the same geographical base, provide a spectacular added value.

*Reclassification and Aggregation:* Manipulation tools allow the user to select and re-select subsets of data for display (Cassettari, 1993). This results in the isolation of resources

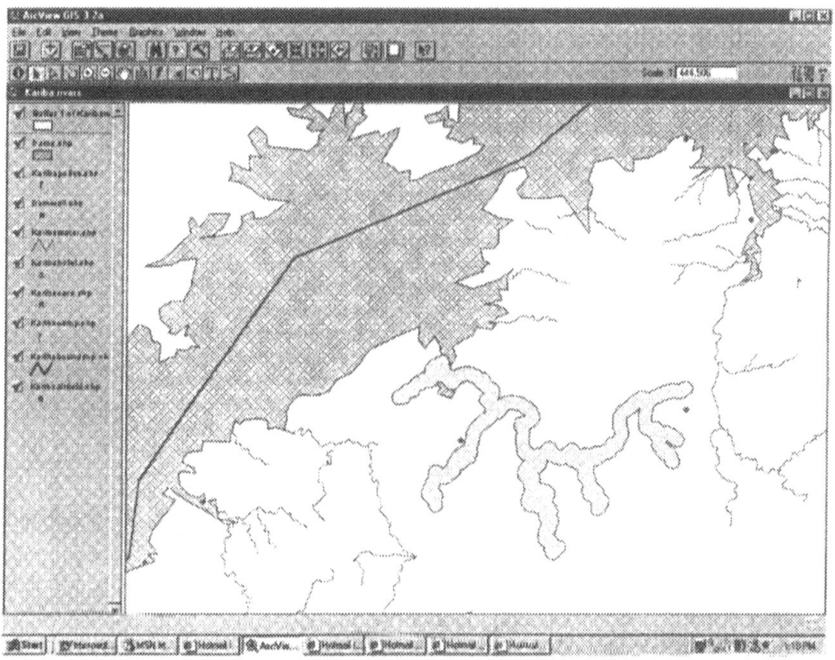

Figure 6: Analytical technique buffering extent of influence of a river within a five kilometre radius in the Kariba area, Zimbabwe

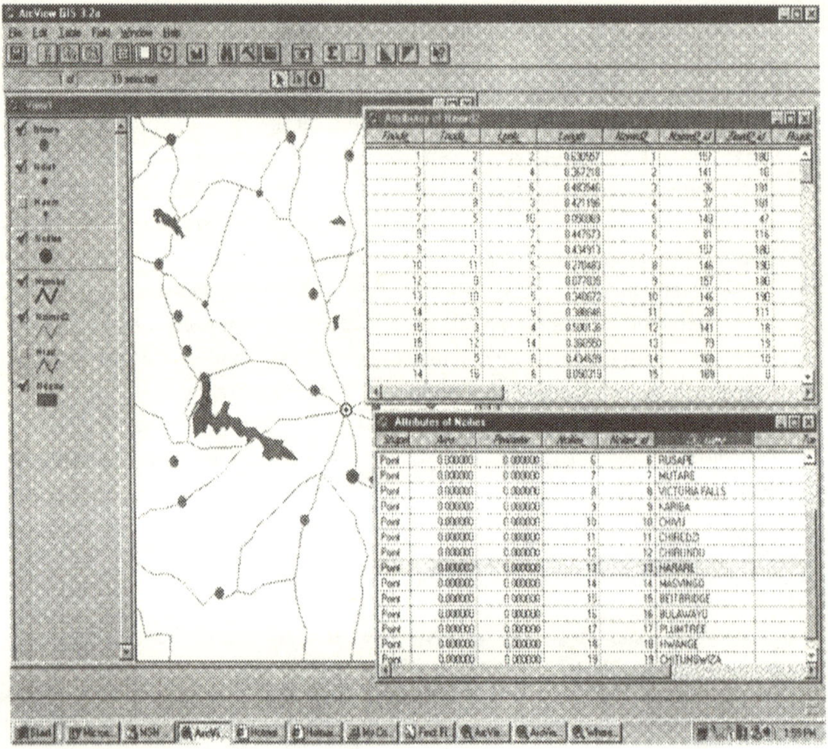


Figure 7: Interrelating spatial map and attribute table in a GIS point analysis

with a common attribute or uniting two resources that share an attribute. For example, in a study to isolate areas that were susceptible to erosion along a river network, a buffer of five kilometres was constructed, highlighting areas that required more management activity within the zone (Figure 6).

In this area, it is necessary to look at other influences, such as slope and vegetation, by uniting/combining with buffered zones to effectively highlight areas for increased attention in managing erosion.

*Geometrical operators:* Geometrical operators, including union *(sum)* and intersection *(minus)*, are used to analyse the effects of integrating and overlaying different spatial datasets. Further quantitative operators such as angular, distance (length) and area measurements are critical in managing the resource.

*Spatial operators:* Spatial operators provide the bridge that links fundamental data models to GIS technology, with the result that applications are enhanced and research findings are broadened and deepened. Together with attribute operators, they allow interrelation and maximum analysis of the character of point (well), line (river, road, rail), and area (field, plantation, lake) features that constitute common property (Figure 7).

*Connectivity:* Links of common property resources through the available transport network is essential if travelling and communication are to be effectively achieved. Therefore, suitable roads or telephone networks are vital in common property management, combined with connectivity links between resource sites. In an analysis of water flow along a river for example, connectivity is used as an integrity check as all rivers must eventually discharge into a pool, pond, lake, sea or ocean.

*Neighbourhood:* A source of pollutants in natural vegetation environment tends to contaminate nearer areas than those further, when all other factors such as slope, wind direction and human management of environment are constant. Hence, in managing the spread, one analyses the distance from source or adjacency (a feature next to the pollutant source). Neighbourhood analysis provides answers to the influence of regional location on a resource and its impact on others (Figure 8).

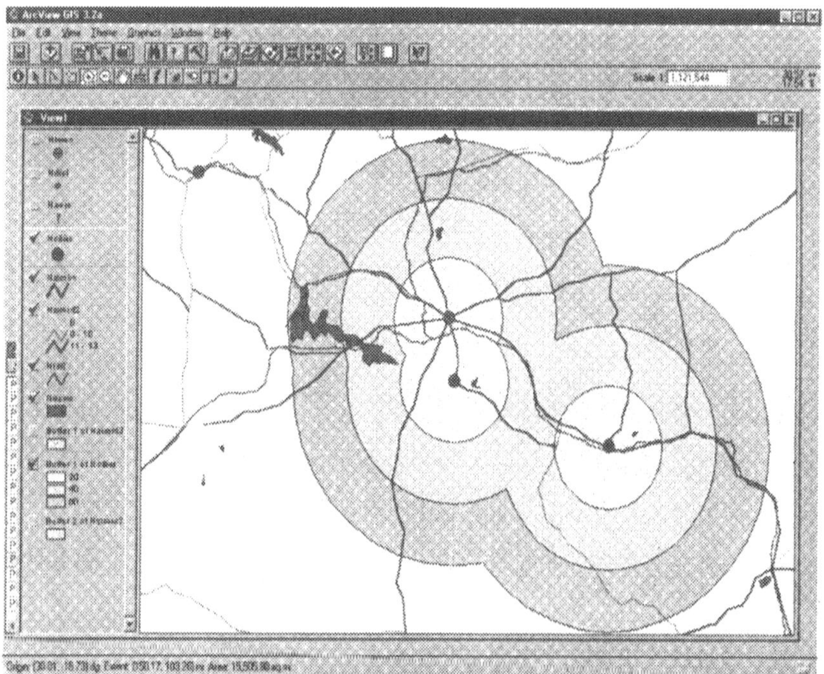

Figure 8: Result of the concentration of fog around major towns of Harare, Chitungwiza and Marondera based on distance attribute only

*Measurement:* Both distance and direction have been used to analyse spatial relations of points, lines and area features in the common property domain; for example, effects of a pollutant that decreases with distance downstream. Although other factors are active, such as discharge rate or the speed of flow combined with distance from source, one can simulate the range of influence. It becomes possible to confirm whether a community 100 km downstream would be affected should they use the water for domestic use.

*Statistical Analysis:* Having postulated a hypothesis that a spatial attribute affects common property management negatively, it can be proven or disproved by GIS using scientific data. The validity of the hypothesis can be based on attribute data while a visual presentation of results can be easily understood. The probability and the extent of reliability of the results are computed and tested against known models. Samples representative of each area are then acquired and compared with the simulation.

*Modelling:* Cartographic modelling (overlay) is a common tool used to integrate various data sets (Figure 9). It is used to combine data layers, provide options and redefine new classes in the combined results. Its use has been mainly in modelling suitability studies for siting, planning and other activities.

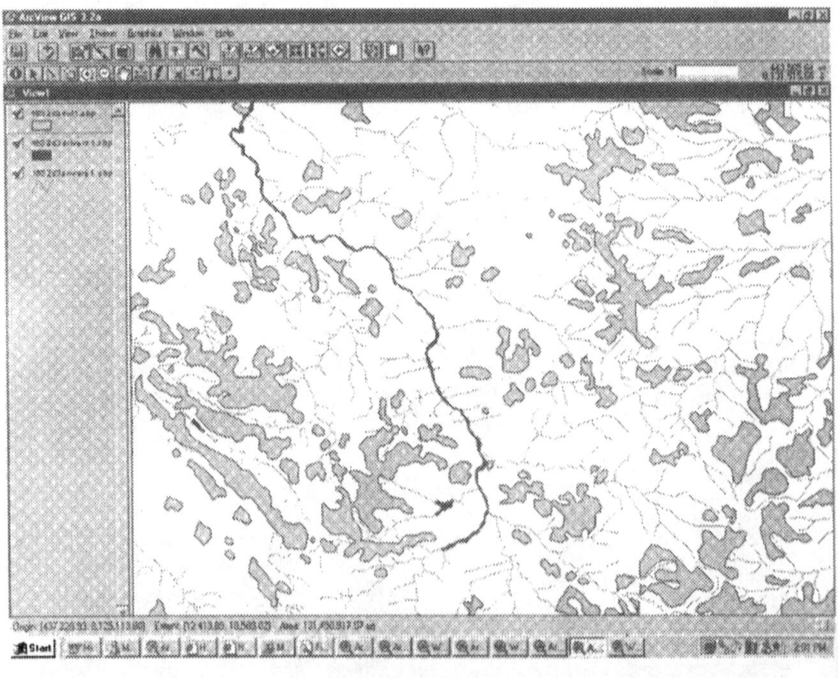


…re 9: An analysis of the land under cultivation, drainage and communal pasture in rura
…owe

In managing CPRs, one aim could be to improve general accessibility of resources by all people and achieve equality of opportunities to and services provided by the same. GIS facilitates this, as it accommodates more sensitive configurations of economic activities and common property regimes. GIS capabilities for handling spatial data allow researchers to develop detailed representations and analysis of the spatial distribution of disadvantaged populations and their access to opportunities and services. In conclusion, it can be said that GIS-based techniques for solving sophisticated and realistic location and distribution problems can allow opportunities and services to be configured to maximise general accessibility and equity.

## *4. Display and Visualisation tools for Common Property Management*

GIS display components explore geographical visualisation techniques that are employed to monitor and manage CPRs in one to four dimensions. Tools are developed and evaluated to ascertain their applicability for visualisation of data associated with specific regions and sites. The aim is to develop new products that improve the effectiveness of the transmission of information and increase the understanding of the process of communication (Taylor, 1991). One-dimensional representation is typical of attribute databases, two-dimensional being the spatial map, three-dimensional displays include models, and the four-dimensional display involves a time series analysis of a 3D product. The most common graphic products of a GIS are maps of various kinds (Star and Estes, 1990). Several other highly-specialised displays with which to systematically depict the earth have evolved, such as digital elevation models (2.5D) and Virtual Reality Models[8] (Figure 10).

Other graphic displays such as bar charts, line graphs, scatter maps and summary statistics can enhance comprehension of the attributes and their spatial locations.

GIS technology has reached the point where non-technical people can comprehend complex data in a format with which almost everyone is comfortable, i.e. maps, thereby making GIS a perfect media for exchange of information among technical and non-technical people. This has provided the key to critically comprehend applications of data benefiting subsequent analysis, processing or decision-making. Of extreme importance is the 3D model of real-life terrain with analytical tools of panning, walk through, fly by, measure and re-scale. Computer-generated terrain is gaining acceptance as visualisation tools in most application areas (Raper, 1989). As CPRs are generally 3D in nature attempts to transform them to 2D lack accurate modelling, analysis and display. Computer-generated terrain is gaining acceptance in Southern Africa in common property resource management, particularly so for meteorology, hydrology, ground water and hazard containment.

---

[8] **Virtual Reality Model** depicts the surface/ object with the third dimension of height and spatial relationship incorporated. It allows the user to interact with the model through fly through, panning, rotating, zooming and walk through abilities, etc.

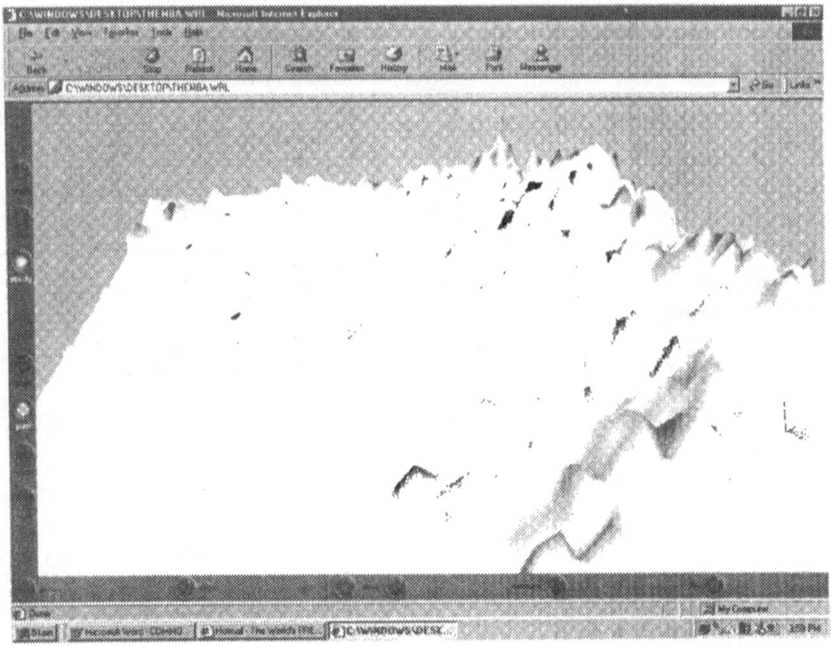

Figure 10: Three-dimensional visualisation of the eastern Highlands in Zimbabwe at a vertical exaggeration of 500 per cent *(Extracted from the Digital Chart of The World)*

## The resultant impact of GIS technology on common property resource management: A southern african perspective

The introduction of GIS technology in Southern Africa involved the complex process of managing change within environments typified by uncertainty, entrenched institutional procedures and little personal motivation. This has affected the opportunities for GIS solutions, particularly for common property applications. However, the GIS diffusion trend has seen increased acceptance, as professionals became more aware of GIS. The old trend of GIS resources being better managed in the developed than in developing countries is slowly fading away. Not only can specialists in distant countries assist in the management of resources using modern GIS and Internet communication, but qualified practitioners are also becoming locally available. TCP/IP technology (commonly known as Internet Protocol) allows remote access to local databases for specialists in Europe, USA and Canada who can contribute to better management of local resources in Southern Africa. The region has significant common property resources because of the prevalence of traditional land tenure systems – village communities who directly benefit from the resources traditionally own most of the land. With the anticipated increased land redistribution in the region, especially in countries like Zimbabwe, South Africa and Namibia, more land and thus resources will fall under the common property regime, demanding increased management of resources. It is pleasing to note that technology is increasingly making it easy to plan land resources utilisation, for now and the future, by few local specialists. We are entering an era of globalised management of resources.

The impact of information technology from acquisition, management, storage and display of land resource information contributes to highly-informed decisions. With increased success in local GIS projects, the diffusion of the technology is gaining momentum and is becoming the fastest growing technology in Southern Africa. The expansion has several advantages, including:

- GIS, being an integrating tool, allows varied source data to be analysed on a common platform. This results in more accurate predictions of future trends as they are based on accurate information. This is more relevant to long-term planning and management of common property resources.
- Spatial consistence is maintained through pre-defined links, making data more effective and manageable. Not only are attribute-based integrity constraints maintained, but the spatial relationships that are vital in the operational, tactical and strategic levels are also upheld.
- Integrated data gives an interdisciplinary perspective to common property resource management. Because several disciplines are involved in the management of common property, there is need to integrate varied source data and present it in a manner that most professionals are comfortable in analysing, this being the map.

The basic benefit is greater awareness of the tasks being performed and the range of information being used (Cassettari, 1993). This is cemented by reduced duplication in data capture, manipulation and storage processes.

## Communication and sharing of the results

The Internet has become a reality even in developing countries through a reduction of the cost of the technology due to economies of scale. Although still largely a privilege of well-to-do companies and research institutes, some businesses have gone to the extent of using Internet Cafes to access regional business and markets. Internet links have been reliable and, as a result, provide specialists with an opportunity to consult interactively on common property management. Coupled with the development of Internet, GIS and Virtual Reality Modelling technology, the availability of reports in both spatial and 3D forms have resulted in better diffusion of the results. The cost of sharing the information has greatly reduced. Moreover, the update is virtually online. The use of local area networks and wide area networks has continued to contribute to a digital communication network, thereby helping to disseminate results. There are a number of resources where this can be applied.

By the end of 1985, Thibault (1986) noted that 1.2 billion people living in developing countries did not have access to clean water. Drought continues to cause famine, particularly in Southern Africa, which adds to the problems of feeding a population with a high growth rate. There is therefore a need to locate, develop, and efficiently manage water resources. Today, Satellite Remote Sensing provides the means for addressing global issues quickly and economically through characterising large areas by their capability to support a variety of human activities. Previously, in developing countries, the cost of satellite data seemed astronomical compared to meagre resources and as yet unproven benefits. With the reduction in the cost of satellite data, projects in catchment management and modelling have increasingly been using GIS. This has resulted in the improved understanding of issues by multidisciplinary teams managing the resource. Notable examples where this has been applied include the Chivero, Mupfure, Manyame and Save catchments. Satellite Remote Sensing increased the understanding of our underground water resource in hydrological unit 3 of Zimbabwe.

Much of Southern Africa is Savannah type vegetation, suitable only for pasture. Two thirds of Southern African land is suitable only for grazing (SARDC 1994). With the increasing number of animals, both wild and domestic, there is an increasing need to understand the changes in vegetation over a period of time. A time series analysis is best undertaken using Remote Sensing imageries of the same area taken over a period of time. The resultant historical report provides evidence that is used to simulate future changes.

Common property management of forests, pastures and wildlife is critical in Southern Africa, for the human and animal population is soon likely to exceed the capacity of the land. One project using GIS and remote sensing in a communal area setting revealed alarming rate of depletion of vegetation and forest cover. No degree of intensive reforestation would match the rate of depletion, which suggests that alternative sources of fuel must be found as a long-term solution. Coupled with a semi-arid climate, GIS was used to integrate the varied attributes in order to model and analyse trends.

## The future role of GIS in common property management

Our communication channels are increasingly becoming digital environments, hence the need to adopt digital innovations. The diffusion of innovative research and development improved tremendously when GIS was integrated with Internet technology. The reduction in the cost of GIS has made it even more appropriate in the light of our low-level needs (based on Maslow's Hierarchy of human needs) and limited resources. Thus more and more organisations are incorporating GIS as part of their business plan, to ensure a competitive edge.

The era of GIS serving tasks and planning rather than more intellectually challenging strategic issues, is coming to an end. Strategic targets are being achieved using GIS because of improved information management, better analysis and better choices. Not only can GIS be specifically modelled to respond to a given problem, but it also allows easy interpretation by technical and non-technical people alike. This enhances the joint participation of local communities and specialised advisers in common property management, in line with the concept of increased community participation in resource management.

The time span between the commencement of a GIS project and its implementation has also been greatly reduced, as has the cost of data acquisition, which was a significant financial component. As the technology was developed in military circles, and civilian use is but a supplementary use, this has led to the overall reduction of development costs in common property resource management.

However, the problems of copyright and data ownership have continually hounded Southern Africa. The copyright law, meant to regulate the use and re-use of digital resources has not developed at the same pace as technological advancement. The data that could be shared is usually re-acquired to ensure compliance to copyright laws. With the exception of data primarily used for research, which carries limited restrictions, GIS has failed to enter the commercial market at the expected rate. As a result, much duplicate data acquisition has continued to unnecessarily increase the cost of new projects, costs that could so easily be avoided.

## References

Burrough, P. A. (1990). *Principles of Geographical Information Systems for Land Resources Assessment*. Oxford, Clarendon Press.

Cassettari, S. (1993). *Introduction to Integrated Geo-Information Management*. London, Chapman and Hall.

Cromley, R. G. (1992). *Digital Cartography*. Englewood Cliffs, New Jersey, Prentice Hall.

Davis, E. B. and R. Williams (1989). *The five dimensions of GIS, GIS/LIS* proceedings V1; November 26-30 1989, Florida, Marriott Orlando World Centre.

Ingerson, A. E. (1997). Urban Land as Common Property, *Land Lines*, Vol. 9 (1), January 1997; http://www.lincolninst.edu/landline/1997/march/commonp.html

Kennedy, M (1996). *The Global Positioning System and GIS - An Introduction*. Michigan, Ann Arbor Press.

Laurini, R. and D. Thompson (1994). *Fundamentals of Spatial Information Systems*. London, Academic Press.

Mather, P. M. (1993). *Geographical Information Handling - Research and Applications*. New York, John Wiley and Sons.

Phillips, W. E. (1986). 'Developing the Use of Remote Sensing for Managing Natural Resources and the Environment.' *Remote Sensing for Development: Proceedings of the International Conference in Berlin (West), 1-6 September 1986*. Technical University of Berlin.

Raper, J. (1989). *GIS - 3D Applications in GIS*. London, Taylor and Francis.

SARDC (1994). *State of the Environment in Southern Africa*. Harare, Southern Africa Research and Documentation Centre (SARDC), World Conservation Union (IUCN) and Southern African Development Community (SADC).

Savory A. (1991). *Holistic Resource Management*. Harare, Gilmour Publishing.

Star, J. and J. Estes (1990). *Geographical Information Systems, an introduction*. New Jersey, Prentice Hall.

Taylor, F. (1991). *Geographical Information Systems*. New York, Pergamon.

Thibault D. A. (1986). 'Satellite Data – a cost-effective tool for Ground water exploration and Water Resources.' *Remote Sensing for Development, Proceedings of the International Conference in Berlin (West), 1-6 September 1986*. Technical University of Berlin.

Zeiler, M. (1999). *Modelling our World: the ESRI guide to geodatabase design*. Redlands, ESRI.

# Chapter 9

# Prospects for transboundary natural resources management in the Southern African Development Community

*Godfrey Chikowore*

## Introduction

Sustainable management of natural resources in countries belonging to the Southern Africa Development Community (SADC) remains an important development goal at the beginning of this new millennium. The challenge is to ensure that the environment is able to socially and economically sustain the population without suffering undue negative consequences. The poor state of the environment, the under-performance of most SADC economies, having an average annual growth rate of 3 per cent per that is surpassed by an average annual population growth rate of 3.5 per cent (SADC, 2001:11), as well as increasing poverty levels, do not make the challenge any easier. The fact that these problems exist in a region that is endowed with a wealth of natural resources (*SADC Review*, 2001:90) makes one conclude that it is the institutional capacity to redress the situation that is lacking. This paper analyses the institutional capacity of SADC countries to sustainably manage the natural resources that fall into two broad categories. First, the focus is on those resources that straddle national boundaries, known as transboundary resources. The second type concerns natural resources that occur within national boundaries and would benefit from a common management approach. The paper examines the viability of the various institutional frameworks that have been and continue to be put in place to manage inland fisheries, wildlife and water resources in an age where globalisation is fast gathering pace throughout the world.

It must be said that SADC appears to be succeeding in addressing the challenge of preserving common natural resources. Its member states are signatories to regional and international conventions, treaties and agreements on such diverse issues as ozone depletion, climate change, biodiversity, desertification and land degradation, and persistent organic pollutants – the controversy surrounding their implementation notwithstanding (World Bank, 2000:88; Smith, 1993:4-6). SADC has also made positive efforts in addressing transboundary natural resource management by creating sector co-ordinating units (and the relevant protocols on the utilisation and management of the resources in question). Some examples will suffice. Namibia co-ordinates the Legal and Marine Fisheries Resources Sectors. The Livestock Production and Animal Disease Control Sector is managed by Botswana. Malawi co-ordinates the Inland Fisheries, Forestry and Wildlife Sectors. The Water Sector is managed by Lesotho.

To engage in a meaningful discussion there is need for a common vocabulary (Berkes and Folke, 1998), hence the need to define key terms and concepts used in this paper. One key concept in this discussion is *effective management*. Carney and Farrington (1999) and Alaev (1983) define this as the ability to productively control and/or handle the use of life-supporting limited resources in a manner that meets present demands without compromising the ability of future generations to meet their own needs. Effective management implies the absence of threats to the ecological, social, environmental and economic factors that affect the coexistence of society and nature. In general terms, the challenges of and prospects for effective management of shared natural resources would, according to Tevera (1994), mean that major concerns about rapid environmental degradation are addressed, and the opportunities of reversing such trends already exist or can be created. This could not be more true for transboundary natural resources, which can be perceived as common property resources that recognise no political boundaries. They are therefore a critical inter-state political issue, one which should be optimally managed within a given set of mutually agreed protocols and agreements. An example of such an arrangement was the signing of the Protocol on Wildlife Conservation and Law Enforcement in 1999, which was meant to establish common approaches to the conservation and sustainable use of wildlife resources in the SADC region (*SADC Review*, 2001:88).

According to Treshnikov (1988), natural resources constitute components of nature that can be used for both production and consumption. Natural resources can be divided on the *principle of their nature of exhaustiveness*. There are exhaustible renewable natural resources (e.g. biological, land, water) and exhaustible non-renewable natural resources (e.g. minerals, ore). There are also non-exhaustible natural resources (e.g. climate, solar energy, energy of flowing water). Whether renewable or not, all transboundary resources require a common management framework.

Common property resources are also another important term to define. According to Dalal-Clayton (1996:23) common property resources include marine and inland fisheries, wildlife, lakes, ponds, rivers, the sea, forests, pastures, and wastelands. While this definition itemises the constituent elements of the commons, it has conceptual shortfalls – it omits the dimension of conservation. The World Bank (2000), define the commons as that class of spillover resources, for which exclusion is difficult, while joint use involves subtractability.

An analysis of the challenges standing in the way of better management of natural resources in the SADC region enables the adoption of more progressive approaches in addressing this real developmental challenge. While it is 'natural' to think that transboundary natural resources are better managed under bilateral, regional or international frameworks, this paper argues that this is not in fact the first critical requirement. A necessary and crucial step is for nation-states to 'look after their own backyards' by putting in place what are called, in this paper, National Development Plans (NDPs) that take account of each country's specific socio-economic circumstances. NDPs must be based on a sound Comprehensive National Development Concept (CNDC). This paper illustrates this point by examining the institutional challenges facing inland fisheries, wildlife and water resources. This discussion is preceded by a theoretical overview of common property resources management in the SADC region.

## Management of commonly-owned natural resources in SADC: a theoretical overview

### *The new conservation paradigm*

Moyo *et al.*, (1993) noted that it was unlikely that contradictions surrounding unsustainable development in Southern Africa would be solved in the coming decades. This was deemed the case because of unsustainable development practices, such as destruction of the tropical moist forests, the loss of endangered species and the threat of the greenhouse effect. However, environmental issues in SADC member countries are undergoing substantial changes and have been articulated at international, regional, national and local fora. Practical remedial measures, however, have yet to emerge.

Despite increasing worldwide calls for sustainable management of the environment, conflicts involving the use of commonly-owned natural resources have been reported. Carney and Farrington (1999) attribute this to three factors:

- While in many cases the ownership of forests, range lands and water resources is vested in the state, the state does not have the capacity to enforce rules governing their access and use.

- The management of such resources by individual users is problematic, principally because of the difficulty of defining boundaries and the high enforcement cost to individuals.

- Private management, that is commercial or individual management of such resources, tends to benefit one group only and is therefore likely to result in unacceptably high inequalities in resource access and utilisation.

These problems have led to new developments in the theory of natural resources and common property resources management in SADC. Murphree and Hulme (1999) noted that over the last decade conservation concepts, policies and practices in Africa have been challenged by a set of radical alternatives. There is now a discernible movement towards 'community in conservation', hence the reference to community-based conservation or community conservation. This is, however, more complex than simply shifting responsibility and authority from the state to community, as is commonly thought. Community conservation of common property resources management does not only incorporate local society into conservation but actually introduces the factor of the market place and in the process redefines the content of conservation. These challenges of conservation make up what is currently referred to as 'new conservation', a paradigm that attempts to connect the theory and practice of conservation beyond the colonial and neo-colonial construct of 'fortress conservation', which shaped the management of natural resources and the commons in the past.

The 'new conservation' paradigm has contributed a three-pronged approach *vis-à-vis* natural resources and commons management in SADC. The first is that conservation of natural resources should be shifted from being a state-centric activity to one based in society, and at the local level in particular. Local society is usually understood to be the community. It is because of this notion that the idea of community-based conservation of natural resources has been mooted. The notion also encompasses the concept of indigenous knowledge (which can be used interchangeably with traditional ecological knowledge), referring to a cumulative body of knowledge and beliefs handed down through generations by cultural transmission. At its core is the rejection of the idea that African communities are degraders of the environment; indeed, the indigenous technical knowledge of rural Africans indicates a possession of sophisticated understandings of the environment. The new conservation paradigm should recognise rural Africans as 'citizens not criminals', with rights and responsibilities over the nation's conservation estate (be that of species, habitats or bio-diversity in general). Since conservation no longer requires that man and nature be kept separate by coercion, a community-centred approach to conservation ideally transfers all responsibilities and full property rights over natural resources to communities at the local level. Rihoy (1995) concurs on the utility of community-based natural resource management and point out that such ideas have informed practice in Namibia as well as in Zimbabwe, where CAMPFIRE is credited with enabling communities participate fully, not just in the management of resources, but also in benefit-sharing. This approach seems to form the basis of the community conservation programme at Tarangire National Park in Tanzania.

The second prong of the new conservation theory, as argued by Murphree and Hulme (1999), relates to the conceptualisation of conservation. Over time this has witnessed shifts as the idea of conservation as preservation has been challenged by the notion of sustainable development, where both conservation and development goals are achieved simultaneously. As natural elements that need to be conserved, biological resources are not exactly set aside but are viewed as renewable natural resources that can be utilised as long as sustainability is not compromised. This shift in the meaning of conservation was due to the realisation that much conservation thinking was, in fact, environmental imperialism that prioritised Western conservation goals over African development needs. The concept of sustainable development is also at the centre of the debate. In the first instance it is argued that sustainable utilisation calls for a careful utilisation of natural resources so that key natural processes are not compromised. This view recognises that significant environmental change is acceptable, including species loss and reductions in bio-diversity, especially where the costs of retaining these environmental characteristics are judged to be excessive by local resource users. The other view argues that sustainability means that utilisation must not threaten the existence of any species, thereby keeping utilisation indigenous. This approach has been criticised for equating indigenous resource users with being primitive, and is criticised as being detrimental and blocking development.

The third prong has a pronounced neo-liberal inclination, arguing that uncontrolled markets give individuals the greatest freedom in what to produce and consume, and that patterns of natural resource use, including conservation, are best determined by market forces. It is argued that if species or habitats are to be conserved, they must not be protected from market forces, as this promotes rent-seeking behaviour on the part of public officials. In the market place the uniqueness and scarcity of the resources will lead to high economic values being placed on them, thereby enhancing the likelihood of their conservation. Consumers, such as trophy hunters, the media, and people who intrinsically value species or a habitat, will bid higher prices for wildlife products, which may serve to discourage alternative uses of the environment that are damaging, such as agriculture. Notwithstanding the polemical and conceptual propositions argued above, Murphree and Hulme (1999: 283) correctly observed that proper management of natural resources and the commons depends on governance processes that allow all the actors to wield influence. The arrangements should be flexible enough to permit relationships, policy and practice to evolve as environmental, economic and social conditions change.

A useful insight into the management of natural resources and the commons in the SADC region has been provided by Murombedzi (1999). In spite of the fact that Zimbabwe's CAMPFIRE was widely regarded as one of Africa's most successful contemporary conservation initiatives, permitting residents of communal lands adjacent to wildlife areas to share benefits generated through wildlife utilisation, Murombedzi notes that the programme still faces some challenges. For example, the development strategies of households in CAMPFIRE areas were characterised by practices that were incompatible with wildlife management, namely population in-migration and the extension of cropping and increased livestock activities. It was further noted that CAMPFIRE had only decentralised authority over natural resources from central government to rural district councils rather than to producer communities.

### *Institutional aspects*

Carney and Farrington (1999) analysed problems of resource management from a historical perspective. Between 1950 and 1980, natural resource and commons management were state-controlled. This was relatively unchallenged. With the emergence of the 'New Political Economy ' during the 1980s there was a liberal backlash where the state was regarded as innately incapable of doing its work. The argument was that civil servants were motivated by self-interest, and thus came the view that imperfect markets were better than imperfect states. As pointed out by Carney and Farrington (1999), the yet to be confirmed success of these market-oriented programmes strengthened, among other things, the case for market-oriented reform in the management of natural resources and the commons. In support of this it can be pointed out that over the past 40 years or so markets in developed countries have done a fairly good job compared to the controls imposed by governments of developing countries. Nonetheless, it is not always true to say that economic growth occurs only when the state is rolled back. Economic growth has been registered in south-east Asian countries where the state was not rolled back, showing that there can be a pluralistic approach where the state closely works together with the NGOs, the private sector and the local communities. The degrees of control by each player over the resources as well as who benefits most, are the key issues that need to be resolved.

Baden and Noonan (1998) discussed the classic tragedy and the problematic conceptions of the management of commons. Based on his research experiences on attempts to reverse marked salmon fish declines in the Pacific Northwest, Ruckelshaus (1998) observed that the maintenance of salmon fisheries could benefit from opportunities afforded to people with diverse backgrounds to meet in working groups to discuss the issues, establish a shared vision of the future, and identify ways of overcoming obstacles to fulfilling that vision. Acknowledging the delicacy of the problem of natural resources and commons management Ruckelshaus further noted that imposition of court orders, tighter regulations or political interference in decision-making could work but had limitations. Success, it was said, could only be guaranteed where there was a broader public education and participation in the decision-making processes, especially by local people. This, however, does not say how well the task could be successfully linked-up to national, regional and international levels without prejudicing both the commons and the relevant communities.

The World Bank (2000) placed emphasis on linkages between national and global environmental issues. The argument was that protection of the local environment would also contribute to addressing global environmental problems. Another area of emphasis in the World Bank contribution was the need to move from national to international action, since the complexity of environmental issues lies in the unique configuration of scientific factors, stakeholders, costs, benefits and policy implications, which were seen as being beyond the capacity of the state. A milestone in the successful management of natural resources and the commons, according to the World Bank, was the adoption of the Convention on Biological Diversity in 1992 by 169 ratifying states. Signatories to the Convention are obliged to conserve and ensure the sustainable use of their own biological diversity. The challenge of the management of natural resources, such as biodiversity, according to the Biodiversity Convention, was regarded as being urgent in developing countries, regardless of the problems faced in implementing these agreements. However, all global environmental management arrangements have one thing in common; there is a lack of sufficient incentives to act on environmental problems because not all countries, especially developing ones, capture all the rewards of so doing. The usefulness of these treaties and conventions should therefore not be over-estimated. According to Smith (1993), such is the position because the agreements are not legally binding. It is taken on trust that parties will abide by them. Even when some of these agreements or conventions are legally binding they remain very difficult to enforce. In the final analysis the problem is that there remains a distinction between upholding the letter of an international agreement and abiding by the spirit of that same agreement.

## *Concluding remarks*

There are widely varying theoretical approaches that have been applied to the management of natural resources and the commons in the SADC region. These should be applied selectively, taking account of the specificities of the resources themselves as well as of the participating countries. SADC has made great strides in addressing the challenges of the management of natural resources and the commons in the region, in the form of mutually-adopted and legally-binding protocols and Sector Co-ordinating Units for which each member state assumes ultimate responsibility. In the remainder of the paper it is argued that the effective management of transboundary resources in southern Africa should begin with a clarification of management systems at national level; it is doubtful that individual countries will succeed as a collective where they are failing as individuals to craft management systems that include all stakeholders. In the concluding section of this paper I emphasise the point that the potentially rewarding management of transboundary resources by SADC states should be guided by the adage 'charity begins at home'.

As this volume clearly illustrates that there is much sweeping to be done in the backyard *vis-à-vis* the unfinished business of elaborating a framework for sustainable natural resource management at national level in Zimbabwe.

## Making transboundary resources management a reality in SADC

### *The environment: the base of common property management*

To underline the importance of natural resources and the commons as the basis of livelihoods, prosperity and development, the SADC Treaty signed in 1980 has as one of its objectives to achieve the sustainable utilisation of natural resources and effective protection of the environment. As already said, the SADC region is endowed with a wealth of natural resources, including arable and grazing land, lakes and rivers, forests and woodlands and precious minerals. There is also an impressive diversity of wild animals and plants, which are to a large extent found in their natural habitats (*SADC Review*, 2001: 90; *SADC Review*, 2000:17).

A high average annual population growth rate of 3.5 percent, against a backdrop of weak economic performance in many countries, is placing huge demands on the environment on which many people, particularly the poor, depend for their livelihoods. Moreover, the region is experiencing environmental problems such as deforestation, soil erosion and general degradation of agricultural land (Tevera, 1994; *SADC Review*, 2001).

The creation in 1985 of the Environment and Land Management Sector (and its attendant Sector Coordinating Unit), which after the 2001 restructuring of SADC became part of the Food, Agriculture and Natural Resources Directorate, gives hope that these problems will eventually be addressed. The sector has the mandate to facilitate the transition towards environmentally sustainable development within SADC countries.

In the early 1990s, the Environment and Land Management Sector adopted a policy strategy to bring about a shift from the previous approach of managing the environment in a fragmented manner to one that took account of other sectors. In 1996, the SADC Council of Ministers approved the SADC Policy and Strategy for the Environment and Sustainable Development. According to the *SADC Review* (2001), it provides the basis for implementing Agenda 21 (the global action plan for environment and development adopted at the 1992 Earth Summit) in the southern African context. The goals of the Environment and Land Management Sector, as articulated in the SADC Policy and Strategy for Environment and Sustainable Development for the region were to:

- Protect and improve the health, environment and livelihoods of the people in southern Africa, especially the poor.
- Preserve the natural heritage, biodiversity and life-supporting ecosystems in southern Africa.
- Support regional economic development on an equitable and sustainable basis for the benefit of present and future generations.
- Strengthen the analytical, decision-making, legal, institutional and technological capacities for achieving sustainable development.
- Increase public information, education and participation on environmental and development issues.
- Expand regional integration and global co-operation on environmental and natural resources management.

The biggest challenge relates to the establishment of competent management regimes for natural resources and the commons. This implies re-constituting institutional arrangements with other SADC sectors. The result will be a consolidation of the development and implementation of harmonised policies, strategies and action programmes, regional guidelines and standards as well as regional protocols. In 2002, two major programmes were adopted, namely Environment Management and Land Management, which would receive benefit from the RIO+10 Conference scheduled to be convened mid-2002. In essence, the Environment Management programme is meant to enhance the capacity of the sector to monitor, assess and report on environmental conditions and changes in the region, mainly through environmental awareness and facilitation of environmental education campaigns. The Land Management programme is meant to cater for production-oriented conservation, building on indigenous and traditional knowledge and institutions, as well as applying more modern approaches. A Land Degradation and Desertification Control Programme is one of its tasks. This latter programme aims to combat land degradation and desertification and mitigate the effects of drought in the SADC region.

### *Institutional Changes*

Strong and credible institutions are needed for effective management of commonly-owned natural resources in SADC. The setting up of the various sector co-ordinating units was (according to the *SADC Review* 2001:76-93), meant to address in a co-ordinated manner, the concept of optimum management of natural resources and the commons. Co-ordination would be done within national, regional and international contexts, through a system of respective protocols and Sector Co-ordinating Units.

These are:

- Legal sector
- Livestock production and animal disease control
- Marine fisheries and resources
- Inland fisheries
- Forestry
- Wildlife
- Environment and land management
- Water

After the restructuring of SADC in March 2001, all these sectors would be clustered under the Food, Agriculture and Natural Resources Directorate (*SADC Today*, 2001). The issue of stakeholder participation, however, was not adequately dealt with. Most of the key stakeholders, such as the private sector, industry, poor rural and urban communities, local and foreign NGOs, are ignored by most Heads of State and governments and other ministerial officials determining the conduct of business in the Sectors and their respective Co-ordinating Units. The absence of a cohesive and fully representative stakeholder structure at national and regional level, has resulted in a loss of focus and consistency in the management of commonly-owned natural resources, at all three levels. However, the national level has been most severely affected. Moreover, synchronising the optimum management of commonly-owned natural resources at the national, regional and international levels in this age of globalisation is a challenge in itself.

### *Legal Sector*

Perhaps the main challenge of managing common property relates to the provision of legal advice and assistance to the institutions involved, i.e. sectors and their respective sector co-ordinating units, which are responsible for the management of commonly-owned natural resources across the region. An important element of managing any natural resource, especially if it used by more than one user, is conflict management (Manzungu, 1999). This is a crucial issue, especially where a resource such as water is exploited by several member states. Water raises important challenges: its exploitation within the confines of national boundaries can have direct effects on downstream countries in the catchment area. Overall, the challenges faced by the Legal Sector in the light of the current debate are:

- Provision of legal advice to SADC and member States in matters relating to the interpretation and implementation of the SADC Treaty, Protocols and other subsidiary instruments pertaining to the effective management of natural resources and the commons.

- Provision of legal advice and related legal services to other functional SADC sectors on the environment and commonly-owned natural resources.
- Promotion of the adoption of mutual assistance agreements and arrangements in conflicts, criminal and civil matters relating to the proper management of the environment and commonly-owned natural resources.

*Inland Fisheries Sector*

SADC's inland waters cover nearly one million square kilometres and produce 450-500,000 tonnes of fish from capture fisheries and aquaculture, making the region one of the largest sources of freshwater fish on the African continent. This demands proper management of the common fisheries of SADC, which are dependent on the environmental conditions of the water bodies. To promote regional management, the Fisheries Sector adopted an Inland Fisheries Programme of Action with the objective of increasing fish production through aquaculture and capture-fisheries development. To effectively manage this resource, this Sector was divided into three units.

The first is the Information Section, which co-ordinates the management of fisheries information within the framework of Regional Fisheries Information Programme (RFIP). This programme enhances the relevance of the delivered information and is vital to the decision-making process at regional level.

The training section caters for human resources development and is meant to assist in the development of the human resources base, which is crucial to the well-being of the people and the resources in the region. This it will achieve by equipping the majority of people in the fishing communities, who are either illiterate or semi-illiterate, with knowledge and skills via its training programmes that are tailor-made made to suit the capabilities and needs of these communities. Equally, resource managers and scientists are also afforded on-the-job management training so that they become key players in the aquaculture and capture-fisheries development campaign. The section has already started training programmes through the Regional Fisheries Training Programme.

The third, the Research and Development section for capture fisheries, co-ordinates research programmes on shared fish resources in the effort to achieve better resource management. This adds more information to the knowledge of the resource base. It also identifies the indigenous species that make the best candidates for aquaculture in preference to directing research efforts into exotic species that could potentially alter the delicate ecosystems to the detriment of the existing stocks. The section further implements efficient fish resource utilisation, and improves resource management and effective control mechanisms. It also undertakes research on both the socio-economic environment and economic environmental issues in order to adequately address the sector's complex nature.

The effort by the Fisheries Sector to improve the management of the fisheries as a common property resource in the SADC region was clearly spelt out in the SADC Inland Fisheries Sector Policy and Strategy. The mandate covered the promotion of sustainable exploitation, the utilisation and marketing of fish resources and the effective protection of the environment to sustain development (*SADC Review*, 2001:83).

The main challenges for the Inland Fisheries Sector involve:

- Increasing fish production through aquaculture and capture-fisheries development.
- Training human resources in fisheries development across the region.
- The co-ordination of the management of fisheries across the region.
- Research and development of capture-fisheries.
- Research and identification of suitable indigenous species.

*Wildlife Sector*

Nearly 2,000,000 square kilometres or 35 per cent of the region's land is comprised of wildlife-rich protected areas and communal lands, which in many cases straddle national boundaries. The area provides large blocks of habitats where elephants, large predators and a plethora of birds, local plants and other forms of bio-diversity thrive. With nearly 40 per cent of all African elephants living in this region, implementing programmes on the conservation and rational utilisation of the resource is a matter of urgency. The political will to manage these resources from a transboundary perspective, which brings together a number of countries into co-ordinated conservation and sustainable development programmes, is visible as attested by efforts towards setting up common management arrangements. However, there is a need to bring on board communities and the private sector so that agreements on natural resource management are widely shared by society. For example, the mutual arrangements cited above, where there was a regional consensus attained on the Convention on International Trade in Endangered Species (CITES) Appendix listing (in which the elephant populations of Botswana, Namibia and Zimbabwe were transferred from Appendix I to II where trade in elephant ivory is allowed), was not just a great step in the conservation and rational utilisation of resources but a benefit to all communities and people involved (World Bank, 2000).

The new system, the MIKE (Monitoring of Illegal Killing of Elephants), which was designed to monitor the poaching of elephant populations throughout Africa, should not lose this focus. Notwithstanding the strengths of CITES I and II in the conservation campaign for the wildlife natural resources and the commons, CITES (COP11) has its own comparative advantage over the former in that while wildlife can be listed to Appendix I or II they all still remain equally furnished with CITES approval for annual quotas for the disposal of elephant ivory.

According to the *SADC Review* (2001:89), the Regional Wildlife Policy and Strategy and the Protocol on Wildlife Conservation and Law Enforcement have been adopted as key documents with which to govern the conservation and management efforts of wildlife. This will be achieved through sustainable and rational utilisation of wildlife resources in a manner that brings benefits to the communities living alongside them. Wide-ranging programmes to prop up these efforts have taken the form of programmes that include regional wildlife training, which is meant to optimise socio-economic returns from the SADC region's natural resource base. This is done by upgrading the professional competence of the staff of wildlife management agencies. Regional programmes on the development of community-based management and utilisation of wildlife resources, as alternative land uses e.g. on marginal lands, are also being promoted.

This will increase the productivity of the lands, which will directly benefit the rural communities. One example is the SADC regional rhino conservation programme, put forward as a long-term conservation measure of the region's biodiversity. It targeted two key species, the black rhino and the white rhino. Another is the wetlands conservation programme aimed at promoting awareness of the role, value and appropriate uses of wetlands amongst policy-makers, resource planners and managers, extension workers, and wetland users. It also offers training in wetlands planning and management and protection.

There are a number of community-based natural resource management programmes that are being implemented under this sector. One example is CAMPFIRE in Zimbabwe, meant to allow the residents of communal lands, especially poor black people, to share the benefits generated by wildlife utilisation, such as commercial hunting. The Gaza-Kruger-Gonarezhou Trans-Frontier Park (GKG TFP) and Trans-Frontier Conservation Area (GKG TFCA) are other initiatives aimed at co-ordinating tourism activities in Mozambique, South Africa and Zimbabwe (see Vassileva, this volume). This will result in increased revenue for these three countries, as well as sustainable management of the shared resources. Notwithstanding the merits of this initiative, controversy still remains as to whether this is a priority for all stakeholders from the three countries. The plight of the affected communities in the three countries is still a cause for concern.

In spite of all the contrasting views, the above-mentioned strategies constitute a significant departure from traditional ways of managing wildlife. At the moment the challenges facing the sector include:

- The different laws and tenure systems in various member states.

- Preservation of wildlife-rich protected areas across the region.
- Protection of the regional bio-diversity.
- Implementation of the regional wildlife training programme.
- Development of a regional community-based management and utilisation of wildlife resources.
- Development of a regional rhino conservation programme.
- Conservation of wetlands and the training of personnel in wetlands planning management and protection.

*Water Sector*

The establishment of both the SADC Water Sector and a Protocol on Shared Watercourse System in the new millennium (*SADC Review*, 2001) was recognition that water is a critical factor towards the achievement of strategic development objectives. For example, water is useful in improving food security and alleviating poverty.

Some of the challenges facing this sector are:

- Control of floods and coping with their effects.
- Mitigation of drought.
- Combatting water pollution.
- Provision of and ugrading sanitation systems.
- Improving water supply systems for both the urban and rural people.
- Definition of water rights for both upstream and downstream users.
- Protection of the environment that yields this precious and finite resource.

Some of the challenges may be beyond the capacity of the region, as is the case with flood-induced disasters. The effects of Cyclone Eline upon the region in 2000 is a case in point. In such instances international help is required. But SADC countries can take appropriate measures to monitor various aspects of water resources in their region. To this end, the adoption of the Regional Strategic Action Plan (1999-2004) is a welcome development. In the plan are a number of programmes and projects, including the SADC Hydrological Observing Systems (SADC-HYCOS), the groundwater management programme, the regional project to control infestation and translocation of aquatic weeds, and the programme on water supply and sanitation.

These regional initiatives should not, however, lose sight of the poor. While governments and NGOs can provide them with water and water-related services, it is important that the affected people are consulted as much as possible. The input of the poor into Protocol Agreements or the adoption of certain aspects of Regional Strategic Action Plan is critical to the sustainable development and management of water resources in the region.

## Global dimensions of natural resource management

While there is merit in international arrangements and fora on the management of commonly-owned resources, there still remains the challenge of making these work on the ground. This is due to a variation of priorities between nation-states and the failure to effectively address critical environmental problems because of socio-economic considerations. In developing countries, the problem is often a lack of human and financial capacity; in developed countries vested economic interests tend to hold sway.

The setting up of global fora (in the form of conventions, treaties, etc.) on environmental problems has provided platforms for debate on the optimum management of natural resources and the commons, even though much controversy surrounds most of these international conventions and treaties (Smith, 1993). Such platforms include the United Nations Law of the Sea, Ozone Depletion, Climate Change and Biodiversity Protection, to name but a few.

SADC countries should exploit the opportunities these platforms offer, to strengthen their efforts in optimal management of natural resources and the commons to the benefit of their national economies as well as the poor communities. In fact, this possibility is a reality if one considers the existence of the Global Environmental Facility, which is meant to provide grants and concessional funds to cover the additional costs incurred when a development project undertakes global environmental objectives in biodiversity, climate change, international waters, or the depletion of the earth's ozone layer. As desertification is one of the pronounced environmental problems in the SADC region, there could be cause for soliciting funding or promoting research to combat this menace under such a facility.

There are, however, many contradictions and problems that characterise these conventions, treaties and agreements. Smith (1993: 5) highlighted some of the limitations:

- Funding for biodiversity and climate change projects has to be commensurate with the level of responsibility. Most developed countries have to essentially show responsibility, in practical terms, for the magnitude of global environmental degradation they have brought about, climate change in particular, which has been attributed to greenhouse gases produced by most industrialised states.

- Deforestation has been attributed to the demand for hardwood products by most consumers in developed countries and to the need for poorer states to exploit their natural resources for foreign currency earnings.
- Even if mutual agreements are reached, there still remain substantial difficulties to be overcome as regards implementation as most are not legally binding – parties are taken on trust that they will abide by the provisions of these conventions.
- Even if there is a considerable degree of legal accountability involved, it is notoriously difficult to enforce breaches of international law.

## Coming down to earth: the importance of a national agenda

It is essential that achievements made in the optimum management of natural resources and the commons by each SADC member state be used as stepping stones for regional programmes. According to Chikowore (1998), a Comprehensive National Development Concept (CNDC), in which the SADC governments both individually and as a community articulate their priorities and goals on the optimum management of natural resources and the commons, should be developed with the aid of all prospective stakeholders. Figure 11 shows the proposed model.

This concept can be seen as a key in the Natural Resources and the Commons Optimum Management Paradigm, where emphasis is placed on the National Development Plans that span a 2-3 year period. In such plans there has to be a definition of the relevant natural resources and the commons, which in most SADC countries comprise land, minerals, livestock, marine fisheries and inland fisheries, forests, wildlife, water, atmosphere, seas, places of natural interest (*SADC Review*, 2001). National development plans must articulate the priorities and goals regarding optimum management of the commons. These priorities and goals could turn commons into viable economic entities, generating income through rational utilisation in a specific locality at district and provincial or at national level.

On the developmental and operational level (B) (see figure 9.1), there should be an arrangement of institutions for the rationalisation of the optimal management of the commons. Legal and ownership rights within the context of decentralisation and devolution of powers to the local people at district and provincial levels, which are seen as being cost effective and beneficial, must be elaborated. The fact that globalisation places its own demands requires that all action plans, agreements, treaties and conventions be grounded in the priorities and goals determined at national level. Where prejudicial and retrogressive tendencies are apparent, mostly on the welfare levels of the poor, corrective measures must be taken. This will necessitate a revisitation of the National Development Plans in terms of targeted goals. The goals may include raising incomes of the people, promoting improved access to health and educational facilities, recreation and cultural development

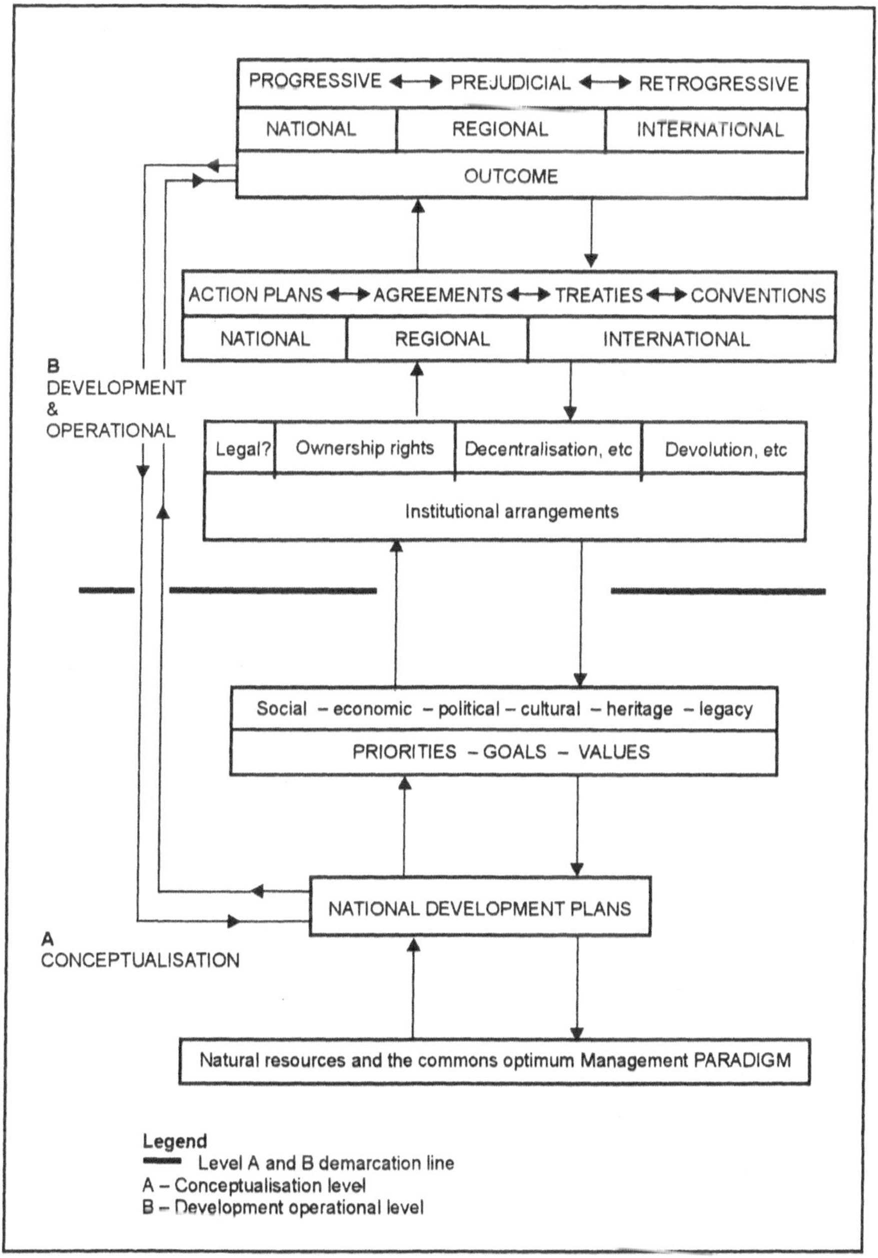


Figure 11: Model on Optimisation of Natural Resources and the Commons Management in the New Millennium.

centers, and employment and self-employment generation levels. The conservation of resources remains an important focus.

## Conclusion

The challenges and prospects of transboundary management of natural resources and the commons in SADC can be addressed within the framework of the treaties, conventions, action plans and agreements mutually adopted at regional and international levels. It must be remembered that most of the regional and international treaties, conventions, etc. are not legally binding, and that the costs incurred for irresponsible use of the commons at any location, especially in developed countries, can intensify the rates of impoverishment of the poor of the SADC region. However the agreements represent a good beginning and in this regard SADC appears to be making progress – member states are signatories to a number of regional and international conventions, treaties and agreements.

The member countries within these areas are likely to benefit from such arrangements if these arrangements are grounded in the priorities and goals of each SADC member state. The successful articulation of these priorities and goals can only be achieved within the framework of Comprehensive National Development Concepts, which find expression in National Development Plans, which have well-balanced inward and outward looking policies. Such NDPs can counteract the tendency to make uniform priorities and goals at regional and international levels for countries with distinct socio-economic differences.

## References

Alaev, E. B. (1983). *Socio-economic Geography*. Moscow, Miscle.

Baden, J. A. and D. S. Noonan (1998). *Managing the Commons*. Bloomington, Indiana University Press.

Berkes, F. and C. Folke (1998). *Linking social and ecological systems: management practices and social mechanisms for building resilience*. Cambridge, Cambridge University Press.

Carney, D. and J. Farrington (1999). *Natural resources management and institutional change*. London, Routledge.

Chikowore, G. (1998). 'Theoretical aspects of regional co-operation'. *SAPEM* Vol. 11, (12) Oct Nov p. 25-32.

Dalal-Clayton, B. (1996). *Environment and Ecology in Southern Africa: Current Trends and Scenarios to 2015*. Southern Africa – Project 2015. Stockholm, SIDA.

Manzungu, E. (1999). 'Conflict management crisis in the Umvumvumvu Catchment, Eastern Zimbabwe.' In E. Manzungu, A. Senzanje and P. van der Zaag. (eds) (1999). *Water for Agriculture in Zimbabwe: Policy and management options for the smallholder sector.* Harare University of Zimbabwe.

Moyo. S., P. O'Keefe and M. Sill (1993). *The Southern African Environment: Profiles of the SADC countries*. London, Earthscan.

Murombedzi, J. C. (1999). 'Devolution and stewardship in Zimbabwe's CAMPFIRE Programme', *Journal of International Development*. Volume 11 (2), p. 287-93.

Murphree, M. and D. Hulme (1999). 'Communities, wildlife and "New Conservation" in Africa', *Journal of International Development* Vol. 11, (2) p. 272-86.

Ruckelshaus, W. D. (1998). *Managing Commons and Community. Pacific Northwest people, Salmon Rivers and Sea*. Bloomington, Indiana University Press.

Rihoy, E. (ed.) (1995). The Commons without the Tragedy? Strategies for Community Based Natural Resources Management in Southern Africa. Lilongwe: USAID.

*SADC Review*: Trade, Industry and Investment (2000). 'Wildlife Protocol'. Gaborone, SAM Co. Ltd.

*SADC Review*. Trade, Industry and Investment. (2001) 'Protocol on Wildlife Conservation and Law Enforcement'. Gaborone, SAM Co. Ltd.

'SADC puts on a new face as restructuring starts'. (2001). *SADC Today*. Vol. 4 (4), April, p. 16.

Smith, R. (1993). International Treaties, Conventions and Agreements relevant to Biodiversity Conservation. New Series discussion Paper No. 36. Bradford, University of Bradford.

Tevera, D. S. (1994). 'Population, the environment and resources in Zimbabwe' in Ezekiel Kalipeni (ed.). *Population growth and environmental degradation in Southern Africa*. Boulder, Lynne Rienner Publishers.

Treshnikov, A.F. (1988). *Concepts and Terminologies. Geographical Encyclopaedia Dictionary*. Moscow, Soviet Encyclopaedia Publishers.

World Bank (2000). Entering the 21st Century: World Development Report, 1999-2000. Oxford, Oxford University Press.

# Chapter 10

# Global or local commons? Biodiversity, indigenous knowledge and Intellectual Property Rights

*Morris Mudiwa*

## Introduction

This chapter discusses issues surrounding Intellectual Property Rights (IPRs) in relation to biological resources and Indigenous Knowledge Systems (IKS), highlighting the salient features that are a source of contention between developed and developing countries. The former create wealth by exploiting biological resources found in developing countries, but do not pass on the commensurate benefits to the latter. The problem is that although developed countries lack the biological diversity that they need within their own territories, they nevertheless possess the technology to make marketable products from resources found in developing countries. This chapter also makes a case for respecting the rights of local communities, who do not receive their due share from either developed countries or governments of developing countries.

The uneven distribution of the world's biological resources contributes to the problem. Egziabher (2000) states that biodiversity increases towards the equator and decreases towards the poles. Industrialised countries tend to be located in biodiversity-poor regions whilst developing countries are found in biodiversity-rich regions, which fall mostly within the tropics. The geographical location of developed and developing nations has led to the use of the terms North and South in describing these nations respectively. More than two thirds of the world's plant species – at least 35,000 of which have medicinal value –

are found in developing countries (Crucible Group, 1994). Nijar (1996) states that today's global food supply rests essentially on biological diversity developed from the wild plants and animals, savannas, and the forests of the developing countries.

The distribution of resources within national territories themselves also has implications for the design of benefit-sharing mechanisms. A good example is miombo woodland, which generally has a higher species diversity than acacia woodland (Biodiversity Support Foundation, 1993; Campbell, 1996). It extends over 2.7 million sq. km in central, southern and eastern African countries including Angola, the Democratic Republic of Congo, Malawi, Mozambique, Tanzania, Zambia, and Zimbabwe. Within these individual countries there is uneven distribution (Frost, 1996). The question is, how are benefits from such a resource going to be distributed, given the regional, national and local dimensions?

Problems have also arisen from the unfair legal systems governing access and exploitation of biological resources. Laws, conventions and agreements tend to disadvantage developing countries. The TRIPs Agreement, to which most developed countries are signatories, allows patents and other IPRs on biological resources or knowledge of use to be granted to any applicant in any country without the knowledge or consent of the country where such resources are found. There is no provision under TRIPs for a patent holder who had exploited certain biological resources or related knowledge to share the benefits with the state or communities in the countries of origin. Under this arrangement developed countries can invoke property rights, which they use to patent the manufactured products and by so doing can prevent others from deriving benefits from them and without paying for the intellectual rights. Such property rights disregard property-holding regimes of developing countries. Developing countries have more to lose under this system of property rights, not just through the direct exploitation of biological resources in their territories, but through the diminution or trivialisation of their innovations and knowledge associated with the native biological resources in question. Local communities suffer most in this regard as they are directly affected by the exploitation of biological resources.

For sustainability it is necessary that biodiversity be conserved, in line with its internationally recognised significance to social, economic and environmental issues. Fortunately, this is gaining support worldwide: biodiversity conservation has gained and continues to gain greater prominence in all environmental agendas. All countries agree that environmental issues are a global concern and need a global approach. In this regard each country has a role to play as it has a share of global resources, whose use has an effect on the global environment. However, when one takes into account the inequitable distribution of benefits derived from the use of biological resources between developed and developing nations, one is tempted to ask which of the two should bear the cost of conservation. What justification is there for a developing country to undertake biodiversity conservation programmes at its own expense when developed countries develop products based on such resources, attach IPRs to their use and derive huge benefits therefrom?

Financial resources made available through global facilities, such as the Global Environment Facility (GEF), are supposed to be used for conservation purposes but do not seem to be easily accessed by developing countries to ensure the success of their conservation programmes. Given the vested interests involved on the part of developed countries, one sees a role for independent environmental organisations that deal with biodiversity issues to set up country-specific programmes, through which funds from global facilities can be channelled towards conservation projects and programmes. Bodies such as the United Nations Environmental Programme (UNEP) and The World Conservation Union (IUCN) can play this role.

Nonetheless, the vexing question is whether there is truly an independent and neutral broker in issues of biodiversity.

This chapter focuses on the need for a just benefit-sharing system, and looks at ways of overcoming some of the identified challenges. The question that runs throughout the paper is: are the biological resources found in developing countries global or local commons?

Before looking closely at the controversies involved, it is important to clarify some of the terms used .

## Definition of terms

### *Intellectual property rights*

Property is a claim to a benefit or income stream. Property rights constitute claims to a benefit stream protected from interference by other potential users through institutionalised arrangements (Kameri-Mbote, 2000). The relationship, rights, and responsibilities between a holder or non-holder of the property and the property itself are also defined. Intellectual property rights are designed to confer ownership and specify rules of access over inventions, processes, and ideas (George and van Staden, 2000; Swinson, 2000). They are private legal rights that acknowledge and protect the intangible contribution of people in the production of technologies.

A distinction is made between tangible and intangible property, as well as the rights pertaining to each. Tangible property refers to real property that has a physical character. An example would be a house, a building or land. Intellectual property, on the other hand, deals with information services that are intangible and are not readily susceptible to either possession or delineation (Kameri-Mbote, 2000). It is argued that real property is relatively scarce and therefore expensive to protect and capture, whilst the value of intellectual property is associated with creation of a shortage of information by limiting the capacity of non-owners to capture it. A major distinguishing factor between property rights, in relation to their tangible and intangible nature, is that of time. Rights to an intangible property, such as intellectual property, are limited by time. After the time allotted elapses, the rights of the holder of intellectual property no longer hold, meaning that anybody wishing to use the property can do so without fear of incrimination.

Information generated through intellect has the general characteristic of being liable to use by others without payment, hence the concept of IPRs. Since the production of an intellectual good requires considerable resources in the form of time, effort and money, and that these resources have an opportunity cost, the person producing an intellectual good needs compensation for their investment. Intellectual property rights are designed to protect investments made in the production of such information, in order that users are obliged to reward the inventors for their creativity. IPRs also enable companies and individuals to legally protect themselves against counterfeiting of their products, technologies and services (Nick, 1999). IPRs generally fall into the following categories: copyrights, trademarks, trade secrets, industrial designs, geographical indications, and patents (Kameri-Mbote, 2000). Products and technologies that are protected by property rights are major exports of most developed countries, as are the rights themselves in the form of licenses on patented processes, techniques and designs, copyrights and trademarks.

Copyrights are extended to scientific publications, and computer software and databases, and generally require no formalities to obtain. In most countries, as soon as one writes factual information, it is protected by copyright (Swinson, 2000). Trademarks protect symbols, words and marks and are designed to distinguish goods and services of one person or company against those of another (Kameri-Mbote, 2000; Swinson, 2000).

Trade secrets are used to protect subject matter that is unpatentable due to its failure to follow the requirements for patenting, or because the holder of such information does not want to publicly reveal the subject matter in case a competitor may commercially use the information to their disadvantage. Examples of information that can be protected through trade secrets are scientific information or traditional healers' knowledge. Trade secrets differ from patents in that they do not prevent others from developing and using the same information in a different way.

Plant Breeders Rights (PBRs), an example of a patent, are rights granted to plant breeders to exclude others from commercialising material of the plant varieties that they have developed (Mpofu, n.d.). For a plant variety to be eligible for protection through PBRs, it must be clearly distinguished from other protected varieties, and be uniform and stable. PBRs are designed to attract the private sector into plant breeding activities. They are also designed to allow other plant breeders to use the protected plant for their own breeding activities and research, as long as they refrain from selling the protected plant itself.

Patents confer exclusive rights to an inventor and, for fixed period, prevent others from producing, using, or engaging in commercial transactions involving the invention. A patent requires that an invention be novel, or recent and original, and not previously known. Nor should the product or process be a trivial extension of that which is already known. When a patent is granted, the inventor is given a private monopoly for a fixed duration to restrict others from making, using, or selling the invention. The application for a patent must include a full written description of the invention. In exchange for the patent, the patent's subject matter should be published. The TRIPs agreement stipulates that the term of patent protection should be no less than 20 years from the filing date of the patent application (Kameri-Mbote, 2000).

Utility Patents provide protection for agricultural research products such as herbicides, insecticides, fungicides, transgenic plants, plant cells, plant genes, plant DNA sequences, plant tissue cultures, transgenic seeds, plant varieties and host vector organisms. Within the category of Utility Patents are Plant Patents, which apply to single varieties of plants. However, biologists are not happy with single plant patents, arguing that they do not provide protection for broad inventive concepts, especially in biotechnology where new traits, such as insect resistance for example, cannot be confined to a single plant variety (Duffey, 1993).

### *Indigenous Knowledge*

Indigenous Knowledge refers to local knowledge held by indigenous people that is unique to a given culture or society. It forms the basis on which local decisions in fields such as agriculture, education, health and natural resources management are made. Such people's livelihoods depend on specific skills and knowledge that have been generated by internal creativity and experimentation over a long period of time (Warren, 1991; Flavier, *et al.*, 1995). While such knowledge is of value to the owners, it is also of value to the world as it forms part of global knowledge and contributes to the world economy. A major distinguishing characteristic of indigenous knowledge is that it is intergenerational. Those who hold the knowledge 'keep' it in trust for future generations. Such knowledge has been preserved, transferred, adopted and adapted in many situations as development processes interact with it . Indigenous knowledge has recently gained prominence because of the role it has played in the preservation of biodiversity. Mayet (n.d.) describes traditional knowledge as any knowledge, innovation, or individual or collective practice of an indigenous population or local community, that has real or potential value that is associated with a biological resource, be it protected or not by intellectual property legislation.

The term 'indigenous', and sometimes 'traditional knowledge', seems to refer to the body of knowledge held by people who are not regarded as 'developed' as far as modern science and civilisation are concerned. Wherever this term is mentioned it is usually in relation to natives of a country or region whose history involves some kind of marginalisation, at one point or another, by 'modern civilisation'. Indigenous knowledge is therefore a term based on a value judgement of its quality, complexity and origin. This type of knowledge does not command the same status as what is termed 'formal scientific knowledge'. The question is, who classifies knowledge as indigenous or formal? Matose and Mukamuri (1993) argue that knowledge is constructed in relation to history, culture, economics, politics, and most importantly, power relations. Those who are politically, socially and economically disadvantaged, i.e. the powerless, are forced to accept the knowledge of the powerful. What the powerful know thus becomes the yardstick against which all other knowledge is measured. The rich and powerful therefore bestow upon themselves the prerogative of acknowledging or recognising knowledge as knowledge or as something else.

The packaging of knowledge into what is called 'indigenous', 'local' or 'modern scientific/formal' influences the value attached to it; knowledge systems are framed within discourses of power, where the powerful subdue the weak (ibid.). Matose and Mukamuri also argue that the way knowledge attains value is dependent on the world's hierarchies, which define the knowledge of 'the other' (for instance 'rural, illiterate people') as inferior to the knowledge of 'the self'. How then can Intellectual Property Rights derived from the superior domain benefit the poor and powerless?

It is quite apparent that traditionally, Intellectual Property Rights regimes attached no value to indigenous knowledge as regards warranting its protection as property. This is one reason why globalisation poses the danger of impoverishing traditional or cultural societies, as their knowledge is not usually accorded a status befitting any other body of knowledge. Gupta (n.d.) points out that people's knowledge systems need not be considered informal just because the rules of the formal system fail to explain innovations in others.

The diminution of indigenous knowledge has highlighted the fact that developing nations are involved in a competition for biological resources with an opponent (developed nations) who is both player and referee. Fortunately, developing nations are realising that there is much to gain in having a common approach to the problem. At the Convention on Biodiversity in 1992, developed countries accepted the view that biodiversity be regarded as a common heritage that should be exploited and conserved for the benefit of all mankind (Kameri-Mbote, 2000). However, these international agreements tend to be cosmetic; they do not hide the contrasting views on common heritage held by developing and developed countries. Indigenous communities in particular, and developing nations in general, have always regarded biological resources a heritage that should be shared for the benefit of all. Developed nations, on the other hand, advocate a position where benefit is limited to access to biological resources as raw materials but not what is derived from them.

One other dimension where there are differences lies in the documentation process. In developed countries, biological resources and intellectual property are defined and controlled in terms of either individual or corporate ownership. Most resources can be traced back to either of the latter entities. Traditional communities, such as those found in Africa, do not keep their knowledge documented in written form. Their knowledge is orally-based, passed on through word of mouth from one generation to another. There has been an effort not to consider written documentation as superior. For example, in the 'African Model Legislation for the Protection of the Rights of Local Communities, Farmers and Breeders for the Regulation of Access to Biological Resources (2000)' farmers' varieties and breeds are to be recognised and protected under the rules of practice as found in, and recognised by, the customary practices and laws of the local farming communities concerned, whether such laws are written or not (Mpofu, n.d.). This shows how developing countries are taking a unified stance as a way of having their knowledge accepted as property. In fact, the rules governing the development of international law do enable states, especially when they function as a voting block, to influence its evolution (Egziabher, 2000). The possible options that emerge from the quagmire of Intellectual Property Rights that developing countries face are:

1) To transform the laws that establish the current IPR regimes, or

2) To transform the institutional structures which have to do with IPRs, e.g. local communities, and their relationship with biodiversity and indigenous knowledge, to fit in the current framework of IPRs; or

3) Both of the above.

*Community*

The social organisation of people has relevance to the management and exploitation of biological resources. In developed countries people tend to live as individuals, whereas in developing countries people live in communities. Consequently, the conferment of Intellectual Property Rights in developing countries is more complicated as this touches on how a community is defined.

The definition and identification of a community is difficult. Can one just go into the countryside and point out a community? Much depends on how a community is defined. Not only is there is great diversity within and among communities, there is no a standard community that can be used as a stereotype. The relationship between a particular community and its environment and biological resources also differs from one to another.

Mayet (n.d.) indicates that there is no single definition of a local community. It can be defined in terms of shared social and economic relationships, or the transmission of knowledge, values and customs. Some communities are said to define themselves in territorial terms, or in terms of a particular natural resource or set of natural resources, or in terms of shared activity. In Zimbabwe there are two contrasting institutions at local level. One is the government-designed Village Development Committee (VIDCO), which is the basic unit of development planning. Before the creation of VIDCOs people were organised into communities headed by traditional lineage leaders. This other unit of organisation still exists alongside the state-created VIDCO system. VIDCO leadership is based on elected representatives whereas that of traditional leaders is based on heritage or descent. Both types tend to command varying degrees of legitimacy from the local people, depending on the issues under consideration. Matose and Mukamuri (1993) observe that VIDCO boundaries often have no relevance to the community's socio-economic dimensions and so bear little relation to resource management terrains. In most cases VIDCO boundaries are said to have ignored cultural and social boundaries, splitting families and ignoring traditional grazing areas. The traditional unit of organisation is a reality however, one which confuses the management of resources as development agencies are officially supposed to work within the context of the state-created boundaries of VIDCOs. Since sustainability in locally-based resource management is guaranteed where and when there is local participation, local people should be consulted as to how they would want to organise themselves. It does, however, seem more appropriate to use the traditional structures since they relate more directly to resource distribution.

## Transformation of laws and institutions

The equitable sharing of the benefits from biological resources between developing and developed countries that is being advocated here, cannot be accomplished without some major transformation of the laws and institutions that currently shape these transactions.

### *Transforming international IPR laws*

Africa has already begun exerting pressure on the evolution of international law in order to meet its own needs. For example, in the Conference of the Parties of the Convention on Biological Diversity, Africa's delegations argued that the Convention should have supremacy over TRIPs, which it was hoped would influence the development of TRIPs and WTO. The other fora where Africa has made co-ordinated efforts to present a common stance on aspects of biodiversity are:

- OAU Summit in Ouagadougou in 1998
- The African, Caribbean, Pacific and European Union Joint Assembly in 1998
- The United Nations General Assembly
- The World Trade Organisation Ministerial Conference in Seattle in 1999

- The Biosafety Protocol in Cartagena in 1999
- The International Undertaking on Plant Genetic Resources for Food and Agriculture in 1997 and 2000

Another way to strengthen Africa's advocacy in order to influence international law is to form professional task-force teams to deal with biodiversity issues on a thematic basis. Such teams can be constituted on the basis of countries where particular biological resources are found and could define the broad regional frameworks from which individual countries could develop their own access and benefit regimes. This recommendation is made in the light of the observation made by Egziabher (1996), when he attended an intergovernmental negotiation session on Biological Diversity in 1992, Nairobi. There, he observed that the delegates of the South were often too few in number to be effective. They also had to deal with a multitude of disciplines without the requisite educational background. Meanwhile, delegates from the North came in large multi-disciplinary teams, equipped with comprehensive databases.

The rationale for Africa to advocate for changes in international laws and conventions is that international efforts are not always compatible. For example, the Convention on Biological Diversity (CBD) and TRIPs have different objectives. The CBD is driven more by the need to conserve biodiversity and acknowledge the role of traditional knowledge and is sympathetic to the plight of developing countries. TRIPs, on the other hand, is a commercial treaty with commercial objectives that largely benefit large private firms (Third World Network, 2001). Some of the provisions in CBD are not in the interest of TRIPs. There is therefore a need for a merger of CBD and TRIPS to form a global organisation that addresses both issues under one umbrella and includes all stakeholders.

Issues of sovereignty also come into play. Under CBD the sovereignty of countries is enshrined, which tends to counter the thrust towards globalisation. If a biological resource is defined as being local as far as conservation and utilisation are concerned, sovereignty will have the effect of limiting the impact of globalisation. If there is a universal agreement about the need to conserve a specific biological resource, such as preserving elephants and banning trade in their products, how does one interpret national sovereignty, as enshrined in the CBD?

### *Transforming local institutions*

Individuals, households, communities and indigenous groups all articulate historical and cultural claims over access to and control of territorial resources with the purpose of securing livelihoods from their local environmental inheritance. A community has historical attachments and entitlements to environmental resources, indigenous institutions and customary rights. It is important to state that community rights regarding the control of natural resources, including bio-diversity, knowledge and technologies, existed before any private rights were conferred (Mayet, n.d.).

Western IPR systems are based on private rights. Collective knowledge or rights are only recognised if the community is a company. This demonstrates the shortfalls associated with the system of granting IPR to traditional communities that is based on 'modern' societies. Traditional communities come from and are characterised by a background of sharing, where, for example, genetic resources are treated as common property. Africa's people have long depended upon free and open access to a diversity of seeds, food, fuel and medicine. Information has always been shared between farmers. Knowledge and experience are also communally owned. The concept of property rights did not exist in traditional African societies (Berg, n.d.). Gupta (n.d.) highlights the fact that a large number of local communities across the world have unhesitatingly shared their knowledge about local biodiversity and its different uses with outsiders, including researchers, corporations, gene collectors and activists.

As if sharing was not enough, a large number of herbalists will not even accept any compensation when offered (ibid). In some cases the communities have cultural and spiritual taboos against receiving compensation because, for example, of the fear that the effectiveness of their knowledge would cease if they received any payment for it. Because of their inability to comprehend such complex community structures and how they relate to their biological resources, many colonial authorities in African countries removed rights to resources from communities and vested them in individuals as a prerequisite for legal protection (Kameri-Mbote, 2000). In other words, as long as resources are not owned by an individual or company there are no binding ownership rights, hence access to such resources is open to all.

The problem faced by most local communities in developing countries is that most national governments inherited systems of governance from colonial regimes that had removed responsibility for the management of natural resources from indigenous people to the state. Local people, who had for centuries managed their resources through local institutions, were removed from their dwelling places in order to give way to tenurial systems based on private rights. This interfered with the system of management of biological resources that local people had developed in their original areas. Colonial and post-colonial governments enacted various pieces of legislation that diminished traditional conservation practices, which were then considered to be ecologically unsustainable. The legislation enacted was authoritarian in form and process.

In Zimbabwe there have been some changes since independence. There has been some acknowledgement of the role local people play in the management and control of resources, trees for example (Nhira, *et al.*, 1998). As regards natural resource management, the government has attempted to decentralise power to local government through community-based approaches towards natural resources, including wildlife and water resources (ibid). The government is, however, reluctant to devolve the governance of resources to local level (Masiiwa, this volume). This is unfortunate as the more communities are able to control land and other natural resource use, the less government is able to dictate economic practices of local people (ibid), which in the end will enhance good local governance. Governance has only been decentralised to Rural District Councils (RDCs), which have little appreciation of the concerns and conditions at local levels (see Mamimine, this volume). Ironically RDCs are not satisfied with the level of devolution (Sithole, 2000). Empowering local communities to manage the resources is difficult in the face of existing legislation. The net result has been disappointing because mistrust is rife. According to the Biodiversity Support Foundation(1993), the historical antecedents of today's protected area system in Sub-Saharan Africa mean that the attitudes of local people living near national parks and reserves often reflect suspicion and mistrust of conservation policies and practices (Mamimine, this volume).

Is the state, therefore, in a position to be entrusted with the management and conservation of biological resources and the distribution of benefits derived from their use to the local people? Nhira, *et al.*, (1998) state that the government has neither the capability nor the means to effectively manage natural resources at local level. Gupta (n.d.) points out that most governments have very weak commitments to making the machinery of government accountable to local disadvantaged communities. Entrusting the task of compensating local people from national or international funds through the state machinery is seen as retrogressive. In Zimbabwe, the CAMPFIRE programme has provided important lessons about what the state is able and not able to do. There is clearly a need to decentralise responsibility for benefit-sharing beyond the Rural District Councils (see Mamimine, this volume). The state should therefore take the initial responsibility of protecting all biological resources from exploitation by outsiders and also establish the right institutional environment for local participation. An important question is, how should traditional institutions be transformed to conform to current IPR legislation?

Since some traditional communities still have ethics prohibiting the acceptance of compensation for knowledge or for granting access to biological diversity, there is need for a serious re-consideration and discussion of this position. This can be effected through local awareness-programmes on the realities of globalisation and its implications. Given that most communities are now dependent on a cash economy one does not expect much resistance.

On the issue of knowledge and resources, whose ownership and management responsibility is the community's, this paper recommends that communities be assisted to register as trusts (see Sanyanga, this volume). This makes the community eligible for benefits as a legal owner of resources, in conformity with the current IPR regime. Since African countries have already made presentations (through the OAU at the 1998 Conference held in Ouagadougou) for recognition of community rights and on access to biological resources, countries can begin the implementation of such initiatives. Trustees can be appointed by the community to both represent and assist them in managing the biological resources. The trustees will have two basic responsibilities. Firstly, their duty will be to have communities recognised as the legal proprietors of any biological resources under their jurisdiction. They should document all such resources as properties for and of the community. Legal expertise (which can be contracted out) is also a prerequisite, in order that legally-binding documents can be produced to protect the interests of the community. The second responsibility is to ensure that benefits from the use of community resources flow back to these communities. In this regard the trustees can borrow relevant strategies from CAMPFIRE. In most countries in southern Africa, there are Community-Based Natural Resource Management (CBNRM) programmes that have already been and are being implemented with the support of NGOs and other development institutions.

The rationale behind engaging legal expertise is that while local communities may not have any problems in managing the biological resources within their territories, they do lack the intellectual and technical capacity to deal with the legalities, and in the short term. They therefore need support in order to draft access rules and benefit sharing mechanisms.

One important point to note is that all households in the community will be eligible to join the trust, which becomes responsible for all community property in its jurisdiction. The shares allocated can be used as the basis for distribution of benefits arising from commercial use of resources owned by the trust. Whilst there may be certain requirements for registration of a company, it must be clear from the onset that we do not immediately envisage a sophisticated organisation. Instead, these will be special community natural resource trusts that are nationally and internationally recognised as the legal owners of biological and other resources within their jurisdiction. Developing countries are encouraged to develop legislation covering the formation and management of such trusts. The important thing is to set up a legally recognised body for the ownership and control of these biological resources, including indigenous knowledge. This will help in closing the gap through which resources are pirated without compensation, under the allegation that there is no owner.

## Piracy of indigenous knowledge

There are several incidences that show that indigenous knowledge is being pirated by developed nations who possess superior technology, the lack of which causes developing countries to lose out on the full benefits of their resources.

Nijar (1996a) points out that three quarters of the plants that provide active ingredients for prescription drugs came to the attention of researchers because of their use in traditional medicine. He states also that of the 120 active compounds currently isolated from the higher plants and widely used in medicine today, 74 per cent show a positive correlation between their modern therapeutic use and the traditional use of the plant from which they were derived.

The current value of the world market for medicinal plants derived from leads given by indigenous and local communities is estimated to be US$43 billion (ibid). Nijar (1996b) further states that the value of crop varieties improved and developed by traditional farmers and contributed to the international seed industry is estimated to be US$15 billion. The contribution from the traditional knowledge resources was never acknowledged; the North viewed the contribution of indigenous knowledge with little regard. The North's classification of indigenous knowledge as unpatentable can be seen as a strategic ploy to guarantee them free access to 'global commons'.

In Zimbabwe, debate is under way involving the University of Zimbabwe, the Zimbabwe National Traditional Healers Association (Zinatha), the University of Lausanne in Switzerland and an American pharmaceutical company, Phytera, over a patent on the use of the root of a certain plant, *Swartzia madagascarensis*, which is found throughout tropical Africa. According to a press statement of August 2000 (Community Technology and Development Association, *et al.*, 2000), a patent on antimicrobial diterpenes was granted to a professor at the University of Lausanne. The patented invention relied on traditional knowledge found in Zimbabwe regarding the use of the root of *Swartzia madagascarensis*. As a result, the agreement signed between the University of Zimbabwe and that of Lausanne stipulating that 'in the event of finding any product which may require the application of Intellectual Property Rights, this will be subject of joint negotiation and application' was negated.

In 1997 an addendum to a material transfer and confidentiality agreement between the American pharmaceutical company, Phytera, and the University of Lausanne, is reported to have been signed under which the two parties agreed to a royalty payment of 1.5 per cent of Phytera's net sales of the specific product. The researcher was obliged to share 50 per cent of any royalties with the National Botanic Garden of Zimbabwe, the University of Zimbabwe and Zinatha. Neither the University of Zimbabwe nor Zinatha were involved in the negotiations between the University of Lausanne and Phytera. It is quite clear from this case that Zimbabwe, as the country of origin of the biological resource, was not going to benefit greatly from such an arrangement. Zimbabwe challenged this arrangement through several NGOs, demanding that an Access and Benefit Sharing agreement be negotiated to include all the main stakeholders in Zimbabwe, and that the contract between the University of Lausanne and Phytera be cancelled and the patent withdrawn. The negotiations are still under way.

Zimbabwe also faces the problem of an insufficient legal framework with which to cover such cases. No legislation is in place to adequately address the issues of access to and benefit-sharing of biological resources found in her territory. As a result, anybody can access biological or other resources, including indigenous knowledge, and develop and patent products, yet still be guiltless as far as national laws are concerned. Whilst international provisions, as enshrined in bodies such as the CBD, stipulate that access to genetic resources and indigenous knowledge be subject to the prior informed consent of the country of origin, developing countries such as Zimbabwe still need to develop relevant legislation in this regard.

Berg (n.d.) discusses two situations where biological development stock was taken from Africa and new varieties developed to the advantage of those countries without any benefits accruing to the source countries. In the first case the International Centre for Tropical Agriculture (CIAT), based in Columbia, has a forage-breeding programme that targets needs in Latin America. This centre works with African species. When the centre started a breeding programme on a Brachiaria species they found locally-available materials to be genetically narrow and therefore unsuitable as source materials for breeding. They collected new accessions from Africa to broaden the genetic base of local varieties through breeding programmes at CIAT. The source countries in Africa never received any benefits from this development.

The other case involved the Nile tilapia (*Orichromis Niloticus*), a particular type of fish found in the Nile. This species was introduced to Asian countries from Egypt some 40 years ago. Aquaculture candidates in Asia were highly inbred and uniform and were not responsive to selection. A programme of breeding to improve farmed tilapia was started at the International Centre for Living Aquatic Resources Management (ICLARM), and fish farming with the African species soon became a major industry. Fresh introductions from streams and lakes in Ghana were made available to broaden the genetic base of *O. Niloticus*. Today, the Nile tilapia is the basis of a multi-million dollar aquaculture industry in Asia, but neither Egypt nor Ghana has benefited from this development.

Chitsike (1997) highlights biopiracy involving quinoa, a high protein cereal which forms an important part of the diet of millions of indigenous people in the Andean countries of South America, and turmeric, an orange-rooted plant found in India. In the quinoa case, he reports how the people of the Andean countries have long cultivated and developed different varieties of this plant. Because of its nutritional value – it has twice the protein content of maize or rice – quinoa has started to enter the US and European markets. Every year Bolivia is reported to receive US$1 million from the sale of this product. In 1994 two researchers from the US received a patent which gave them exclusive monopoly control of male sterile plants of the traditional Bolivian 'Apelawa' quinoa variety. The researchers are said to have admitted that they did nothing to create the male sterile variety. It was, in fact, 'just part of the native population of plants'. The patent covers any quinoa hybrid derived from the Apelawa male sterile cytoplasm, including 36 traditional varieties. Once the patent finds its way into corporate hands, Bolivian exports of quinoa to the US can be prevented. Quinoa can be grown commercially elsewhere with the permission of patent holders.

Turmeric, a plant which is a magic cure-all for many people in India, is orange-rooted and an ancient component of Ayurvedic medicine. It is native to the Indian subcontinent and has been used for thousands of years in the treatment of sprains, inflammatory conditions and wound. In 1995, two US scientists from Mississippi were granted a US patent on the use of turmeric for healing wounds. Though the government of India filed a challenge to the patent, the appeal can only be upheld if India provides proof that turmeric has been used in India specifically for healing wounds. This proof should be in the form of an academic paper that predates the patent application. The US researchers are said to have acknowledged in the application for the patent that turmeric has long been used in India as a traditional medicine for treatment of various sprains and inflammatory conditions, but they argued that there was no research carried out to that effect. So, if the patent could be granted on the basis that the process that had led to its discovery and use by the people of India was not regarded as research, this then means that no traditionally-based knowledge can be patented. The implication is that any scientific researcher who can take traditional knowledge, verify it through a recognised scientific research process, without adding anything more, can apply for a patent to their benefit.

The neem tree, which is also found in India, has now more than 35 US and European patents for its pesticidal properties (Chitsike,1997). Local communities who have used this plant and have preserved it for generations are already marginalised because of the reduced access to this resource due to high market demand. If the 35 patents were for Indian nationals or corporations, nobody would raise the question of biopiracy, querying instead the distributional aspects within the country.

Some research agendas and programmes carried out in the context of development institutions such as universities, NGOs and other rural development institutions, through various bilateral and multilateral co-operative programmes, are flow channels through which indigenous knowledge is siphoned to developed countries where it is used to develop marketable products. Dery, *et al.*, (1999) highlighted the fact that knowledge of traditional medicine is a treasured secret of specific individuals. This means that, given the chance, such individuals could patent such knowledge. Western laws of property rights have mechanisms for protecting such treasured information, as trade secrets for example. In order to elicit this treasured information from local communities in developing countries special extractive tools were and are being developed, tools commonly referred to as Participatory Research Methods. These methods have in-built mechanisms to tease out valuable information from local people. No payment is made for this knowledge for it is implied that such knowledge is common heritage. The best publications from such acquired knowledge are patented by the authors. The communities supplying the knowledge may receive no more than a mere acknowledgment.

The hospitality of local people is also sometimes exploited. In research studies conducted in Tanzania, Dery, *et al.*, (1999) established that people from Shinyanga Region relied heavily on over 300 tree species for treatment of a variety of diseases. From these people some researchers were able to ascertain and list the trees used, in terms of local name, botanical name, the part of the tree used as well as the disease treated. Such valuable information was provided at no cost and the people who supplied the knowledge received no reward for it, let alone a patent. The authors actually admitted that they were greatly surprised at the eagerness with which many traditional healers were willing to release information on the medicinal values of the tree species.

The objective of this exercise, which resulted in the availing of such knowledge by local farmers, was to identify and document the wealth of knowledge on medicinal trees, to domesticate the identified priority medicinal trees, and to evaluate ways of integrating them into existing farming systems in the miombo woodlands of southern Africa. This was expected to increase the availability of scarce medicinal products to traditional healers and farmers, which would raise their incomes as well as reduce pressure on wild tree populations. In turn, this would contribute to better healthcare. And to a scientific researcher it is priceless research for developing commercial products.

Chitsike (1997) also reports on a case of biopiracy involving a West African berry called brazzein. This berry contains a protein that is 500 times sweeter than sugar. A natural substance that does not lose its sweetness when heated, it is therefore valuable in the food industry. Researchers at the University of Wisconsin have received US and European patents for the protein isolated from this berry. Subsequent work on the protein focussed on making transgenetic organisms to produce brazzein in the laboratories, thereby eliminating the need for it to be collected or grown commercially in West Africa. The University of Wisconsin is said to have reported that corporate interests in brazzein are very strong, adding that the worldwide market for sweeteners is US$100 billion a year The university was quite clear that their brazzein was an invention of a University of Wisconsin researcher and that there were no plans for benefit-sharing with the West African people who discovered and nurtured the plant. This clearly shows how local indigenous people lose out.

In most of the cases of biopiracy, such as have been highlighted in this chapter researchers from developed countries apply for patents on inventions resulting from research conducted on biological resources using indigenous technical knowledge from developing countries. How do these researchers manage to access these resources? There are many co-operative programmes that take place in developing countries involving researchers from the North and nationals from the South. The latter may just act as research assistants in identifying and collecting specimens whose analysis will be carried out in the North. Discoveries from analysis of such resources are then patented in the North, as happened with Zimbabwe's *Swartzia madagascarensis*. Developing countries should therefore set up surveillance mechanisms that will enable them to know what research activities are going on and exactly what materials are involved. Until such surveillance mechanisms are put in place, developing countries will remain as unwitting accomplices to the evils of biopiracy within their territories. With the option to register communities as trusts, such surveillance mechanisms would be easy to implement at a more local level. The trustees of community trusts can be mandated with the responsibility of sanctioning research conducted in, or using resources from, their areas of jurisdiction. They will also need to monitor results from such activities to ensure that communities get a fair share of any benefits.

There is also a need for awareness campaigns within the developing countries themselves, to alert their nationals as to how their biological resources and indigenous knowledge can be accessed by other countries in order to develop valuable products from which they derive no benefit. Such campaigns will help predispose people in developing countries against innocently declaring their knowledge to strangers without knowing how they should benefit from such information-sharing.

## Conclusion

This chapter has shown that globalisation can have negative consequences for some communities, in this case those in developing countries, while at the same time benefiting other communities in developed countries. The challenge is how to strike a happy medium between the two. In the case of biological resources in developing countries the question that needs to be answered is, are the resources global or local commons? If it is argued that they are global commons, as vaunted by developed countries, then the question arises as to how the benefits can be globally shared. The appropriation of resources, through Intellectual Property Rights, which in many cases is blatantly exploitative of the innovations and knowledge of locals, whether they be communities or researchers, is a prime example of inequitable global sharing of benefits. Consequently, there is a need to come up with other paradigms for managing and exploitation of biological resources. The issue is not simply between developed and developing countries. Local communities who live with the natural resources and therefore tend to suffer most from irresponsible exploitation of resources are often forgotten by their own governments as well as developed countries. Communities in developing countries cannot and will not be forever spectators of the exploitation of their resources. Soon conflict will arise and with it all the treaties that have been signed will go up in smoke.

## References


Berg, Trygve. (n.d.). Sharing of Benefits (mimeo).

Biodiversity Support Foundation (1993). *African Biodiversity: Foundation for the Future. A Framework for Integrating Biodiversity Conservation and Sustainable Development*. Beltsville, Biodiversity Support Foundation.

Campbell, B. (ed.) (1996). *The miombo in transition: woodland and welfare in Africa*. Bogor, Centre for International Forestry Research.

Chitsike L. T. (ed.) (1997). *Report on Indigenous Knowledge Workshop held in Madrid, Spain: November 1997*. Convention on Biological Diversity.

Crucible Group (1994). *People, plants and patents: the impact of intellectual property on biodiversity, conservation, trade and rural society*. Ottawa, IDRC.

Dery, B. B., R. Otsyna, C. Ng'atigwa (eds) (1999). *Indigenous Knowledge of Medicinal Trees and Setting Priorities for their Domestication in Shinyanga Region, Tanzania*. Nairobi, International Centre for Agricultural Research.

Duffey, W. H. (1993). 'Intellectual property laws and their impact on agricultural research' in Weaver R.D. (ed.) *U.S. Agricultural Research: Strategic Challenges and Options*. Maryland Agricultural Research Institute.

Egziabher, T. B. (1996). *A Case for Community Rights*. Study Report 1. Addis Ababa, Institute for Sustainable Development.

——— (2000). *Intellectual Property Rights in Biological Diversity and Trade Agreements*. Addis Ababa, Institute for Sustainable Development.

*Flavier, J.M.* et al *(1995) 'The regional programme for the promotion of indigenous knowledge in Asia' in Warren, D.M., J.L. Slikkerveer and D. Brokensha (eds) The cultural dimension of development: indigenous knowledge systems. London, Intermediate Technology Publications.*

Frost, P. (1996). 'The ecology of miombo woodlands' in Campbell, B. (ed.) *The miombo in transition: woodland and welfare in Africa*. Bogor, Centre for International Forestry Research.

George, J. and J. van Staden (2000). 'Intellectual Property Rights: Plants and Phyto-medicinals – past History, Present Scenario and Future Prospects in South Africa.' *South African Journal of Science*. Vol. 96 (8), 433-44

Gupta, A. K. (n.d.). Rewarding Creativity for Conserving Diversity in third world: Can IPR Regime Serve the Needs of Contemporary and Traditional Knowledge Experts and Communities in Third World? Ahmedabad, Indian Institute of Management. (mimeo).

——— (n.d.). Compensating Local Communities for Conserving Biodiversity : How much? Who will? How and when? (mimeo).

Kameri-Mbote, P. (2000). Community Rights, Farmers and Breeders Rights in Africa: Towards a Legal Framework for Sui Generis Legislation. Nairobi, African Centre for Technology Studies. Draft Working Paper Presented at the FAO/IUCN Regional Workshop on Community Rights, Farmers' and Breeders' Rights, Nyanga, Zimbabwe, October 29 – November 1, 2000.

Matose, F. and B. Mukamuri (1993). 'Trees, people and communities in Zimbabwe's communal lands' in Scoones, I. and J. Thompson (eds) Beyond Farmers' First: rural people's knowledge of agricultural research and extension practice. London, Research Series Vol 1. No. 2. Intermediate Technology Publications.

Mayet, M. (undated). Securing sustainable livelihoods: Imperatives underpinning the development of an appropriate regime to protect community rights to biodiversity. mmayet@global.co.za (mimeo).

Mpofu, B. (n.d.). *Farmers' and Breeders' Rights.* (mimeo).

Nhira, C., S. Baker, P.Gondo, J. J. Mangono, and C. Marunda (1998). *Contesting Inequality in Access to Forests*. Policy that works for forests and people series, No. 5. Harare, Centre for Applied Social Sciences (CASS) and Forestry Commission; London, International Institute for Environment and Development.

Nick, M. (1999). *Intellectual Property Rights: a battleground for trade and biodiversity?* Gland, Switzerland, IUCN.

Nijar G. S. (1996a). *In Defence of Community Knowledge and Biodiversity. A Conceptual Framework And The Essential Elements of a Rights Regime*. Paper 1. Penang, Third World Network.

——— (1996b). *TRIPs and Biodiversity. The Threat and Responses: A Third World View*. Paper 2. Penang, Third World Network.

Sithole, B. (2000). *Telling it like it is: devolution in the water reform process in Zimbabwe*. BASIS CRSP Project.

Swinson, J.V. (2000). 'Intellectual Property.' *Australian Science Teachers' Journal*. Vol. 46 (3), 36-40

Third World Network (2001). Intellectual property rights, TRIPS Agreement and the CBD. Statement to the 2nd meeting of the Panel of Experts on Access and Benefit Sharing, Montreal, 19-22 March 2001.

Warren, D.M. (1991) Using indigeous knowledge in agricultural development. Washington DC, World Bank Discussion Paper no. 127.

# Conclusion:

## Whither common property management in Zimbabwe?

*Godfrey Chikowore, Emmanuel Manzungu and France Maphosa*

### Introduction

Globalisation has generated and continues to generate passionate debate about how the world as we know it today is changing. It is a process that is ordering the world in a way that, in many respects, is epoch-making. Maphosa, in the introduction to this book, argues that in Africa the effects of globalisation are as far-reaching as were those of slavery, colonialism and neo-colonialism. While this characterisation of globalisation may seem rather harsh, especially to globalisation enthusiasts, it is nevertheless a widely-shared perception. In their book, *Globalisation and the Third World,* Kiely and Marfleet (1998: 11) say that 'it is not the case then that some parts of the world are effectively incorporated while others are insufficiently globalised; rather, it is *the actual processes of globalisation that have been intrinsically uneven, and unstable'* (emphasis in original). There is, therefore, a growing consensus – at least in civil society and some academic circles – that globalisation is bad news for developing countries. This is particularly worrying given that by the year 2025, 80 per cent of the estimated eight billion people in the world will be living in developing countries (van Hofwegen and Svendsen, 2000).

A look at some of the titles of a book series produced by Zed Books, in collaboration with a number of other publishers and NGOs, proves that this skepticism is not diminishing but increasing. *The Myth of Development: Non-Viable Economics of the 21st Century: Brave New Seeds: The Threat of GM Crops to Farmers* and *Hungry for Trade: How the*

*Poor Pay for Free Trade* are but three books, among others, that show that the so-called advantages offered by globalisation come at a heavy price. And unfortunately, it is the world's poor who pay this price. In this respect, the contributors of the chapters in this book are in good company. The contributors display a healthy scepticism of globalisation *vis-à-vis* its impacts on the management of common property resources, and upon the livelihoods of the people that are affected.

Despite the differences in the perceptions of the effects of globalisation, the fact remains that it is a reality that has far-reaching effects. The various social actors, especially those in the South, should seek to explore the maximum opportunities offered by globalisation while at the same time making an effort to minimise its negative impacts. This book sets out to explore this very possibility by delving into the challenges facing the management of common property resources in Zimbabwe, a developing country whose experiences are relevant to other developing countries in southern Africa and beyond.

Herein we try to synthesise the findings of the book; not by way of presenting an abridged version of the conclusions, but by presenting what we believe is the connecting thread that runs across all the chapters. To this end, we emphasise that managing common property resources in an age of globalisation is essentially about relations, be they political, social, economic or cultural, and between and among various actors. Power defines who gains and who loses in any relationship. This includes access to common property resources and gives credence to the political economy approach to natural resources management and use. This approach is best placed to provide answers to the different types of access to natural resources as well as common property (Kiely and Marfleet, 1998: 10). We observe that governance is a central issue be it at the local, regional or international level.

After characterising the findings contained in the various chapters of the book we will proceed to suggesting the way forward for common property management in Zimbabwe. While this is first and foremost a Zimbabwean experience, those countries with similar experiences, particularly in southern Africa, can benefit from some of the lessons learned.

## Cascading and interlocking relations in common property management

This book has presented issues facing common property management in Zimbabwe, in two sections focusing on local and regional aspects of common property management. We argue that there cannot and should not be such a strict separation between the local and transboundary dimensions of common property management if enough light is shed on the dynamics of common property management. This is because there is no regional dimension that does not have a local dimension or vice versa. Neither is there a transboundary issue without local or international dimensions.

This then brings us to the argument that managing common property in an age of globalisation must be understood in terms of the relationships between the different actors and aspects of common property resource management. These include international, transboundary and local actors. It is futile to think that there are strictly local solutions to the management of local common property resources, as what are sometimes termed local solutions are, in fact, international solutions that have been internalised, re-packaged or presented as local. Similarly, international or transboundary philosophies or practices are in many cases local philosophies/practices that have been translocated to another culture or country, which also underlines the need to deconstruct international/ transboundary/local philosophies and practices in order to understand the processes at play. Without unpacking these processes we run the risk of mystifying the global-local divide in common property management. In short, local, transboundary and international dimensions *vis-à-vis* common property management are three pieces of the same jigsaw puzzle and can be understood as a cascade of relations that are in many cases interlocking. In the paragraphs below we will illustrate this in the development of our argument.

A good starting point is to recap the question that Mudiwa posed in Chapter 10: are common property resources global or local commons? This question lies at the heart of the whole globalisation debate. Using the issue of Intellectual Property Rights, Mudiwa shows that the definition was to a large extent dependent upon self-interests that are really local interests. Thus, developed countries view biological resources in developing countries as global commons that can be exploited. However, the goal posts are shifted when it comes to sharing the benefits of the modified resources, whether substantially or insubstantially. To safeguard *their* local interests developed countries redefine the global commons as *their own*. The modified global commons are then commodified as Intellectual Property Rights, which developing countries have to pay for. Mudiwa and Masiiwa emphasise this point in their respective contributions.

Uneven power relations mediate this unfair transaction, and are themselves products of local considerations in the first place. For example, the need to protect local employment influenced the US against the ratification of Agenda 21. It is also for the same local reasons that the US is disputing the Kyoto agreement.

An important issue to note is that local interests in developed countries are not always as inherent in local people as they are in communities in developing countries. The local constituency may in fact be a transnational corporation that has a strong voice and may want to exploit global commons. This means that international dimensions are more dependent on the local interests of those in power than on regional or transboundary concerns. We suggest that common property management in an age of globalisation must be seen as being mediated by a cascade of relations incorporating local, transboundary and international dimensions. In the developed world strong local lobby groups are institutions that ensure that their governments legislate to their advantage. In such cases, the cascade moves from local to the regional level and then to the international level. The relations, it can be seen, are interlocking as one does not function without the other.

Unfortunately, in developing countries the relations tend to be disjointed. Sometimes nation-states commit themselves to certain aspects of common property management without much involvement from other stakeholders. In such cases it can be said that the problem is one of governance, in this case poor governance, where states assume that they are always acting in the best interests of their people. Masiiwa, Matose, Mamimine and Sanyanga all make this same point in their respective contributions.

The reference to the differences between what 'local' means in developed and developing countries, as illustrated with the reference to the United States, raises an important issue about the lack of appreciation of heterogeneity in the management of common property resources. We therefore caution against the rather pervasive mentality of seeing people as 'communities' and 'local people'. Such labels including 'third world' or 'developing countries' are blunt characterisations of reality and do not take into account the heterogeneity that exists. With respect to people in the developing countries and common property resources, the issue of livelihoods is paramount. This, perhaps, is one drawback to the book. There are few descriptions of what happens at local level, for example the contestations over resources that occur locally. Only Matose does some justice to this issue. He shows that different forest products are exploited by different categories of people. This point cannot be stressed strongly enough, as there is a need to move away from stereotypes in natural resource management, which in the end yield only half-baked results and solutions. In other words, discussions of common property resources must move beyond the common clichés.

In this regard we particularly want to caution against one development that is happening in Zimbabwe. For some reason, there is a strong cultural revivalism that advocates for a return to what are called 'our traditions'. Even in resettlement areas where there have never been chieftainships such positions are being created. Furthermore, institutions such as traditional leadership structures are being entrusted with the management of commons. For example, under the Traditional Leaders Act, traditional leaders now have some power over the allocation of land. Under the Environment Management Bill traditional leaders will have the power to declare certain areas as requiring environmental protection.

Another example of this cultural revivalism is the concept of *zunde ramambo*. The idea is touted as an answer to drought for local people under a particular chief who will till a common field with the proceeds being distributed to the needy by the chief (Mararike 2001). This romanticisation of the glorious past is, however, at odds with the reality of the ground. Mukamuri (2000) observes that communal land tenure, considered a bastion of traditional land tenure, is increasingly being privatised. Moreover, state-created local institutions are becoming marginalised.

More importantly, Mukamuri notes that traditional institutions are losing their local legitimacy, although there are local variations. This observation casts doubt on whether traditional institutions can be relied upon as custodians of the commons with the people as obedient subjects of the Chief. The call to rely on traditional authority in the management of common property at local level is juxtaposed with increasing demands for democratic elections as the basis for legitimacy at national and international levels. The singing of some of these traditional and cultural mantras (see Zharare and Mudavanhu, 2000; Tyynela and Mudavanhu, 2000) needs to be tempered by the realisation that this may well short-circuit the efficient management of common property resources.

## The way forward

In many chapters of this book there has been a call for the state to devolve the management of common property resources to local communities. While this road may be paved with good intentions, it does not always lead to the intended results. The social circumstances prevailing in many rural areas in Zimbabwe have raised and continue to raise some ugly scenarios against which community management has to take place. This has to do with the fact that, apart from other issues, the community itself is changing.

The challenges facing common property management in Zimbabwe today have as a backdrop increasing poverty levels and the impact of the HIV/AIDS pandemic. Poverty is known to expose the biological environment, which constitutes the commons, to unsustainable exploitation as people strive to make a living (Chenje and Johnson, 1996). The statistic that over 70 per cent of rural households are poor presents a huge challenge to the efficient management of the commons. Common property management should therefore incorporate strategies for poverty alleviation.

The impact of the HIV/AIDS pandemic is also a serious matter. The scenario of child-headed households in Zimbabwe, in the light of the HIV/AIDS pandemic, raises or should raise new questions about how community management of natural resources can be achieved. Bourdillon (2000), on the basis of the inter-census survey conducted in Zimbabwe, gives some chilling statistics. Persons under the age of twenty head one in every 70 households nationwide. Under the traditional authority structure, decision-making is vested in adults, mostly males. The question then becomes: to what extent will the child-headed households be part and parcel of the new community-based natural resource management strategies? If they are not included, how will they survive? If they are included, what will be the type and tempo of their involvement?

Still on the issue of community participation there is the vexing question of proprietorship of indigenous knowledge, and its relation, Intellectual Property Rights, as discussed by Mudiwa in Chapter 10. We suggest that the debate must be taken beyond developing versus developed countries. There is need to examine the relationship between the state and the people as well as between the various people in determining proprietorship of knowledge. The power differentials between these various actors determines whose knowledge counts.

Yet the challenge of managing common property in Zimbabwe is also an international one, as the country is an integral part of the global community and should have equal voice. This, of course, is not the case, not only for Zimbabwe but also for other developing countries. This is why they need to lobby as a group, as suggested by Mudiwa. There is, therefore, merit in the international dimension of proposals for the creation of new United Nations structures for regulating intra- and inter-state activities, such as an Environmental Court of Justice. Commonly endorsed mechanisms for monitoring mutually adopted arrangements such as Agenda 21 and international environmental treaties and conventions should simply be regarded as starting points. Other advocacy efforts include the establishment of a third generation world organisation to handle new global environmental problems. In this new dispensation, the state would play a pivotal role of legislating for the desired change while other functions would be decentralised and devolved to civil society, local communities and the private sector. While this input is viable, it is equally vital to consider the implications generated by the distinctly varying socio-economic, political and cultural levels of development between developing and developed countries.

Transboundary resources represent a difficult proposition for local management and create greater prospects for co-operation between countries sharing the resources. The challenges should not, however, be underestimated. Co-operation in many cases involves different political, social, economic and ecological systems, as well as systems of utilisation and management. There is therefore a need to harmonise these management systems; this is no easy task.

Even if governments were to achieve harmonisation, what of the issue of participation of communities across national boundaries? In other words, the protection and sustainable utilisation of resources has to extend beyond government-to-government co-operation. It must involve all stakeholders. Such an undertaking necessitates designing physical plans that have their basis in social systems, as suggested by Vassileva. In short, planning of the commons should be a dynamic process that strengthens and protects local communities who should be regarded as full participants in as much as their livelihoods are at stake. As argued by Muzondo, technology plays a crucial role in this process.

While physical plans and technological designs are easy to produce, viable social systems that involve local communities are more difficult to generate. It is important to note that there are no typical societies 'out there', whose experiences in managing a certain resource can simply be replicated. In this respect, a degree of action research is necessary when incorporating local people as part of the management structures or procedures. As suggested previously, investigation is needed into how much local people across boundaries are enabled to participate in programmes.

As suggested by Chikowore, transboundary resource management of the commons should be established within a system of priorities and goals, and articulated from the basis of National Development Plans (in the image of Comprehensive National Development Concept). These policies, in turn, should be well-balanced, both inward- and outward-looking, and consistent with the development-oriented objectives. The priorities and goals should also incorporate what the local communities uphold as guiding principles of the management of the commons with respect to fisheries, wildlife, land, water, livestock, forestry, etc., and in an optimum manner that generates immediate benefit.

While it is agreed that in the final analysis the success of any development programme depends on the extent to which it incorporates the local communities, the way to achieving this is not clear. It may be achieved through decentralisation and power devolution processes. In this regard Mamimine made a critical observation. He argued that CAMPFIRE, and any other such programmes with a national or regional dimension seeking to empower poor black people in the communal areas, cannot be secured by tendencies of power retention abetted by the myth of lack of capacity at grassroots level. As reported by Sanyanga, the Manyuchi Fisheries Project represented an attempt to correct this problem by providing an alternative way of implementing the CAMPFIRE Programme by diversifying from traditional wildlife, (especially mammals) to common fisheries as well as drawing the communities, local authorities and the donor into the consultative process. Local participation in formulating, implementing and asserting ownership of the project through a trust may provide the answer to what local participation means in practice.

This is not an unimportant point given the efforts of the Government of Zimbabwe to devolve power to rural communities as a measure of ensuring effective management of local resources. The shortcomings of the decentralisation drive have been well documented in Section1 of this book. There is no need to labour this point. What is important is that globalisation is likely to increase the problems, chiefly because legal and policy pronouncements have either not been matched by corresponding action on the ground or they do not exist. For example, the current Intellectual Property Rights regime segregates not just national governments but local communities, who in many cases are custodians to commons, as they participate in the conservation of biodiversity, resulting in sustainable management of natural resources. It is therefore vital that strong and sincere co-operation between the rural common people, national government and international institutions be fostered in order to stop the marginalisation of the poor and rural communities.

One other crucial aspect of the local participation question relates to the global ideologies often bandied about by international agencies and taken as gospel truth by the local social actors. Manzungu illustrated this point with regard to the water reform process in Zimbabwe. This was based on the Rio-Dublin principles and included such concepts as water as an economic good and full-cost recovery. However, these were found to have irreconcilable inconsistencies with local realities. The problem was identified as arising from the shortcomings at the conceptual, administrative and human capacity level. The most promising alternative is to craft local solutions for local problems. There is no harm in drawing upon international experiences – as long as they are not the determining factor in the conceptualisation and implementation of the reforms.

Last but not least, a crucial element in the local participation dimension of the management of the commons in Zimbabwe is that boundaries between and among states are often tinderboxes, places where conflicts incubate and hostilities erupt. An example of this is the small-scale mining and alluvial panning activities that are widespread in eight Zambezi Basin riparian states. This haphazard activity, one that is poverty-driven, has caused and continues to cause siltation, a deterioration in water quality, and flooding. The existing SADC protocol on management of shared resources is inadequate and cannot stem this problem. This raises the point about conflict resolution *vis-à-vis* the utilisation of common property resources.

One possible solution is to put in place innovative policies and laws. This could involve formulating strategies for the adoption and adaptation of customary laws and traditional institutional structures to fight this impending threat. However, as argued above, th traditional card should not be overplayed.

## The final word

This publication has explored several interlocking dimensions of common property resourc management. It represents a practical effort to make the management of commons benef local communities in Zimbabwe, of whom the majority live in dire poverty. For this to b a reality, we need to operationalise concepts such as 'communities', 'local level', an 'traditional' as applied to particular situations. One impact of globalisation is that it rende these concepts very fluid and open to various definitions. At a theoretical level the objectiv was to understand the dynamics of common property resource management by linking with the distribution of power among the different actors at local, transboundary an international levels.

The success of managing the commons in Zimbabwe is dependent on the strength of national institutions capable of articulating national priorities and goals, and on the participation of local communities. Yet there must be an awareness of the global dimension, which is increasingly getting stronger and being worsened by the marked disparities in socio-economic levels of developing and developed countries.

## References

Bourdillon, M. (2000). Introduction. In M. Bourdillon (ed.) *Earning a life: working children in Zimbabwe*. Harare, Weaver Press

Chenje, M. and P. Johnson (eds) (1996). Water in Southern Africa. Maseru/Harare. SADC/IUCN/ SARDC.

Kiely, R and P. Marfleet (eds) (1998). *Globalisation and the third world*. New York, Routledge .

Mararike, C.G. (2001). 'Revival of indigenous food security strategies at the village level: the human factor implications'. *Zambezia*, 28. No. 1.

Mukamuri, B.B. (2000). 'Local institutions and management of indigenous woodland resources in Zimbabwe'. In Virtanen, P and M. Nummelin (eds) Forests, chiefs and peasants in Africa: local management of natural resources in Tanzania, Zimbabwe and Mozambique. *Silva Carelica*. No. 34.

Tyynela, T. and H.T. Mudavanhu (2000). Management and species diversity of a sacred forest in a deforested area: the case of of Dzete Mountain, north-east Zimbabwe. In Virtanen, P. and M. Nummelin (eds) Forests, chiefs and peasants in Africa: local management of natural resources in Tanzania, Zimbabwe and Mozambique. *Silva Carelica*. No. 34

van Hofwegen, P. and M. Svendsen (2000). *A vision of water for food and rural development*. Paper presented at the Secnd World Water Forum, The Hague, 17-22 March.

Zharare, G.E. and H.T. Mudavanhu (2000) Forests, chiefs and peasants in Africa: local management of natural resources in Tanzania, Zimbabwe and Mozambique. *Silva Carelica*. No. 34.

www.ingramcontent.com/pod-product-compliance
Lightning Source LLC
LaVergne TN
LVHW090358210926
848480LV00002B/376